SUSTAINABLE ENERGY BRANDING

Sustainable energy branding has become one of the hottest topics in business. As climate change and market liberalisation—the greatest environmental and economic challenges of our times—are prompting the world's power companies to transform on a scale never seen before, the eyes of the world are firmly upon them.

By introducing new business models, as well as new ways of generating power, energy-sector giants are aiming to dramatically cut harmful emissions over the next few decades. Crucial to the success of this transition is the support of energy consumers and political decision-makers, and this challenge should not be underestimated. Power companies are, therefore, developing new marketing and communication strategies around renewable energy, sustainable growth, co-operation with customers and environmental protection. Fridrik Larsen, the world's foremost expert on energy branding, looks at the role of branding and marketing in the energy transition through a series of interviews with senior energy-sector executives.

These compelling insights from industry leaders make this book a must-read for marketing and C-suite executives at energy companies who are wanting to communicate sustainable and renewable energy solutions effectively to make a difference.

Fridrik Larsen is an associate professor of marketing at the University of Iceland. He is the leading authority on branding within the energy space and the first person to hold a PhD in energy branding. Larsen holds graduate degrees in finance, economics and psychology and a postgraduate degree in marketing. He is the author of three books on energy branding, a sought-after public speaker and the founder of the CHARGE conference.

"Fridrik Larsen has opened up a new area of study within energy marketing. In these fascinating interviews with some of the world's most influential energy sector executives, branding comes alive, fully justifying its importance for the current low-carbon transition."

Kevin Lane Keller, *Professor of Marketing and author* of Strategic Brand Management

"Traditionally, branding was considered of secondary value to the energy business. Liberalisation and the fight against climate change upended such views. As a branding expert I recommend this book to everyone working in energy, sustainability and marketing."

Jacob Benbunan, *CEO of Saffron Brand Consultants*

SUSTAINABLE ENERGY BRANDING

Helping to Save the Planet

Fridrik Larsen

LONDON AND NEW YORK

Cover image: © Getty Images

First published 2023
by Routledge
4 Park Square, Milton Park, Abingdon, Oxon OX14 4RN

and by Routledge
605 Third Avenue, New York, NY 10158

Routledge is an imprint of the Taylor & Francis Group, an informa business

© 2023 Fridrik Larsen

The right of Fridrik Larsen to be identified as author of this work has been asserted in accordance with sections 77 and 78 of the Copyright, Designs and Patents Act 1988.

All rights reserved. No part of this book may be reprinted or reproduced or utilised in any form or by any electronic, mechanical, or other means, now known or hereafter invented, including photocopying and recording, or in any information storage or retrieval system, without permission in writing from the publishers.

Trademark notice: Product or corporate names may be trademarks or registered trademarks, and are used only for identification and explanation without intent to infringe.

British Library Cataloguing-in-Publication Data
A catalogue record for this book is available from the British Library

Library of Congress Cataloging-in-Publication Data
Names: Larsen, Friðrik, author.
Title: Sustainable energy branding : helping to save the planet / Fridrik Larsen.
Description: Milton Park, Abingdon, Oxon ; New York, NY : Routledge, 2023. |
    Includes bibliographical references.
Identifiers: LCCN 2022038034 (print) | LCCN 2022038035 (ebook) |
    ISBN 9781032396712 (hardback) | ISBN 9781032397122 (paperback) |
    ISBN 9781003351030 (ebook)
Subjects: LCSH: Energy industries—Marketing | Renewable energy sources—
    Marketing. | Branding (Marketing) | Customer relations—Management.
Classification: LCC HD9502.A2 L394 2023 (print) | LCC HD9502.A2 (ebook) |
    DDC 333.79—dc23/eng/20220901
LC record available at https://lccn.loc.gov/2022038034
LC ebook record available at https://lccn.loc.gov/2022038035

ISBN: 978-1-032-39671-2 (hbk)
ISBN: 978-1-032-39712-2 (pbk)
ISBN: 978-1-003-35103-0 (ebk)

DOI: 10.4324/9781003351030

Typeset in Joanna
by Apex CoVantage, LLC

To all the progressive industry practitioners who had the foresight that energy is not just a meter-to-meter business, but a human-to-human relationship.

CONTENTS

Acknowledgements	ix
Introduction: Energy Branding versus Greenwash	1
1 Northern Lights and the Power of Brand: Jukka Ruusunen on Energy Monopolies and Public Perceptions	7
2 Brand as a Promise: Magnus Hall on Energy Companies Fulfilling Expectations	19
3 Business to Human: Ryan O'Keeffe on the View from a Seven Trillion Dollar Fund	31
4 The Sound of Brand: Michael Boumendil on the Next Frontier in Brand Collateral	44
5 Branding in America: Mary Powell and Mari McClure on Building and Maintaining an American Energy Brand	55
6 Black Gold and Green Energy: Rahul Malhotra on Marketing Shell in the Age of Renewables	68
7 Oil Companies: Henrik Habberstad and Tom Van de Cruys on Sovereign Energy Brands in the Social Media Era	80

viii CONTENTS

8 The Italian Job: Antonio Cammisecra on Enel's Power
Distribution Branding Strategy 95

9 A Solar Collaboration: Anthony Ainsworth on Turning E.ON
into a Pop Brand 107

10 In the Big Country: Paula Gold Williams on Leading
America's Largest Municipal Utility 120

11 A Model Island: Hordur Arnarson on Going Beyond Full
Sustainability 132

12 Finding the Right Balance: Jacob Benbunan on Branding
between IQ and EQ 146

13 Virtual Power: Nic Kennedy on the Meeting of Energy and IT 159

14 Who You Are and Who You Want to Be: Hando Sutter on
Brand as the Tip of the Corporate Strategy Iceberg 171

15 Liberalisation Bonanza: Stephen Fitzpatrick and Kevin
McMinn on "Energy Minnows" Becoming Big Fish—or
One of the "Big Six" 184

16 From Product to Service: Ana Busto on Engie Post-Rebrand 198

17 Harder Than Rocket Science: Kevin Lane Keller on the
Theory and Practice of Energy Branding 209

ACKNOWLEDGEMENTS

I would like to use this opportunity to thank the colleagues without whose participation this work could literally not be written. In the order they appear in the book, they are Jukka Ruusunen, Magnus Hall, Ryan O'Keeffe, Michael Boumendil, Mary Powell, Mari McClure, Rahul Malhotra, Henrik Habberstad, Tom Van de Cruys, Antonio Cammisecra, Anthony Ainsworth, Paula Gold Williams, Hordur Arnarson, Jacob Benbunan, Nic Kennedy, Hando Sutter, Stephen Fitzpatrick, Kevin McMinn, Ana Busto and Kevin Lane Keller. I would also like to thank Nick Medic, researcher on this project.

In addition to these experts who were so generous with their time and advice during the writing of this book, there are all the others I have had the privilege to meet over the years, at industry conferences, academic seminars and specialist events – in person and online. I think of you as my "energy branding friends", and I am particularly grateful to Joao Duarte, Paddy Young, Elisabet Brusse and Aki Koskinen.

And, of course, to Agnar Lemacks, Akif Papas, Anders H. Lier, Björgvin Sigurdsson, Caroline Kamerbeek, Deryl Brown, Einar Snorri Einarsson, Florian Frömberg, Guðmundur Ásmundsson, Hans Petter Kildal, Kenneth Black, Kevin O'Donovan, Knut Aasrud, Koen Noyens, Magnus Bach, Magnús Kristjánsson, Marc Cloosterman, Marc Cloosterman, Matt Judkin, Robert Stulle, Rolf Olsen and Wayne Burke.

ACKNOWLEDGEMENTS

With all of you I have had many thought-provoking conversations, useful email threads and quick message exchanges that have nudged me towards a better understanding of the value of branding to the energy sector. I hope my dedication of this book "to all the progressive industry practitioners" goes some way to repaying this debt of gratitude.

Mentioning one such progressive CEO, the late Jim Rogers of Duke Energy, is a special honour. His passing precluded an interview, hence he is without a chapter in the book. And yet, his ideas on the energy business permeate every page. I got to know him when I was planning my first Charge Energy Branding conference in Reykjavik. I will always remember our first call. I asked him why he wanted to come to such a remote place like Iceland to talk about energy branding, a topic no conference had covered before. After all, he was an executive of great stature in the industry, Duke Energy being one of America's biggest power producers and retailers. He simply said: "I've been waiting 20 years for someone to do this." Jim made his mark on the energy space as one of the most influential energy executives of modern times. His assertion, championed throughout his long and illustrious career, that electricity is a basic human right, will surely stand the test of time. And I am privileged to say that he was a good friend.

Finally, I would like to thank my colleagues at the University of Iceland, the pleasant and nurturing environment of which has been so conducive to my academic career. In particular, Jon Atli Benediktsson, the University's President and Rector, whose support over the years has been greatly appreciated.

INTRODUCTION

ENERGY BRANDING VERSUS GREENWASH

Energy branding is the theory and practice of marketing and branding as it applies to the energy sector. Rather than a *niche* within a wider area of study, I prefer to think of it as a *terra incognita*, a vast new land waiting to be explored by practitioners and academics alike. If I may extend the metaphor further, the reason this landscape had not been surveyed earlier is that, to a large extent, it didn't exist. It emerged as the stale waters of energy-sector monopolism began receding under the incessant winds of liberalisation.

To put it more prosaically, over the last 30 years both power and oil and gas companies worldwide have been transforming from state owned monopolies into businesses competing in an open market. For example, where there was one company controlling the generation, distribution and sales of electricity, there could now be multiple operators and suppliers, each holding their own power stations, or supplying their own customers. In the coming chapters, as the need arose, we have described this trend, sometimes synonymously termed "energy-market liberalisation" or "deregulation". It is one of the themes of this book.

DOI: 10.4324/9781003351030-1

INTRODUCTION

From the customer's point of view, liberalisation introduced a new element in the process of purchasing energy, one that simply could not exist before—the element of choice. By definition, where there is a monopoly, there is one supplier. In an open market, businesses are competing for customers and they, in turn, are free to choose. To be successful in such a market, companies need to differentiate themselves from one another, and where there is a need for differentiation—there is a need for branding.

I hasten to add that, although energy branding is modern phenomenon, branding as such is not. As a number of examples in this book illustrates, branding is indelibly connected to trade, which seems to be an inherently human activity. History of branding and notable examples of its practice today, particularly as they apply to the energy industry, are another theme of the book.

This brings me to the title. Ours is an age of big words, strong statements, powerful soundbites, striking taglines . . . There is hyperbole everywhere and I can perfectly imagine the reader wondering, "No doubt there are many things that can help save the planet, but is energy branding really one of them?" You might have been reinforced in your scepticism by the preceding paragraphs: energy branding could be of great importance to companies in the energy sector, but hardly beyond.

Then, noting that the writer holds a PhD in "energy branding" and is a professor of marketing, you would be excused in assuming that here is another academic suffering from a severe case of professional myopia (in addition to being—at least where his own book is concerned—a foot-in-the-door marketer). To this I can only admit that it is easy to get immersed in your area of study, to the extent that it expands in significance, disproportionate to everyone's perception but yours.

As to the suspicion, however, that I am "panic-marketing" my book by peddling hyperbole, I invite you to consider the following example. In 2016 the government of the United Kingdom introduced a moratorium on the development of onshore wind farms. They were excluded from bidding for subsidies, leading to a severe decline in new projects.

In the run-up to the ban, there was widespread criticism of both the technology and its promoters. Wind turbines were *perceived* as unsightly and developers *insensitive* to the *feelings* of local communities. There was widespread *sense* that the English countryside was overrun by wind turbines, with little *benefit* to the nation as a whole. *Aesthetically*, the turbines didn't *seem* to fit in. Project promoters were *seen* as profit motivated, their technology an example of *greenwash*.

Following this example, it is not difficult to imagine other beneficial low-carbon technologies or projects, in other parts of the world, meeting with opprobrium despite the contribution they make to energy security and the fight against climate change. A public pushback, just when we need all the renewable energy we can get. But, why should there be such a reaction by the media, the general public and political decision-makers?

I have italicised some of the words in the penultimate paragraph to draw your attention to the type of language used in the debate. It is the language of emotion and perception, very similar to the one used in talking about brands and branding. The final word in italics, *greenwash*, frequent in media reports and public debates at the time, proved to be especially potent.

The concept of greenwash, having gained wide currency in the 1980s, has now come to mean at least three different things: firstly, measures introduced to protect the environment, which in fact are either ineffective or cause more harm than good; secondly, measures which are to some degree effective, yet purposely divert attention from a much greater problem, which needs to be addressed first or in parallel.

Finally, measures designed to create a sense of smugness, complacency and inner satisfaction in the consumer (something we could call "environmental righteousness"), despite their questionable effects on the environment. To these three meanings some add a "harder" definition which considers greenwashing the deliberate spreading of disinformation on environmental matters by large companies looking to profit from despoiling the planet.

Among the most detrimental consequences of greenwashing is the undermining of public trust in measures which really make a difference to energy security or the fight against climate change. And because it requires two industries to come together, that of energy and the environment on the one side, and marketing, branding and public relations on the other, anytime those two worlds intersect a dark miasma of greenwash-doubt clouds their meeting.

On their part, energy businesses have responded to suspicions of greenwash by erring on the side of caution. They have tightened their communications materials in the direction of greater numerical accuracy and technical detail. This is in keeping with a communication style favoured by the energy sector, which has been traditionally led by engineering professionals. However, you could argue that something was lost in the process—assuming that it was there in the first place.

Going back to our example of onshore wind farms in the United Kingdom, the "technical arguments" in favour of this technology, though correct from an engineering point of view, had largely fallen on deaf ears. To politicians the technology was a vote-loser; local people could not see beyond the immediate disruption and the media latched on to a source of controversy that just kept giving.

All of this was despite the statistical evidence. In the years prior to the moratorium the UK had one of the lowest number of onshore wind turbines per square kilometre out of all the countries in north or west Europe.[1] Yet, in those countries there was little controversy over deployment, leading to onshore wind energy becoming a significant contributor to each nation's electricity supply (at the time of writing it is 31 per cent in Ireland, 26 per cent in Portugal, 24 per cent in Denmark and Spain, and so on).[2] In other words, the technology stacked up, but communicating its benefits was a matter beyond engineering.

Many energy companies around the world face similar problems. For instance, electricity from new renewable sources such as offshore wind farms was more expensive than electricity from coal-fired plants for most of the previous two decades. To the challenges of developing, constructing and maintaining these new technologies, energy companies have to add the task of justifying the cost hikes. Furthermore, energy storage technologies and devices such as solar panels require greater consumer participation in the generation of electricity, while intrusive measures on energy efficiency might require both investment by the customer, and behavioural change.

All of these initiatives are necessary in terms of combatting climate change and advancing energy sustainability. For example, since 1990 the carbon intensity of the EU power sector has declined from 524 grams of CO_2 per kilowatthour to just over 200, a fall of over 50 per cent.[3] Renewable sources—chiefly hydro, wind and solar—now account for close to 40 per cent of Europe gross electricity consumption.[4] But, more needs to be done, as the European Union aims for power sector carbon neutrality by 2050.

I contend that only strong energy brands can see through this energy transition. Theirs is a great responsibility: unlike in the old days, when they just had to deliver electricity, they now need to educate, motivate and inspire not just consumers, but stakeholders and the media alike. Otherwise, the alternative is unthinkable. We are looking at continuing dependence on an ever diminishing supply of fossil fuels, and a steady increase in the concentration of atmospheric greenhouse gasses.

Hence, finally, the title of this book and also its overall purpose. If I had thus far alluded to its themes, then the purpose of this volume would be to suggest energy branding, normatively, as a mode of communication in the energy sector, that avoids the pitfalls of greenwash, but also the disengaging communication styles pursued by energy businesses the world over. Because, if there was ever a need to engage with energy consumers it is now.

A few more words on its gestation. It all started on a balmy evening in May. I was in Florence for the Eurelectric's 2019 Power Summit. Traditionally, the event starts with an eve-of-conference reception and on this Sunday, we were gathered in the Torrigiani Garden. The seventeen-acre site is one of the largest privately-owned gardens in Europe, and there among the exotic shrubs and spring flowers I saw Magnus Hall, the CEO of Vattenfall.

In any kind of gathering Magnus is pretty hard to miss. At over two meters tall, he might as well be known as the gentle giant of the energy industry, particularly as his stature is matched by his friendliness. For a CEO of a company which employs close to 20,000 people and generates €16 billion per year in revenues, Magnus is immensely approachable and unrushed. Having spoken to him before, I decided to say hello.

Invariably on such occasions, conversation turns to business. I reminded Magnus of my PhD thesis. Published as a book titled *Energy Branding— Harnessing Consumer Power*, it forms the basis of my subsequent work. Between teaching marketing at the University of Iceland and running the world's only event dedicated solely to energy branding, Reykjavik's *Charge* annual conference, I have developed the auditing instrument which examines energy brand effectiveness.

However, as I went over my views, Magnus seemed unconvinced. He said: "Fridrik, I know what you do, but I need more evidence. What are other people in the industry saying? What do they think about the value of branding? What problems are they trying to solve and how can branding help? What can it really do for us?"

The gauntlet was well and truly thrown down and the challenge accepted head on. I decided to interview professionals from the realms of energy and branding, with questions expanding on the themes of my previous book. As to the format, the idea was to have the theory and practice of branding interwoven together in each chapter, and placed within the wider context of branding and energy-related research. Let the reader be the judge of how successful I was in bringing together these two endlessly fascinating fields of study.

Notes

1. RenewableUK. "International Comparisons: Turbine Densities and Capacity Factors." *RenewableUK (British Wind Energy Association – BWEA)*, 2011, as quoted in OECD. *Linking Renewable Energy to Rural Development – Green Growth Studies*. OECD Publishing, 2012, pp. 148, (doi:10.1787/9789264180 444-en).
2. WindEurope Business Intelligence. "Wind Energy in Europe 2021, Statistics and the Outlook for 2022–2026." *WindEurope*, 2022, Fig. 9, pp. 20, windeurope.org/intelligence-platform/statistics/.
3. European Environment Agency. "Greenhouse Gas Emission Intensity of Electricity Generation in Europe." 14 Jul. 2022, eea.europa.eu/ims/green house-gas-emission-intensity-of-1.
4. Eurostat. "Renewable Energy on the Rise: 37% of EU's Electricity." 26 Jan. 2022, ec.europa.eu/eurostat/web/products-eurostat-news/-/ddn-2022 0126-1.

1

NORTHERN LIGHTS AND THE POWER OF BRAND

JUKKA RUUSUNEN ON ENERGY MONOPOLIES AND PUBLIC PERCEPTIONS

The last Grand Prince of Finland, and the last Russian Tsar of the Romanov dynasty, Nicolas II was fourteen when, in the southern regions of his principality—in the town of Tampere—electric lights went on for the first time. The year was 1882 and the earliest permanent power station in Finland, built by the Finlayson textile mill on the nearby Tamerkoski rapids, lit up the factory's 150 incandescent bulbs. These were ordered directly from the Edison Electric Light Company in New York, and were the first incandescent lights to be installed in any of the Nordic countries.[1]

Soon, the whole of Tampere (official town slogan *Tampere—All Bright!*) was on a 110V volt DC grid. In 1884 the first power station in Helsinki was on line, the same year as in Berlin. To the east, however, the Russian Empire, encumbered with the legacy of outdated institutions—the 700-year-old system of serfdom had been abolished only 20 years prior to the lights coming on in Tampere—was struggling to keep up with the

DOI: 10.4324/9781003351030-2

industrial revolution, its economy predominantly agrarian. As Jonathan Coopersmith writes in his book *The Electrification of Russia, 1880–1926* "electrification suffered, as did most economic activities in Russia, from the government's restrictive procedures . . . utilities, like other industries, suffered from state overregulation and involvement in almost every area of operations."[2]

And the empire was becoming increasingly politically unstable. Calls for reform of absolutist tsarist rule were getting louder, and dissenters more violent. In 1881 the grandfather of Prince Nicolas II was assassinated by an anarchist's bomb. Finland, on the other hand, economically and culturally aligned with the prosperous Baltic and North Sea trading hubs, was industrialising quickly, while becoming more politically autonomous. As Timo Myllyntaus writes:

> One might expect that the transfer of heavy electrical engineering from industrialised countries to such a peripheral country such as Finland . . . would have been delayed for many years. This was not the case. Heavy electrical engineering arrived in Finland . . . comparatively quickly.[3]

Perhaps, muses Myllyntaus, "electricity as the source of light captured the attention of the Finns at an early date because in winter natural light was not sufficient to workshops, factories, offices, or homes even during the daytime."[4] By 1914, three years before independence, there were utilities in all 38 electrified towns in Finland, and by 1930 production of electricity per capita stood at 350 kilowatthours (kWh). Way below USA's 931 kWh, and yet more than Netherland's 313 kWh or Italy's 261 kWh.

In rural Finland, as the supply of paraffin dried up during the 1918 Finnish Civil War, enterprising villagers set up their own electricity utilities. The number grew from around 100 to 400 in just a few years. The expansion was so intense that it went down in history under its own name: *sähköistysvimma* or "electrification frenzy". In the rush to get connected barbed wire was used for overhead transmission lines and bottle-necks for insulators.

The frenzied love of electrical energy has continued undimmed, so to speak, into the present age, the Fins being the only nation, as far as I am aware, with a term of endearment for their main high-voltage transmission line. Reading affectionate reports about a recent refurbishment of this

560km 110kV installation you could be mistaken in thinking they were about a distinguished national figure:

> When I tell my colleagues from other countries that the matriarch of our main grid—Rautarouva—is turning 90 this year, they are always amazed and full of admiration: Wow, how is that possible! The Iron Lady combines many positive aspects of Finnishness. The key mottos have been: Do it well and keep it in condition.[5]

Concluding his scholarly essay on the transfer of electrical technology to Finland, Professor Myllyntaus says: "How Finland managed to electrify its economy faster than the other late-to-industrialise countries with a similar standard of living is a puzzle."[6] Interestingly, he lists positive attitudes towards industrialisation and innovation in the late nineteenth century as possible factors. New technologies were seen by the Finns as supporting their national aspirations.

I wonder, following Professor Myllyntaus's cue whether Jukka Ruusunen's views on branding are deep down motivated by a social consciousness, an awareness of the colossal role his company plays in the day-to-day life of every single resident of Finland.

Jukka is the chief executive officer and president of Fingrid, the country's transmission system operator (TSO). On the face of it, you will find his enthusiasm for branding as puzzling as the rapid adoption of electricity in his home country. Fingrid, a national transmission monopoly, was formed long after the Fins had abandoned their experiments with barbed wire, bottle tops, and 400 different energy co-ops. It has no competitors, having been formed in 1996 by government decree. Following purely commercial logic, or marketing orthodoxy, one would think that Fingrid does not need to worry about branding. It stands all alone in the field of national transmission like a tall electrical pylon. There is no Pepsi to its Coke, nor a Lyft to its Uber.

Its assets came from two vertically integrated energy companies, which had to comply with European Union energy market liberalisation guidelines, by divesting their power transmission assets. The Finish government still holds a majority share in the company, with the remaining 30 per cent of stock held by five pension mutuals and insurance companies. And yet I remember the evening when, at the Charge awards ceremony I host every year in Reykjavik, Fingrid won the "Best transmission and distribution" trophy. The Fingrid delegation leapt on stage to receive the award with great alacrity and good cheer. At that moment I overheard a snippet of conversation at the next table, where two delegates from the United Kingdom were seated. "Have you ever seen a happy Finn?", said one. "Well, you have now!", answered the other.

It is to this question—why should transmission companies care about branding—that I have returned to in my conversation with Jukka over the years. Why compete for the award? Of course, I was glad that they did, and I would always invite Fingrid back, but really—why care? As things stand, there will always be only one Iron Lady.

Jukka a genial, bespectacled man in his sixties, sets out his views, characteristically for many Finns, with good humour and quiet intensity. Something of an academic heavyweight (with a PhD in Technology and previous jobs at Helsinki University and the Helsinki School of Economics on his CV), Jukka talks about branding in terms of a "social licence to operate". Yet, behind this accepted notion of branding as a social-commercial enabler, there is the view that, paradoxically, branding is almost more important to monopolies than to open-market actors. If any-thing, monopolies should worry more about it.

> Whether you are interested in branding or not, the outside world has an opinion about your company. For monopolies it is especially sig-nificant what society and your customers think, as they have all the tools to control you, through political means. If, on the other hand, you compete as a business with other businesses on purely commer-cial, open-market terms, you have a lot of opportunity, a lot of leeway, to make your own business decisions, even mistakes. Customers will make their judgements about you, but much needs to happen before the unlikely event of politicians getting involved. And they generally don't like getting involved. A strong brand, sending our message that we are working for society, that we are reliable and the best option for Finnish citizens is our social licence to operate.

In the occasional blog posts he publishes on Fingrid's web-site Jukka puts it in starker terms:

> From Fingrid's point of view, the trust and support of society is a mat-ter of life and death. Society can intervene in the TSOs operations at

any time by changing regulations if the company fails to fulfil its task. As a result, TSOs must be especially careful about their reputation.[7]

Jukka was an advisor to Imatran Voima in 1996, when it was one of the two vertically integrated Finnish companies directed by the government to spin off their grid assets. The deal was driven by the liberalisation of the European energy market in the 1990s, which itself was provoked by the sense that large European utilities were complacent towards their customers, and ill-equipped to deal with societal challenges such as climate change, or energy security. In other words, these companies were becoming weak brands, symptomatic of an outdated way of doing business, in an era of wholesale privatisation and fierce competition. The liberalisation of the telecoms industry in the 1980s and the early 1990s, driven by new technologies such as mobile telephony and the internet, had proved that opening up markets could be a good thing. It gave customers a better deal, accelerated innovation and drew in fresh capital. At the same time, at regulatory level, the European energy sector was being subsumed under the single market agenda, also designed to drive down prices and foster EU-wide competition.[8]

In Jukka's view, the cross-border openness and the new laws governing the energy sector, imposed not just a greater degree of transparency, but also greater customer interest in how the energy companies went about their business—their pricing and business practices, their generating portfolios and their social role.

> In the past, when we were part of vertically integrated companies, nobody knew what we were doing. A company such as Fingrid, which in the past would have been a department within a larger company, or a subsidiary, would have just been part of the value chain. We were in the Nordic system, where nothing ever happened and everything was fine. What we have to get to grips with in this new world is how to relate to people. Rather than being seen as arrogant technology experts, we now have to build good relationships. Building those relationships is the best way to protect ourselves against undue interventionism.

I always found this notion, that by becoming better at what many in the energy sector (but I hasten to add not Jukka) see as the energy company's non-core activities, you actually protect the fundamentals of your business, particularly fertile. The logic seems to go something like this: juxtaposed to engineering, branding, marketing and even customer relations are "soft" sciences. But, if you are a monopoly, then by becoming softer, you are protecting the hard-core of your business, because you are able to relate better to your customer base, most whom do not have your technical nous. You are, in fact, shielding your business against intervention by politically motivated non-experts, who understand neither what is best for the business, nor, by extension, what is best for those whom the business serves.

An important stage in softening up an energy technology company is training up your staff to become more "brand aware". Such initiatives are often greeted with much eye-rolling and huffing by the engineering staff, but Jukka's proposition is that, in addition to being prudent, it is another way of upskilling your people.

> Training your employees how to talk to clients or external stakeholders, ultimately increases their employability. It increases their value both as actual and potential employees on the job market. Then there is the intangible, yet real benefit of this kind of training improving internal communications. It is worth understanding, though, that this kind of training has nothing to do with overcoming the old and, in my view, cliché dichotomy in technology companies, between the supposedly introverted engineers and extroverted sales, marketing or communications people. We would never force someone to do something they would not want to do, for instance, be more extroverted. What I am saying is that even when the training that we offer is not focused on branding, this awareness permeates the training agenda.

With Fingrid this focus on brand goes to the extent of having a public website subdomain brand.fingrid.fi setting out the company's brand fundamentals, visual identity, web design and applications over a total of 8 sub-menus.

The underlying brand philosophy was formulated, in Jukka's view, gradually, by considering how Fingrid should respond to climate change; but, also, how the organisation should respond to greater societal expectations of responsible corporate behaviour. It is this Nordic vision of a monopoly as a kind of social enterprise, a vision far removed from the paradigm of a monopoly as an exploitative and rapacious business venture, that deeply influences Fingrid's branding strategy. As a social, even communal enterprise, it is defined by how it is perceived by the community at large. To put it another way, it is defined by how the community perceives the company's staff.

> The word brand is a very difficult word for engineers. It is thought to be for marketing people, for those who are on television or wherever else. This is why going into the deeper meaning of the concept of branding is more important than getting fixated on the word. When I wanted to cut to the definition I asked the question internally: should we be interested in how society at large and our customers see us? Everyone agreed that, of course, this was important. So, this is the brand!

For engineers, Jukka thinks, "brand" is a Hollywood-styled word:

> When they studied physics no one ever mentioned brand. However, when you talk about reputation and reliability everyone understands what you mean. We don't call it brand, but we mean the same things.

Or, as Jukka writes on his blog:

> The existence and success of monopolies, just like any other organisation, is in the hands of external stakeholders. Reputation has a direct bearing on people's trust in the organisation and willingness to work with it. A company with a good reputation gets better employees, more satisfied customers, cheaper capital and the support of society.

To illustrate to colleagues what he meant when referring to Fingrid's brand, Jukka came up with a schematic now referred to internally as "Jukka's House". He is fond of flashing it up as a slide during presentations. The foundation of this house is "personnel and expertise", the ground floor "internal processes", and the first floor "finance". The roof and a kind of apex of this conceptual structure is "customers and society". Underneath those words you will find an explanation: "We secure reliable electricity and a well-functioning electricity market for society. We offer affordable services that meet our customers' needs."

But then, Jukka reflects on an interesting phenomenon which I find particular to the energy industry.

There are many who don't like to call customers—customers. They prefer to use the term "connecting parties" or "loads" or whatever technical term they are using for the connection point to the end user. These companies are only now starting to realise that they really have customers who pay their salaries.

Why would they not want to call them customers?

I don't know. I think it is partly because it is easier to hide behind technical terms, then talk about customers as customers. Because, when you do, then all sorts of questions come up: what are we doing with the customers? How are we interacting with the customers? And so on. It is like opening a Pandora's box, because it takes a long time to work through such questions, which sometimes are not as readily answerable as purely technical questions. Others might not agree with your opinions or they might have opinions of their own. It's a lot more complicated then dealing with voltages, loads and kilowatt hours.

In this world-view, where branding is in the final instance a precaution against over-regulation, the choking off of investment streams, or mutinous stakeholders, spending on brand is deeply aligned with the most basic corporate survival instincts. How would you justify spending one million euros on branding?

The first thing to remember is that spending on brand is not separate from your other strategic spend. If, as the owner, you want to protect your ownership and the value of the company; if that value is much more than one million euros, and, finally, if by spending it we could, let's say over the next five years, lower the risk of difficult financial regulation, then we don't need to argue much further that we should spend it. Or think about it this way: if under the process of branding you also consider learning from customers—as part of building your company and preparing for the future—then branding is not separate from what you would normally do in the course of business. It does not mean simply giving branding consultants a lot of money, or conducting an exercise that people will quickly forget. Nor does it mean separating it out from the other strands in your corporate strategy. It is something that you have to keep on talking about, when you talk to your people.

This intuitive view of the cost of branding being greatly outweighed by the rewards of protecting and advancing your business interests is borne out in business practice, even if you take *branding* in its most direct marketing sense. The word "brand"—related to the Old Norse *brandr*, and also to the Germanic word for "burning"—means, originally, to sear a name or image with a hot iron. By extension, in marketing practice, it has come to mean naming a company or its product. When Lexicon, a Californian branding and naming agency, was hired in 1992 by Intel to brand its new microprocessor—developed as model i586—Lexicon came up with the name Pentium. In 1995 Intel sold close to 30 million Pentium chips, against a business plan projection of 3 million.[9] The word Pentium became one of the most recognisable in the whole of the electronics business. As Andrew Grove, former CEO of Intel said in a 2011 interview, "according to our own internal research, in the late nineties Pentium was a more recognized brand name than Intel".[10]

I asked Jukka whether he ever talked about the power of branding to his fellow TSO executives. Was this ever a topic of conversation? He laughed, and admitted that he never mentioned branding at high level TSO meetings.

> Our technical language does not admit the word "branding". But, in saying that, we had recently at Fingrid welcomed a delegation of our colleagues from Hungary, and in talking to them I touched on how we work with our customers, and mentioned our brand. Things might be changing. Interestingly, those CEOs who don't have a long track record in the industry are more likely to start thinking about it.
>
> I guess when I start on branding some of the old guard think I forgot to take my morning medicine. But, if I explained that it means we have to think about how others see us, that we have to listen, it would be a much easier conversation. Let's just say I wouldn't use the word "branding" at first, but would come to it later in the conversation.

And if they pressed you, I asked, to sum up your views on why it is important for TSOs to develop a brand, in a few short words, as if it was one of those formulas engineers love so much, or perhaps even a bite-sized quote, ever popular with the media—what would you say? Jukka thought about this for a few seconds.

To combat climate change we have to work for societies. Developing our brand is a way of proving to the people that we are on their side. You know, perhaps transmission is moving to be more of a people business, than a technical business. Across Europe, we are now developing the electricity markets, distributed and on-site generation and we are talking to people all the time. We have to be very credible and we have to be good at talking to people. And to do that you have to upskill your people, to relate to those outside your company who might not have had the same technical background, or technical education.

And what would you say to your fellow executives who are just not interested?

I would say—fine. If it is part of your strategy that you are not interested in what society and customers think about you, if you are not interested in the views of the outside world, tell that to your regulators, to the people who have the power to legislate your business. To be fair, what you have to remember is that the DNA of transmission companies is so much more in technology than in customer relations. But now the world is changing.

And Jukka is right, of course. The age of the big thermal or hydro plants radiating electricity through a centralised network, to faceless private and business users is coming to an end. In 2018, for the first time, renewable sources have surpassed coal in EU's gross inland energy consumption. Compare that with 1990, when coal contributed 5 times more than renewables.[11]

Investment in distributed energy, a fresh challenge for transmission companies, because it requires an intelligent, data-driven grid which dispatches energy to and from millions of households, is set to exceed $1 trillion over the 2020s.[12] These households will be connected into virtual power plants, with peer-to-peer trading capabilities and energy tariffs priced up very differently from tariffs today. How do you take a transmission-company brand such as Fingrid, that traces its roots all the way to the age of the Romanovs, to the birth of the Iron Lady and the rural energy enterprises, into this kind of future? Meaning, how do you future-proof energy monopoly brands?

We can learn from positive examples . . . But, more fundamentally, as an industry we need to be thinking about the role of TSOs in the twenty-first century. That vision surely includes some form of an integrated and centrally regulated system, whatever you understand under those terms. And then we, the facilitators of this system, need strong, reliable branding so that our customers can follow our thinking.

Befitting his professorial tenure at Helsinki University of Technology, Jukka's blog post on Fingrid's branding philosophy is titled, with pedagogic clarity, "When a monopoly's brand and reputation are good, everyone benefits." Starting with a somewhat axiomatic statement, which yet retains a poetic edge—"The brand is born from the union of image and reputation"—he goes on to conclude: "If an operator with a vital role in society says one thing and does another, its reputation will be gone in a heartbeat." If Fingrid (not just the company, but the actual transmission grid) is the nation's electric heart, the bringer of power and light into those long northern nights, then that reputation is indeed everything.

Notes

1. Myllyntaus, Timo. "The Transfer of Electrical Technology to Finland, 1870–1930." *Technology and Culture*, Vol. 32, No. 2, Part 1 (Apr. 1991), pp. 293–317. The article carries a wealth of statistics about the development of electricity in Finland, which this chapter draws on. Myllyntaus postulates that in the early days of global electrical-technology development, the speed of electrification at national level was chiefly predicated either on high GDP per capita, or the abundance of hydro resources. How Finland electrified quickly despite not being blessed with either (in addition to being geographically remote to the world's main industrial hubs) makes the country's rapid electrification "puzzling"—yet, perhaps, understandable, given the climate, the geographical latitude and Finnish national aspirations.

2. Coopersmith, Jonathan. *The Electrification of Russia, 1880–1926*. Cornell University Press, 1992, ch. 2. Coopersmith draws interesting parallels between the development of two nineteenth-century industrial systems in Russia: the railways (a priority under the Tsars) and electricity (less of a priority). Soviet authorities, however, seized total political control over the energy system, realising the significance of rapid electrification to the communist state's industrial ambitions.

3. Myllyntaus, "The Transfer of Electrical Technology to Finland, 1870–1930".
4. Ibid.
5. Kuusela, Kari." A Strong Main Grid Enables Clean Energy Production." *Fingrid Lehti,* 6 Mar. 2019, fingridlehti.fi/en/main-grid-enables/. Executive Vice President Kari Kuusela also wrote with some nostalgia of the "old Iron Lady finally retiring", on the website of Fingrid's company magazine (*Fingrid Lehti*).
6. Myllyntaus, "The Transfer of Electrical Technology to Finland, 1870–1930".
7. Ruusunen, Jukka. "When a Monopoly's Brand and Reputation Are Good, Everyone Benefits." *Fingrid Lehti*, 31 Aug. 2020, www.fingridlehti.fi/en/monopolys-good-brand-and-reputation/#4da74137.
8. See Eberlein, Burkard. "The Making of the European Energy Market: The Interplay of Governance and Government." *Journal of Public Policy*, Vol. 28, No. 1, Jan.–Apr., 2008, pp. 73–92. Burkard writes of how in the early 1990s "global privatisation and liberalisation seized infrastructures and network industries, spilling over from more advanced sectors such as telecommunications, into public utilities."
9. Donald Alpert—one of the first Intel engineers to work on the Pentium—wrote on his website about the development of the Pentium, including 5-year business plan projections and sales figures. See camelback-comparch.com/about/technical-highlights/#p5.
10. Colapinto, John. ""Famous Names—Does it Matter What a Product Is Called?" *The New Yorker*, 26 Sep. 2011, www.newyorker.com/magazine/2011/10/03/famous-names.
11. Eurostat. *Energy, Transport and Environment Statistics—2020 Edition.* Publications Office of the European Union, 2020, (PDF edition), (doi: 10.2785/522192).
12. Data on Distributed energy market projections were taken from the summary of the Frost and Sullivan report, "Growth Opportunities in Distributed Energy, Forecast to 2030", published on 5 May 2020, which can be found on the company's website at https://store.frost.com/growth-opportunities-in-distributed-energy-forecast-to-2030.html.

2

BRAND AS A PROMISE

MAGNUS HALL ON ENERGY COMPANIES FULFILLING EXPECTATIONS

There are mottos, aphorisms and purported quotes we hear many times without quite knowing their provenance. For instance, "What can't be measured, can't be improved".[1] I had heard it in business meetings, seminars and presentations, and in conversations with colleagues. It is sometimes attributed to Lord Kelvin. But the closest he had said—in the lecture on "electrical units of measurement" delivered to the Institution of Civil Engineers in 1883—was actually: "When you can measure what you are speaking about . . . you know something about it; but when you cannot measure it . . . your knowledge is of a meagre and unsatisfactory kind".[2]

Over the years this statement was condensed, and amalgamated with the management philosophy of the Austro-American business guru Peter Drucker. Although in its concentrated form the quote cannot be attributed to either thinker, its sentiment permeates not just the intellectual realms of Kelvin and Drucker—those of applied science and management

DOI: 10.4324/9781003351030-3

theory—but also much of social research, economics and by extension, business and marketing.

In 1990, for instance, the United Nations Development Programme (UNDP) published its first *Human Development Report*, subtitled *Concept and Measurement of Human Development*. Midwifed, among others, by world-famous economists Mahbub uh Haq and Amartya Sen, the report sought to measure development not by "the yardstick of income alone, but by a more comprehensive index". This "human development index" or HDI, reflected "life expectancy, literacy and command over the resources to enjoy a decent standard of living".[3]

Faithful to UNDP's goals of improving the common lot of humanity ("no poverty, zero hunger, good health and well-being, quality education, gender equality . . ."),[4] the authors saw the utility of collecting data as a "genuine measure of socioeconomic progress".[5] The measurements in that 1990 report revealed Sweden as number 2 on the list of countries with the highest HDI, closely behind Japan.

In the intervening 30 years much has changed in the world, not just in terms of country rankings according to the HDI—for instance, comparing the 1990 report with the 2019 report you will notice that Japan has tumbled from number 1 to 19—but, some countries have ceased to exist altogether. The world has witnessed the end of the Eastern Bloc, rampant industrial liberalisation, the reunification of Germany and the economic rise of China.

One thing that remained constant, though, has been Sweden's place in the HDI top 10, its reputation as a "socialist paradise"[6] largely unsullied. And, crucial to the economy of this nigh-perfect country, contributing around 4 per cent of the country's GDP and as many terawatthours (TWh) from its pan-European portfolio as is consumed in Sweden, stands Vattenfall, a nigh-perfect energy brand.[7]

In English *vattenfall* means "waterfall". As a name for an energy company, in this day and age, you can't really do much better than "waterfall". Consequently, when fellow Nordic energy giants Statoil and Danish Oil and Natural Gas (DONG) scrambled for new names in 2017 and 2018, hoping to remove the lingering whiff of soot tarnishing their brand-lustre[8], the branding experts at Vattenfall decided on something less radical: a tweak to the company logo. In fact, there has been no need to fundamentally reconsider the company's name since 1909, when the Royal

Waterfall Board (*Kungliga Vattenfallstyrelsen*) became the world's first state-owned power producer.[9]

But, as it will become clear from our conversation with Magnus Hall, the CEO of Vattenfall, underneath the surface of the brand, behind that impervious name, a dramatic narrative shift has happened, and that shift, or the promise contained therein, became the brand.

Now, it is perhaps far-fetched to think that the foresight of Vattenfall's founders had future-proofed the brand. More likely, the construction of the Olidan power plant at the Trollhätte falls, commenced in 1905, suggested this propitious name. And yet, is it not peculiar that this socialist paradise—also, paradoxically, a kingdom—is the home of so many world-conquering brand-names? IKEA, Volvo, H&M, Spotify—even ABBA, with its perfectly symmetrical name and line up. As the BBC reported in August 2020, it is Max Martin, a Swede, that is third only to Lennon and McCartney in the number of US number 1 hits. It is rumoured that he had discovered a set of formulas for a perfect pop song—the theory of "Melodic Math".[10]

The Swedish-born American economist Lars Sandberg talked about "*financial sophistication*" of nineteenth-century Sweden, noting that the country also had a highly literate populace. It was as a direct result of the "strikingly large stock of human and institutional capital", Sandberg hypothesised, that in the years 1850 to 1910, "Sweden had the highest rate of growth of per capita GNP and the second highest rate of growth of total GNP", among the developing European countries.[11]

The legacy of this sophisticated growth are the successful brands, nurtured by a discerning and educated population, who expect nothing less than both front-end and back-end brand compliance. In other words, both light, modern and aesthetically pleasing design, and the adherence to the highest environmental, labour and safety standards. Perhaps we could also restate it like this: the Nordic consumer has come to expect nothing short of perfection.

Yet, perfection poses its own set of challenges. Not just because you are operating in an imperfect world, where corporate indebtedness, currency crises, regulatory pressure and falling electricity demand prey on your profit margins (in 2013 Vattenfall wrote down the value of its business by $4.6 billion saying there was no recovery in sight for the European electricity markets),[12] but also because it forces you to consider the question of

BRAND AS A PROMISE

"how do you improve on perfection"? Where do you take your successful Scandinavian energy brand, when it is already in the pantheon of the world's mightiest? And how do you know you're headed the right way?

Magnus Hall describes himself as "a typical general manager type". Having completed a combined business and engineering degree at university, he started his career in the pulp and paper industry, where his father and grandfather had also worked. Coming through the marketing side of Holmen, the paper and board manufacturer, he became company CEO.

"I was able to get the most out of people", says Magnus. Having spoken to him over the years, and observed his interactions with industry and company colleagues, I can attest that he is indeed—as they say in popular management speak—"a people person". His stature, and I mean this in the literal sense for Magnus is tall even by Nordic standards, is only matched by his tact and patience. There is genuine warmth, as well as conviction in his words.

The offer to join Vattenfall came soon after he had decided to leave the pulp and paper industry for horizons new, by which point he had been the CEO of Holmen for 10 years. This was in 2014 and it turned out to be a congruous move. "I knew Vattenfall well. My company was quite a big energy consumer, and we had long term deals on buying electricity. We were very energy dependent." Indeed, according to estimates, the Swedish pulp and paper industry accounts for 50 per cent of country's annual industrial energy use.[13] Holmen alone used 4.5 TWh of electricity per year.

> As a customer, I had a special relation to energy in that respect—from an industrial perspective. But, really what I thought I knew before was nothing compared to what I learnt during the previous five years at Vattenfall. I came from a corporate culture where energy meant a lot, to an industry where energy is everything.

Reinforcing his point, Magnus continues:

> In a company such as Vattenfall you are instantly made aware that in our society, actually in any modern society, energy is the key to everything. Despite not being a tangible product as such, it has vast political and business implications—it impacts everyone's lives.

I was glad Magnus had used the word "tangible". It reminded me of coming unstuck at the very start of my PhD course at Aston Business School.

I had proposed to do a thesis on "energy branding", but was told that you could not brand energy. The thesis title, perhaps even the concept, would be misleading. Energy is a commodity, and marketing orthodoxy says that you cannot brand a commodity.

In their 800-page textbook *Marketing Management*, a sort of marketing Bible, Kotler and Keller explain that a brand differentiates a product or service from competitors in the same field, that satisfy an identical need.[14] The American Marketing Association is even clearer: a brand is "a name, term, design, symbol, or any other feature that identifies one seller's good or service as distinct from those of other sellers. The legal term for brand is trademark. A brand may identify one item, a family of items, or all items of that seller."[15]

Now, to give my tutors their due, it would indeed be difficult to trademark energy, if you think about it in the dictionary sense of the word, as the disposition of objects or substances to do work or produce heat. And yet, have we not in the last 15 to 20 years had a proliferation of companies that are very specific in offering renewable energy, intelligent energy, distributed energy, carbon-neutral energy . . . ? Fortunes were made (and lost) on such distinctions.

It turns out that, as with energy, branding too is for Magnus something not quite tangible and yet also critically, almost *morally* important. It is much less concrete than a logo, or even a symbol, but then, on the other hand, more compelling, almost more binding. It is definitely more than marketing.

> Branding is making a commitment to your customers—and to your stakeholders, and the society as a whole. And then you communicate around that and you deliver around it. That's what to me branding is really about, creating expectations, and then fulfilling them. To me the concept of branding is much more than just communicating and creating a strong energy brand towards our consumers.

I find that there is something excitingly polysemic about the word "commitment" in this context, that puts the idea of branding in a sharper relief, than if we think of it only in the sense of "loyalty". For Magnus, behind this dynamic idea of commitment—to your customers, but also to a project, a strategy—there is a promise, and the brand is the guarantor of that promise. Brand loyalty would then mean not just loyalty of customer to company and vice versa, but also a loyalty of both to a common goal, even if it was in the distant future.

Another way to understand such meaning of commitment could be through the quintessentially Swedish concept of *folkhemmet*. In 1928 the chairman of the Social Democrats, and later Prime Minister Per Albin Hansson, had launched, in a famous debate in parliament his vision of Sweden as a "people's home". The *folkhemmet*—a compelling concept of a "solidaristic society"—came to mean a few things: the period from 1932 to 1976 when the Social Democrats were in power, while also the Swedish welfare state. And much more besides: in aesthetics and design— unostentatious and egalitarian comfort, in social policy—the idea of familial cohesion and solidarity between citizens; and, importantly, a promise that the state should take care of everyone's well-being, presently and in the future.[16] It is no surprise then, that such notions should be embedded in the Royal Waterfall Board's corporate culture, for it was for many years, effectively, a state agency.

Of course, this approach to branding can never be half hearted, it cannot just stop at selling a service, or communicating its value. Magnus agrees:

> It comes with a commitment to do the whole thing, because if you create expectations that you don't fulfil, you will get a negative reaction on your branding. This will actually deteriorate the value of your business rather than improve it.

What Magnus has committed to do could be, in fact, his lasting legacy at Vattenfall. "The expectation"—as he puts it—has been summed up for the first time in the headline of Vattenfall's *Annual and Sustainability Report 2017*, which said "Fossil free living within one generation". As a tag line, it now greets visitors to group.vatenfall.com homepage, and appears in internet search results when you enter for the company's name. Hence, brand as a promise—and that promise, as Magnus points out, is now "really the brand".

There are a number of technological and economic developments which have favoured this pledge. One of them is the acceleration of offshore wind deployment over the last twenty years. The technology's downward cost trajectory and upward generating capability, its almost unlimited scope for development—there are many thousands of square kilometres of seabed available for development off the coast of northern Europe—promises cost-competitive and plentiful electricity, sufficient to phase out fossil fuels in many coastal nations, including Sweden.

The example of the UK, a world leader in offshore wind deployment, is instructive: in the third quarter of 2019, coal power stations supplied only around 1 per cent of the nation's electricity.[17] By the mid-2020s the UK plans to phase out coal altogether.

Vattenfall was an early and enthusiastic adopter of the technology. Thanet, its offshore wind farm off the coast of Kent in England, seemed to have spawned its own Hollywood blockbuster, also called "Thanet". But, in Magnus's words, there was something beyond technological savvy and readiness that was required to get people on board:

> When I joined the company, I recruited a few new people, to think-through, amongst other things, the concept of how we tell our story. Considering that the brand is not far from that, it is really what you fill it with, at the level of purpose and commitment.

Taking this new vision of a fossil-fuel free Vattenfall through the layers of management, all the way to the board, was less about convincing people, but rather about, in Magnus's phrase "onboarding".

But, did the perception of what the brand can accomplish actually change in the last few years?

> I think our purpose of "fossil free living within one generation" is being taken seriously. In the first place we see that internally, amongst our staff. Externally, we are seen as a very modern, forward-leaning company. Remember, we are very open and vocal about our commit-ment, it is now part of our brand, but we are also very open about the challenges, about what we are doing. The connection between our strategy and purpose, or between how we communicate and how we build expectations is very strong. We want our customers to feel that this company is committed to something important, and that it will ultimately be their success. If you can get that feeling with your branding you should think "Wow, that's pretty good".

In Magnus's view, which is influenced by the notion of social coherence and solidarity, of individuals and institutions working towards a common goal:

> Branding is also about making society more accepting of our [Vattenfall's] views, of the things that we want to do. If we want to build a wind

BRAND AS A PROMISE

farm in a place where some people are always opposing it, they should at least feel that this company is a reliable and honest company.

In that sense, whether you are a business-to-business (B2B) or a business-to-consumer (B2C) company should have little to do with how you build your brand.

> If you have other companies as your customers, they too want to be connected to suppliers who are strong, who have a reliable brand. This is where branding becomes broader and higher level marketing. It helps us not only in selling our products, but also in creating a good impression of our company: that we are trustworthy, reliable—that we are good citizens. These are things which are important for every company, whether you're B2B or B2C.

As it happens, that can kind of reputational spend is not difficult to justify "if there is this general belief that it is the right thing to do". The counter-vailing question then becomes "how much of the effect of good branding can be achieved with your existing communications capabilities? The com-bination of those things is probably the best", Magnus concludes. And then he remembers a further point:

> If the discussion internally is only about your marketing or brand-ing cost, and not about your beliefs about the branding process, for instance, that it will help you build a platform from which you can launch your business strategy—then you are having the wrong kind of discussion. As a guide, it is helpful to consider two things: the strength of the results and how fast you get them. If you are satis-fied with the answers, spending a reasonable amount on marketing and communications is justified. In a way, if you don't believe your branding or your marketing strategy will help you, then you will always come back to the discussion around money.

He continues on the value of rational versus emotional communication.

> I think you need a good mixture. Emotions will open up your audi-ence, so I think you need both. For example, if you are saying no to our message of "we want to make it possible for you to live without fossil fuels within one generation", then we would like to make this clear: by our pledge we really mean that when the kids born today become

parents—when they have kids of their own in 25 to 27 years—we will be there as a company to supply those fossil free solutions.

In the meantime, we don't want the children of today to worry about climate change. We, as much as other energy companies, should really concentrate on solving this climate change issue. So that is where the emotions come in, when you're talking about generations, rather than saying "by 2045 we're going to be . . ." Expressing it "within one generation . . ." makes it emotional, it connects our message to your family, to your children, and it also reflects the strength of our commitment. I think this combination is necessary.

This line of reasoning seems to be the culmination of a series of bold decisions made as soon as Magnus joined Vattenfall. In an interview given two-and-a-half months after his appointment as CEO, he said:

We have made one decision already: we've started the process of selling the lignite business in Germany. It's a considerable business: 60 TWh, 8,000 people and about 10% of German energy supply. It's about one-third of all our electricity production.[18]

It was the right the decision, as the following year Vattenfall's stock traded at a historic high. But, what about mistakes—branding mistakes? Magnus is diplomatic, but, in the final instance, confident:

I want to make sure that we don't stop communicating our milestones, things that support our purpose. My worry is that people might think we have created a greenwash thing. To be clear, we haven't fallen into that trap, it is not a mistake that we have committed, but I think it's very easy to do something like that. Therefore, we have tried to foresee what we need to concentrate on, in order not to fail. However, I don't see any big mistakes. I think it's been very well handled not so much by me, but internally.

The subtext here becomes clear as Magnus says that in the addition to supplying energy, either as electricity or heat, the world's power producers "must make it their line of business" to fight climate change. An energy company of the future should not try to be anything but green. All the resources, whether nuclear, renewable or biofuel, at the command of such an enterprise, should be geared towards eliminating the use of fossil fuels.

At which point I am reminded again of that introduction to the first *Human Development Report*, and its statement that one of the measures of human development is the "the command over the resources to enjoy a decent standard of living". That decent standard of living in the *folkhemmet* philosophy includes not just present material comfort, but also provisions for the future. These provisions ensure a life free from worry, a social-democratic ideal, for such a life is crucial to your political and social freedoms, as much as for your quality of life.

Translated to branding, this world view deems that the energy company—concerned with customers as citizens—should extend its duty of care to the next generation. It is the long view and the Swedish way. The brand in itself becomes more than a product or service, and definitely more than a trademark. It becomes a promise—a promise that the customer and all those close to them will be looked after.

I wonder, then, whether that is where we should look for the secret of so many successful Swedish brands; whether the function of that light, functional and efficient design, of that unostentatious yet appealing presentation is to transmit this message: you are safe with us. Behind this brand is someone who cares.

Notes

1. "What can't be measured, can't be improved" is chiefly attributed to three people, none of which is on the record as having said or wrote those exact words. Those who put forward Lord Kelvin as the author point to his lecture to the Institution of Civil Engineers (see note 2 below). The other person is the statistician W. Edwards Deming (see Deming, W. Edwards. *The New Economics for Industry, Government, and Education.* MIT Center for Advanced Engineering Study, 1993, p. 36: "It is wrong to suppose that if you can't measure it, you can't manage it—a costly myth"). Finally, there is Peter Drucker, the statement in question being close to his theories of management. My assumption is that Lord Kelvin's quote had been taken up by scientifically minded managerial types, who then found in Peter Drucker's theories a confirmation (rightly or wrongly) that it should be applied to business.

2. Thomson, Sir William (Lord Kelvin). *Popular Lectures and Addresses Vol. 1.* Macmillan and Co., 1889, p. 73.

3. UNDP. *Human Development Report 1990.* Oxford University Press, 1990, p. 1, https://hdr.undp.org/system/files/documents//hdr1990encompleteno statspdf.pdf.
4. A list of UNDP's sustainable development goals can be found at www. undp.org/sustainable-development-goals.
5. UNDP, *Human Development Report 1990.*
6. The debate on whether Sweden is a "socialist paradise" was given a fresh and powerful impetus, especially in America, by US senator and presidential contender Bernie Sanders in 2015. In a televised debate ahead of the 2016 presidential election, Sanders, an avowed democratic socialist, said: "I think we should look to countries like Denmark, like Sweden and Norway and learn from what they have accomplished . . ." You can find the clip titled "Bernie Sanders: Why I'm a Democratic Socialist" at edition.cnn.com/.
7. Statistics on Vatenfall's electricity production are from the company's website, subpage "Our operations", at https://group.vattenfall.com/ investors/understanding-vattenfall/our-operations.
8. Kent, Sarah. "Getting the Oil Out: Norway's Statoil Rebrands." *Wall Street Journal*, 15 Mar. 2018, wsj.com/articles/getting-the-oil-out-norways-statoil-rebrands-1521110218.
9. Information on Vatenfall's history is from the company's website at history. vattenfall.com.
10. For a nation of 10 million people, the Swedes seemed to have exerted a disproportionately powerful influence on the pop music charts. The BBC, perhaps having identified Sweden as one of Britain's chief rivals in this lucrative arena (United Kingdom's Culture Minister Nicky Morgan stated in 2019 that annual music industry exports were worth £2.7 billion), sought to understand "the Swedish Pop Formula" in a documentary titled *Flat Pack Pop: Sweden's Music Miracle.* The programme promised to uncover "centuries old Swedish customs and folklore hidden in the unlikely music of One Direction, Nicki Minaj and Justin Bieber". It was aired in 2020; the quotes are from the programme summary at bbc.co.uk/programmes/ m0002k6k.
11. Fisher, Douglas and Walter N. Thurman. "Sweden's Financial Sophistication in the Nineteenth Century: An Appraisal." *The Journal of Economic History*, Vol. 49, No. 3, Sep. 1989. Despite the accepted view that "the Swedes are good at branding", there is a dearth of academic literature examining the Swedish branding phenomenon (if there is such a thing).

BRAND AS A PROMISE

This article, which advances a more generalist approach by appraising a variant of Lars G. Sandberg's "financial sophistication hypothesis", sheds some indirect light on the issue.

12. A brief summary of Vattenfall's 2013 $4.6 billion write off can be found in Ringstrom, Anna and Geert De Clercq. "Vattenfall Writes Down $4.6 billion in Ailing Energy Market." *Reuters,* 23 Jul. 2013, www.reuters.com/article/us-vattenfall-earnings-idUSBRE96M0B920130723.

13. See Thollander, Patrick and Mikael Ottosson. "An Energy Efficient Swedish Pulp and Paper Industry—Exploring Barriers to and Driving Forces for Cost-Effective Energy Efficiency Investments." *Energy Efficiency*, Vol. 1, No. 1, pp. 21–34, (doi:10.1007/s12053-007-9001-7).

14. Kotler, Philip and Kevin Lane Keller. *Marketing Management*, 15th edition. Pearson, 2016. See Part 4, "Building Strong Brands".

15. This definition can be found on the website of the American Marketing Association, on the subpage titled "Branding", at www.ama.org/topics/branding/.

16. The concept of *folkhemmet* (eng. people's home) has received scholarly attention inside and outside Sweden commensurate to its huge importance in Swedish national life. For a brief introduction see Sunnemark, Fredrik. "Who Are We Now Then? The Swedish Welfare State in Political Memory and Identity." *Култура/Culture*, No. 5, Mar. 2014.

17. Department for Business, Energy & Industrial Strategy. "Statistical Press Release—UK Energy Statistics, Q3 2019", 19 Dec. 2019, assets.publishing.service.gov.uk/government/uploads/system/uploads/attachment_data/file/853580/Press_Notice_Q3_2019.pdf.

18. Van Renssen, Sonja and Hughes Belin. "Exclusive—New Vattenfall CEO Magnus Hall: 'What is True for Eon, Is Pretty Much True for Us'." *Energypost*, 10 Dec. 2014, https://energypost.eu/vattenfalls-new-ceo-magnus-hall-true-e-pretty-much-true-us/.

3

BUSINESS TO HUMAN

RYAN O'KEEFFE ON THE VIEW FROM A SEVEN TRILLION DOLLAR FUND

While I was writing this chapter I spoke to a relative. We were catching up on family matters. He asked what I was doing and I replied that I was writing a book. "What kind of book?", he asked. I said it was a collection of essays, based on interviews with energy executives, from some of the world's biggest companies.

"That's interesting", he said, "and how's this book going?" "Good" I replied, "just now I'm writing up the interview with Ryan O'Keeffe, a Managing Director at BlackRock." "BlackRock? Never heard of them." "Well, it's the world's largest investment fund—managing over seven trillion dollars on behalf of their clients." He paused for a second. "No, you must mean seven billion. Seven billion dollars . . ." "No, I don't", I said, "I mean seven trillion dollars". "But, that is impossible. That is seven thousand billion. The GDP of Germany is not quite 4 trillion." "Yes, I know. But, seven trillion is what BlackRock manages in assets." "It can't be true", he insisted, "why don't you check again? It's probably seven billion." "No, it isn't", I said. The discussion went on for a while longer.

DOI: 10.4324/9781003351030-4

To be fair, if you trawl the internet on BlackRock you are bound to read, sooner or later, that it is "the most powerful company you have never heard of".[1] Thinking about its enormous asset holdings—or as they are technically known "assets under management"—you are squarely in the realm of the hyperbolic and the scarcely believable.

To give an example: seven trillion US dollars is not just more than the GDP of Germany, or even Japan, it is more than the combined GDP of the 150 countries (out of 195) at the lower end of the world's GDP rankings.[2] Or, to put it this way: according to the World Gold Council, by the year 2020 an estimated 187,200 tonnes of gold had been mined since the dawn of civilisation. BlackRock's asset holdings, according to today's gold prices are worth 115,064 tonnes, or over 60 per cent of the gold that has ever been mined.[3] To make it all the more fanciful, the world's top ten "money managers"—of which BlackRock is number one—had by the end of 2018 just under 27 trillion dollars of assets under management.

Even the name BlackRock conjures mythic caches of wealth, power and influence. Perhaps contrary to what is expected of a branding expert, I don't believe that company names are decidedly important to its success (it is rather what you do with the name that matters), and yet, somehow, I doubt that the world's biggest asset manager could ever be called *PurpleCottonBud*. The forcefulness of those capitals "B" and "R", the two monosyllabic words joined together—each one projecting seriousness, solidity and hard intent, as if forming an impregnable rampart adjoined by two vigilant watchtowers—means Business with a capital "B".

In his book *Microstyle: The Art of Writing Little*, Christopher Johnson—former Professor of Practice of Communication at the University of Washington, linguist and a verbal branding consultant known as "the Name Inspector"—draws a distinction between two types of rhythmic contrasts in speech and writing. Most metrical units, meaning groups of syllables, are either *iambs* or *trochees*. Johnson writes:

> Iambs consist of an unstressed syllable followed by a stressed one (dee DUM); and trochees . . . consist of a stressed syllable followed by an unstressed one (DUM dee). Iambs tend to sound lighter and softer, and trochees tend to sound heavier and harder. This is true even in messages as short as brand names. "Feminine" brand names, like Chanel, are often iambs; "masculine" ones, like Black and Decker,

tend to be trochees. Most people "feel" this difference even if they find it hard to pinpoint.[4]

To Johnson, who was also a language data researcher on Amazon's Alexa AI team—focusing on Alexa's ability to interpret contextual references—there is a certain degree of inevitability to how we order syllables, and how we then use those metric units in speech to emphasise points and create mood. His example of why we normally say "salt and pepper", rather than "pepper and salt" shows that "rhythm that characterises poetry also forms part of normal speech. In 'salt and pepper', emphasised syllables alternate with de-emphasised syllables. That's a sort of default rhythm that we fall back on when we're not thinking much about it. It's the path of least resistance, so to speak, for English."[5]

And then there is the historical dimension to a name, a layer of meaning, evolving from an idea into a syntactic mould. In an interview on CNBC in 2017 Steve Schwarzman, the co-founder of Blackstone Group—an early investor in BlackRock, when the new company was called Blackstone Financial—said Larry Fink, the founder of BlackRock, wanted a "family name with 'black' in it". Schwarzman then recalled how Fink suggested the new name for his business should be either "BlackPebble or BlackRock".[6] Predictably, and in accordance with Johnson's conjectures, it was to be the latter.

As there was an inevitability to the name, so there was an inevitability to the rise of the asset manager giga-investors, in the energy sector and elsewhere. In Chapter 1 we have seen how liberalisation separated energy companies from their national-government owners. EU legislation choked off budgetary support. State owned banks, too, were scrutinised for soft loans. It was all for a good cause: the legislative drive to break up telecommunications and energy monopolies was intended to give customers a better deal. There was also the matter of shifting energy off the governments' balance sheets: in any given year the investment in electricity infrastructure across the EU could be $100 billion. When you add mergers and acquisitions (but not the cost of fuels), R&D and other sundry costs, you could be looking at over $150 billion.[7]

Regardless, however, of whether this legislative programme was successful or not, there was a consequence. Cast adrift from their traditional patrons, energy companies, had to look elsewhere for project support. Notoriously capital-intensive, often difficult to build and operate, and with payback periods stretching 10 to 20 years, the hydro-electric dams and offshore wind farms, the coal-fired stations and gas plants needed a new type of investor. Such projects required a big spender, plugged into transnational flows of cash, highly liquid and entrepreneurial.

Liberalisation of the energy sector, in parallel with trading arrangements that increased market liquidity—such as the London Stock Exchange's Big Bang in 1986—set a trend that culminated in the part-sale of Danish Oil and North Sea Gas (DONG), now Orsted, to Goldman Sachs in 2014.

As the report by the Working Group on Infrastructure Finance, convened in 2016 by New York University's Stern School of Business, pointed out:

> Government budgetary pressures have given rise to various innovative finance structures allowing for a greater private-sector role in constructing and operating large-scale public service projects. Such public-private partnerships (PPPs), pioneered by European governments took the form of build operate transfer (BOT), build-own-operate (BOO), and design-build-finance-operate (DBFO) arrangements.[8]

And with flows of capital came the flow of human resources. Ryan O'Keeffe—a Managing Director in BlackRock's London office—worked alternately in both finance and energy. His boyish good looks, and enthusiasm for branding and public communications, belie his experience of 20 years in the energy and finance sectors. He sounds as if he only got started. Describing his professional interests he says:

> In my career there was a lot of diversity of perspective, but certainly my passion is about telling stories, and about mobilizing and influencing the direction of travel of the world. And there are many ways in which you can do that and there are many different seats from which you can do that.

He speaks with the confidence and self-assurance that might be a natural consequence of occupying senior managerial positions throughout his career. But there is also humility, characteristic of those who approach their work with an open mind. His demeanour, personal and polite, reveals a likeable man, in charge of his high-profile job. Prior to joining BlackRock, Ryan served as group director of communications at the Enel Group.

That is how we first met—I was intrigued by his efforts to internationalise Enel's brand, his ideas easing a somewhat conservative, multinational, yet ultimately Italo-focused company into its role on the global stage. An alumnus of the University of Edinburgh, Ryan is an engaging conversationalist, his good humour and focus reassuring, given his role in the control room of the world economy.

He describes himself as a "communications leader", and to this appellation his Twitter profile adds "digital brand-builder, keen sportsman and nature conservationist". Of his time at Enel, Ryan says this:

> One of the most valuable attributes I was able to bring to the Enel executive committee was, first of all, not being Italian. You have to remember that, regardless of the fact that the company is a global leader and present in 40 countries world-wide, it still is a very Italian organisation.

He adds:

> If you went outside of Italy, back in 2014 when I joined the organisation, not many people would have heard of Enel because the Enel brand was not really used in other countries. We addressed that head-on in the 2015 rebranding of the group, because the reality is that Enel delivers light and power to half a billion people around the world. In that context, a non-Italian director of communications, with both professional expertise and an international perspective, was what the chief executive was expressly searching for.

As a South African who has also lived and worked in the UK, US and Europe, Ryan summarises his contribution by saying that he was able "to bring communications and corporate positioning practices from around the world into Enel".

In a contemporary and multinational corporate environment, promoting diversity of views at board level is seen not just as a social obligation, but as sensible commercial practice. The EU's top down, directive-driven market reform programme—the energy sector's slow motion Big Bang—has resulted in "national champion(s)" being superseded "by a few big European players present in several countries", as Leonardo Meeusa *et al.* write in their 2005 article "Development of the Internal Electricity Market in Europe".[9]

They add that "since the collapse of Enron there has been a move away from light asset companies and towards companies that integrate generation with supply activities and also companies that integrate gas supply activities with electricity". The authors call this trend "consolidation and re-verticalization".

In other words, both regulators and consumers now want a liberalised energy market, with ample scope for competition, entrepreneurship and cost-reduction, yet they also want to see powerful energy brands actually doing things: building generating assets, producing electricity, maintaining infrastructure and galvanising development capital. For a communication, marketing or branding professional this poses a specific requirement of joining a project from the outset, to ensure it has *substance*; in a sense, being not just a branding expert, facing a *post-festum* task of slapping a name and a logo on a finished artefact, but also being a development catalyst. This is a task Ryan faced with the launch of *Enel X*.

> With Enel X we were building a new global sub-brand for Enel. Now, it is worth noting that as recently as the 1990s or early 2000s, the argument was that there was no such thing as a global utility, because "a utility" was a fundamentally local thing: you generated electricity, you distributed it down your power lines, and then it went into people's homes. All of this happens at a local, or perhaps regional level. Generally speaking, the only way to think about a global utility was as the sum of lots of little local utilities. Enel X, then, was from the outset more than just a new brand. It was the best expression of how Enel was leading the energy services business into the future.

That vision included the roll out of new infrastructure networks, such as smart charging points for electric vehicles, and decentralised energy systems for homes and businesses. In that sense Enel X is a statement of priority.

> As a brand, Enel X has made the future visible to all of our 65,000 employees around the world, as well as to the ecosystem around the organisation, including to our regulators and clients. It was there to show everyone how the energy sector was going to change and what we needed to do to prepare for that.

Given the worldwide consensus on what is needed in the energy sector—more renewables, more distributed resources, smarter grids, more electrification of transport, more energy efficiency—it is not altogether surprising that, across different business cultures, and across the industries of finance

BUSINESS TO HUMAN　37

and energy, there is a degree of convergence in the soft sciences of branding and marketing.

Asked about the branding culture at Enel versus the one he encountered at BlackRock, Ryan says:

> We use exactly the same language. I found that the way that I talk about brand is the way that BlackRock talks about brand as well, and that everybody at BlackRock was very much aligned with my thinking. There are, of course, many cultural differences between Enel and BlackRock, some of which are rooted in the Italian and Anglo-Saxon cultures, and some of which are specific to those two individual organisations. For instance, decision making at Enel was fairly hierarchical. At BlackRock it is exactly the opposite—nothing is done unless you have fifteen people, figuratively speaking, who all agree on "the way forward". But from a branding perspective I don't see anything significant—in both cases, the company embraces the brand as the expression of who we are, what we do and how we do it.

That there should be no fundamental difference in how multinational companies process their branding is not just down to a broad consensus on development agendas. It has also been ascribed to the phenomenon of "global brand architecture"—how each trans-national company negotiates global expansion versus local adaption.

As Talay *et al.* write in *Global Brand Architecture Position and Market-Based Performance: The Moderating Role of Culture*: while local, or single-market brands appeal to patriotism and ethnocentrism, "mounting evidence seems to support the notion that global brands act as a quality signal". For instance, in Eastern European markets "global brands have been found to be perceived as a passport to global citizenship".[10]

The statistical evidence presented in the article seems to prove that, even discounting for a host of other seemingly relevant variables, the companies with higher-level *global brand architecture* (GBA)—those with not just regional, or multi-regional, but global branding strategies—are able to capture more market share. But, with the proviso that "cultural values moderate the signals brands send". I find this kind of numerical research exciting, as it points out to another factor in the inexorable spread of global brands, and, by extension, to the importance of good branding.

We have seen at the start, following Christopher Johnson's work, that there is a sort of "natural" logic, or an everyday aesthetic, at work in the collateral of a strong brand. We have also seen that the three fundamental forces acting on any company, the forces of technology, markets, and regulation are also important enablers to the rise of strong brands. But, it also seems that once brand development gathers momentum, it is as if the very energy of that development is pushing the brand forward.

In other words, if at first the company is pushing the brand, then, at some point, the brand will start pulling the company. As a brand goes through progressively higher levels of GBA it reaches the marketing equivalent of escape velocity, until it is ensconced in the pantheon of global brands; or, as Talay and his collaborators simply conclude "progressive positions through the GBA engender higher levels of market share".[11]

There is something close to scientific determinism at work here. Equal starting conditions will return the same results. But, as we all know, not all companies are the same. Neither are brands. In a roundabout way, we are back to the seven-trillion-dollar question.

"BlackRock's scale and reach give it an unparalleled ability to drive a positive impact in the world", says Ryan. "To give you an example: in many places today we have aging populations—older, on average, than the generations before them. And we have a greater burden placed upon people in work today by those currently retired." He continues:

> In Europe particularly, our populations are under-invested, with too much money "sleeping" in savings accounts, rather than working hard to help fund people's retirement in the future. I think there is a huge job to be done to get the world to a place where everybody is able to retire into old age with dignity, and I don't think the magnitude of this task is fully appreciated. It is a huge challenge for governments, for civil society, for the private sector . . . Particularly as the onus is moving from the employer to the employee to take responsibility for this.

He sounds emphatic: "BlackRock is uniquely positioned—and therefore has a huge responsibility to its clients and to society—to play its part in tackling this problem."

Which then raises the question of how BlackRock—a company of such resources, reach and responsibility—remains under the radar, a company "you have never heard of". Particularly, as the evolution of BlackRock's brand closely followed the growth of the company. "The asset management business model is B2B, so our brand visibility is very high amongst the investor community, but asset managers are less visible to the man or woman on the street."

Ryan reminds me it was the 2009 acquisition of Barclays Global Investors that had transformed the company's profile. It was reported at the time as a "blockbuster deal", Reuters observing that for BlackRock "a 21-year-old company which relied heavily on acquisitions to grow from a one-room bond investment firm into the largest publicly traded US money manager, the deal will more than double assets to roughly \$2.7 trillion". The company was turning into a global brand, going through the higher levels of GBA. Geoff Bobroff, a leading consultant to money managers and mutual funds, was quoted in the same article as saying: "This gives BlackRock a global footprint which is a substantial thing to have in these markets."[12]

Ryan says that the company's brand profile is in "a very different dimension to how it was seen even just 10 years ago". He continues:

> BlackRock today has the most extraordinary brand profile. It was interesting this morning—I was at an industry event. There was a discussion and I asked a question. As soon as you say that you work at BlackRock, people immediately pay attention. They turned around and looked . . . We are seen as an agenda-setting organization, and that is brand!

At which point I started to think that this could be the finest example of B2B branding I had ever come across. So carefully and precisely tailored that everyone in your line of business sits up when you speak, without the man on the street ever having heard of you. Ryan, however, would have none of it.

> B2B, B2C, B2G—these are all wrong. It's the wrong way to think about corporate branding. The way to think about it is B2H: business to human. These are all human beings that you're trying to communicate with. Don't worry about whether they are consumers, or the business they work for is a client, or they work in a government or as a regulator. They are all people, and so corporate brand-building has to be about engaging human beings. That is what we are all doing.[13]

Every business needs to deliver a value to society, it must have a social purpose. It has to invest in and protect its social license to operate. That is the best way to deliver value to your shareholders, to your clients, to your employees, and to everybody in your ecosystem. And that is what branding is about, not whether you are B2B or something else.

"Business to human" sounded buzzwordy, so I wondered where Ryan had heard it first.

I honestly do not remember who first showed it to me, but it was when I was at Enel, taking the group through the rebranding. And when I heard it, it was just so obviously right. A few years later a colleague tried to tell me that a particular piece of research we were publishing was for a B2B audience, and so there was no need to think about making it warmer, simpler and more accessible.

I thought, "What a short-sighted thing to say!" B2C, B2G and B2B might describe a business model, but we only ever communicate with people. And everyone likes warm, elegantly articulated and nicely presented content. It doesn't matter if you're communicating on behalf of an energy company, an investment manager or an automotive manufacturer. Every single one of your stakeholders is a human being. It's so much easier and simpler—and therefore more powerful and impactful— to think about your comms and branding work in those terms.

In my work as an expert on branding, I too have heard the mantra that B2B communication is of second-grade importance—just as I have heard many times from clients that it is difficult to justify spending on brand, or that it is not a priority. On these points Ryan sounds combative.

I actually find it hard to believe that a CEO of a successful company would ever say something so misguided. I mean, you're destroying value in your business if you're ignoring your brand. You're destroying value for your shareholders, for your employees, for your clients . . . From an investor's perspective, deciding to buy or sell is based on a belief that a company is fundamentally over or under-valued— and the brand informs the perceptions that drive those beliefs. It is about expressing who you are as a company, what you do, and how you do it. So if you can successfully articulate that what the business does is important and will continue to be in demand; and if it's done sustainably, in the true sense of the word—that it will be sustained over time, because it is profitable and fairly delivered to all stakeholders—then your brand becomes a key driver of enterprise value.

Perhaps, following this understanding of business value, a justification of branding-spend, for those who need it, can be found in the framework provided by Gini Dietrich's PESO model of public communication. Ryan reminds me that, according to this model, there are four types of communication channels open to any communicator, regardless whether they work for a global multi-national, the government, an investment fund, an NGO, a small business or an individual. These channels are paid, earned, shared and owned (PESO).[14]

But can any message, can any signal work across these channels, if not supported by a strong brand? Can there be a unifying theme, a direction, can there be any global brand architecture—meaning a coherent growth plan—without an agreement on brand strategy? Importantly, can there be long-term value, or long-term profitability? Can there be sustainability?

The commercial value put on a company is actually a material expression of values invested in the brand—company value equals brand values externalised. These values are based on such feelings, as Johnson puts it, that we find "hard to pinpoint". They are also values we, as societies, attempt to embody in technological development, legislation and business acumen. Even if we have never heard of a brand, we can still feel it.

Notes

1. From Florida (Rogers, Brad. "BlackRock: The Most Powerful Company You've Never Heard of." *Ocala StarBanner*, 8 Jul. 2018. www.ocala. com/story/opinion/columns/more-voices/2018/07/08/shawn-mccoy-blackrock-most-powerful-company-youve-never-heard-of/11574330007/) to Bangkok (AFP. "A Look at Global Investment Juggernaut BlackRock." *Bangkok Post*, 3 Jan. 2020. www.bangkokpost.com/world/1828099/a-look-at-global-investment-juggernaut-blackrock), the internet seems to be in agreement that the trophy should go to BlackRock.

2. Country GDP rankings are based on International Monetary Fund data published on the organisation's website imf.org, subpage "GDP, Current Prices", www.imf.org/external/datamapper/NGDPD@WEO/OEMDC/ ADVEC/WEOWORLD.

3. World Gold Council holds a wealth of intriguing numbers about this coveted precious metal at *gold.org,* including the fact that "over 90 per cent of the world's gold has been mined since the California Gold Rush".

4. Johnson, Christopher. *Microstyle: The Art of Writing Little.* W. W. Norton & Company, 2012, p. 130. Johnson also publishes a fascinating blog, thenameinspector.com, where he discusses, among other things, 37 company names: from Amazon and Apple, to YouTube and Zumobi.

5. Ibid, p. 129.

6. Belvedere, Matthew J. "Blackstone or BlackRock, Confused? CEOs Steve Schwarzman and Larry Fink Actually Did it on Purpose." *CNBC,* 22 Jun. 2017. www.cnbc.com/2017/06/22/blackstone-or-blackrock-schwarzman-and-fink-did-it-on-purpose.html.

7. See here European Parliament, Directorate-General for Internal Policies of the Union, Yearwood, J., Van Nuffel et al., *European Energy Industry Investments,* European Parliament, 2017. data.europa.eu/doi/10.2861/29209. The report quotes International Energy Agency data on "electricity utility investment" in the EU for 2014 and 2015 at between $90 and $100 billion. The consultancy Ernst and Young quotes total "deal value" in Europe's power and utilities sector in 2018 at $126.5 billion. See "European M&A Propels 2018 Power and Utilities Deal Value to All-Time High." *EY,* 19 Feb. 2019. ey.com/en_nl/news/2019/02/european-m-and-a-propels-2018-power-and-utilities-deal-value-to-all-time-high.

8. Walter, Ingo (ed.). *The Infrastructure Finance Challenge, A Report by the Working Group on Infrastructure Finance.* Open Book Publishers, 2016, pp. 55–56, (doi:10.11647/OBP.0106).

9. Meeusa, Leonardo *et al.* "Development of the Internal Electricity Market in Europe." *The Electricity Journal,* Vol. 18, No. 6, July 2005, pp. 25–35, (doi:10.1016/j.tej.2005.06.008).

10. Talay, M. Berk et al. "Global Brand Architecture Position and Market-Based Performance: The Moderating Role of Culture." *Journal of International Marketing,* Vol. 23, No. 2 (2015), pp. 55–72, (doi:10.1509/jim.13.0164). The article posits four hypotheses on the performance of global, multiregional and regional brands across each of Geert Hofstede's cultural dimensions

of power distance, individualism, masculinity and uncertainty avoidance. It then tests those hypotheses statistically.

11. *Ibid.*

12. Herbst-Bayliss, Svea. "BlackRock to Buy BGI, Becomes Top Asset Manager." *Reuters*, 12 June 2009. reuters.com/article/us-blackrock-barclays-idUSTRE 55B06X20090612.

13. The expression "business to human (B2H)" seems to have originated around the turn of the century. The first online reference I could find dates from 2002, and can be found on marcusevans-conferences-australian. com, on a web-page advertising a seminar on "Content Marketing and Brand Equity". It is used in the sentence: "Exploring the future of branding and how to position B2H (Business to Human) into your company".

14. If you are interested in Gini Dietrich's PESO model of public communication there is no better place to start than Ms. Dietrich's website spinsucks.com.

4

THE SOUND OF BRAND

MICHAEL BOUMENDIL ON THE NEXT FRONTIER IN BRAND COLLATERAL

In 1981 Raymond Carver—hailed as one of the great American writers of the previous century—published a wonderful collection of short stories, *What We Talk About When We Talk About Love*. That book, I hasten to add, is not about branding. In the short story that gave the collection its name, now considered a classic example of the form, Carver describes a group of friends talking about love, over a couple of bottles of gin.

In keeping with this elusive subject, the examples of love they proffer in boozy conversation might strike you as mad, touching or profound. Rather than steer his characters towards any kind of agreement, Carver shows that when we talk about love, we could even be contradicting our earlier selves. We could be running in circles, or discovering something new.[1]

Preparing to write about the work of Michael Boumendil I kept going back in my mind to the title of that book. In the light of my academic and professional preoccupations, I hope I will be excused for repeatedly asking myself "What do we talk about when we talk about branding?" Do we talk about branding collateral, the representations of the brand in the media?

DOI: 10.4324/9781003351030-5

Usually, they are the brand's logo, colours, typeface and other aspects of the company's visual identity. For many consumers, and a fair number of business people, the logo is the brand.

Or, do we talk about something we could refer to as *branding philosophy*, an attempt to conceptualise branding as an activity in its own right? This offshoot of marketing theory was given a strong impetus in 1955, with the publication of Gardner and Levy's seminal article "The Product and the Brand".[2] What that article had claimed now seems obvious: that in cases where differences between products are hard to discern, consumers make purchasing decisions based on brand.

In their famous example of six different marketing slogans appended to six different brands of detergent, the authors point out that the products not only fulfil the same function, but they are described in very similar ways. All the slogans, ranging from 6 to 16 words in length, used, for instance, the word "whiter".

Product-marketing cannot then, on its own, account for purchasing decisions. Talking about differentiation further in the article Gardner and Levy mention "other dimensions . . . perhaps of greater importance" and develop their idea that the net result of marketing is "a public image, a character or personality that may be more important for the over-all status (and sales) of the brand than many technical facts about the product".[3]

In conceptually separating product and brand the work of Gardner and Levy had a far-reaching impact on all three constituencies of the marketing business: consumers, businesses and marketers themselves. To describe brands, we now use such attributes as established, aspirational, international, reliable, staid, conservative and many others, over and above those used for their products.

Equally influential was the authors' advice in favour of "long-term investment in the reputation of the brand". As Levy said five years later in his article "Symbols for Sale", honing the ideas from that earlier article, "People buy things not only for what they can do, but also for what they mean."[4]

The question, then, is which aspect of branding does Boumendil's work lean towards? Is he an aesthete or a philosopher, or as so many Frenchmen, a bit of both? With Gallic intensity he says that when, as a teenager (for he was 19 at the time) he hit on the idea of creating a new form of communication for brands, based around their own musical expression or sonic identity, the notion seemed crazy, even unrealistic. Regardless, he went on to form Sixieme Son, a branding agency committed solely to harnessing the emotional and functional power of sound, but not through songs or melodies. Rather, for their corporate clients Boumendil and his team create sonic signatures, short acoustic flourishes that could perhaps best be described as audio logos.

And business is good. As sound quality improved on mobile phones and laptops, audio file storage became more convenient, and internet connectivity spread, Boumendil expanded *Sixieme Son* to a staff of fifty, servicing clients such as Renault, Michelin and AXA.[5] But, it was not just the winds of technology that puffed up the sails of this teenage branding enthusiast. There is also now a universal expectation that when we engage with an electronic device, visual and sound-emitting functionality should go together. Not just in the sense that a product, such as an app, should have a characteristic "ping", but that a company should be able to project itself through sound, across all the various electronic platforms and means of customer engagement.

It is worth reminding ourselves of Gardner and Levy's conceptual separation of product from brand. Sixieme Son does not design pleasing sounds for sound-emitting products. It also does not compose theme songs. As Boumendil puts it he takes the "branding approach", rather than the "musical approach". Finally, the agency does more than transpose the brand's visual collateral into the medium of sound—although that would be work enough. What qualifies Sixieme Son as a branding agency and Boumendil as one of marketing's innovators is his quest for "consistency, coherence and competitive edge when brands are using sound and music to create a relationship with people". If you are a business, he continues, "audio branding is a way to express who you are, with the view of making the brand stronger".

"That is why I created the concept", explains Boumendil. "It was not music to me. It was not brand music. It was branding through audio." His claim to be a progenitor is boosted by the fact that, traditionally—by the nature of available technology—branding collateral was visual. It was a mark, a seal, a schematic, a letter or sequence of letters, and then a combination of letters or words, with a stylised image.

Archaeological and textual evidence places some of the first examples of what we would now recognise as brands in Ancient Greece. As professor

THE SOUND OF BRAND   47

Diana Twede writes in her article "Commercial Amphoras: The Earliest Consumer Packages?", cross-Mediterranean trade in wine, olive oil and processed foods such as fish sauce, dating from 1500 BC to 500 AD, necessitated packaging that "served as 'silent salesmen' to convey information about the contents' origin, type, and grade. Many identified the merchant". She writes that "like brand markings today, the symbol system was understood and appreciated by consumers in order to facilitate sales".[6]

We know from the ancient wine trade that these proto-brands were not just product markings, but part of a reputation-management protocol. For instance, in classical Athens, wine from Thasos was prized for its quality. Classical scholar James Davidson writes:

> A series of inscriptions from the island reveal that political intervention in the wine trade could be intense and far reaching. The overall concern of the laws seems to be for quality, a consideration which benefited not only Thasian consumers of Thasian wine, but exporters too, whose success depended on maintaining the island's reputation for high standards.[7]

Chios, which according to Twede "produced the most famous of all Greek wines" was so protective of the "distinctive and slender . . . trademark shape" of its amphoras that it appeared on the island's coins.

As in the West, so in the East. In their article "A Brief History of Branding in China" Giana M. Eckhardt and Anders Bengtsson claims that the "first recorded complete, symbolic brand was developed in the Song Dynasty (960–1127)".[8] The White Rabbit brand of sewing needles, owned by the Liu family needles' store in the city of Jinan, came with a logo—representing a white rabbit crushing herbs in a pestle—a slogan, and an assortment of branding collateral, including branded packaging paper, and what we now recognise as advertising flyers.

Meanwhile back in Europe, emerging out of the hiatus of the early Middle Ages, long distance trade picked up. To indicate provenance, merchants and guilds started using marks on products, evolved out of ancient Nordic Runes (heraldic symbols deemed unsuitable for commercialisation).

> One theory is that in early times some kind of mark was fixed on the ridge pole of a house as magical protection. By degrees this

house-mark came to be regarded as the personal mark of the owner of the house. Later, it was used as an ownership of mark on his goods and chattels. If he engaged in trade it was natural that he should use the mark to identify his goods. In addition to proclaiming the ownership of goods, the mark came to stand for the integrity of the merchant and the quality of his goods. It was, in fact, the forerunner of the modern trade-mark.[9]

Put this way, the concept of "brand-magic" attains a whole new layer of meaning. It is obvious that, given technological limitations, these merchants of old could have only used visual symbols. But, were they able, would they have used sound? In other words, what does sound add to the brand? Is the innovation in the medium, or in some other dimension of brand experience?

Boumendil says that sound makes "the brand experience more appealing, richer". He talks about the "strong emotional message . . . that can be true to the identity". As an illustration he gives a fascinating energy-sector example of how audio branding can convey more than words of pictures:

> Think about how sound and music was used in energy marketing. As a rule, it was very powerful as energy meant power. But, I believe that today energy is more about empowering people than simply about supplying power. Secondly, if you are talking about the future of the planet, it also means that you are talking about proper use of the planet's resources. And when you have music that is big, powerful, played by a large orchestra, your customers could associate that with waste and extravagance. That would not reflect well on your business.

In lieu of explanation, Boumendil continues:

> The perception that you are using sounds wastefully or extravagantly, will lead your customers consciously or unconsciously to doubt your management of your energy resources. That is what I mean by coherence and consistency. Sound is a means of creating emotional confidence in people. There are things that a brand needs to say, but cannot say it with words, nor with pictures. It can only say it with sound.

THE SOUND OF BRAND   49

I find Boumendil's assertion that music and sound leverage "emotional confidence"—as opposed to something we could term "intellectual confidence", derived from the power of argument and persuasion—in keeping with some of the recent findings on how we are affected by sound. In his book *Musicophilia—Tales of Music and the Brain*, Oliver Sacks writes:

> Listening to music is not just auditory and emotional, it is motoric as well: "We listen to music with our muscles", as Nietzsche wrote. We keep time to music, involuntarily, even if we are not consciously attending to it, and our faces and postures mirror the narrative of the melody, and the thoughts and feelings it provokes.[10]

For these reasons, music has become such an important part of any marketing campaign that a whole cottage industry has sprung around pitching, licensing, composing and—to use a trade term—syncing musical compositions to visual content. It also explains why business are prepared to pay considerable sums of money to get the right song behind a product. As *The Seattle Times* reported in 1995, Microsoft was rumoured to have paid The Rolling Stones $12 million (equivalent to $20.5 million in 2020) for the right to use the song "Start Me Up" in the Windows 95 launch campaign.[11]

But, what Boumendil has in mind is beyond simply matching the right song to the right product. That is why the concept of brand coherence figures in his work—especially as content-sharing platforms such as YouTube, Instagram and Facebook continue to proliferate and attract users. "If a brand has content all over the internet, without a clear tool to say who they are, meaning, an audio signature that works across all the different platforms, they run a risk of appearing incoherent. This is a particularly strong risk for energy brands."

The reason for the added risk is that energy companies are negotiating not just the changing digital media landscape, but at the same time a deep transformation in all areas of their business: from how they generate electricity to how they relate to consumers. "These transformations in the energy business should be part of the vocabulary of the brand, especially to show that their change is beyond cosmetic—that it is real and long lasting. In a word, that it is a change that could be trusted."

It is at this point, in executing such an abstract brief, that Sixieme Son's approach decisively parts ways with those of musicians and composers:

> When considering audio branding many companies supply a music brief. That is a mistake and our biggest challenge. An audio branding brief should start from the brand. When you send your music brief to composers, they will, naturally, try to compose music that will please you.

But, as Boumendil insists, "I'm not here to please you. I'm here to create value for your brand and your customers."

Clearly, adding value to the brand is a rather different process than composing a piece of music. While an artist might hope for a stroke of inspiration, Sixieme Son takes a more business-like approach:

> We have developed a methodology that measures a set of parameters, with the ultimate aim of getting the brand closer and more familiar to the consumer. Whether our client is Renault, Samsung or Coca-Cola we would start by clarifying what aspects of the brand they aim to strengthen. The second part of our research methodology complements the first. With IPSOS we have developed a barometer that assesses consumers' views on around 100 brands, which gives us our own sense of how effective we can be in creating a competitive edge. And finally, we would research customer brand-experience at point of contact.

Boumendil gives two examples of how audio branding can improve customer/brand interaction:

> If you call a brand's customer centre, you might be put on hold. Our research tells us that what people hear during those seconds or minutes, impacts both their experience and opinion of the brand. That is logical. Now also imagine that you are queuing, for instance, to get into Disney World. The right combination of sound and visuals will influence your perception of how long you have waited to get in. If you are entertained while in the queue, although you were waiting for an hour, it might seem like 25 minutes. We constantly update our research to see how effective we are at improving such interactions through audio branding.

There is also a sense that audio signatures are gaining in importance, because they now feature prominently in people's homes. We hear them not just via smartphones and television sets (Boumendil claims that audio logos are particularly effective at diverting our attention back to the TV screen, in case we have stopped paying attention), but also increasingly through devices such as Amazon's Alexa and Google Home. The number of smart speaker users in the US alone is approaching 100 million, with annual percentage growth in double digits.[12] Boumendil's view is that, when to these technological trends we add anecdotal evidence of people walking around with earphones and headphones, sounds are gaining in prominence as tools of communication, at the expense of written words.

Energy companies are not spared these changes. Boumendil notices major shifts in how energy company CEO's view the work of his agency now, compared to 25 years ago when he founded Sixieme Son. As much as taking his work more seriously, his clients are more discerning:

> There is an acceleration of interest in what we do, but also in how we do it. To give you an example, whereas before energy company CEOs would be simply interested in having an audio brand, now they are interested in having a sound that is right for them.
>
> They are also more aware of the pitfalls of using music that is either out there, or composed just to appeal aesthetically to the listener. If you use something off the shelf, you could be using something that is stylistically similar to another brand. And it is also worth mentioning that with some of these astronomical music licensing fees, you are just making the superstar richer, when you could be reinvesting that money in improving your relationship with your customers.

Asked about examples of corporate inertia when it comes to branding, with many companies claiming "it is not for them" (as every branding consultant has heard more than once) Boumendil is adamant that "branding is for everyone". He insists that his work is more democratic and affordable, than the traditional methods of advertising and branding agencies, which sync sound and music from external sources. As proof, he says that his clients are not just for multinational corporations, but also, for example, health care providers. At the other end of the scale in terms of client size, Sixieme Son is part of a project developing an app for the visually impaired. The client, a company in the UK, has ten employees.

THE SOUND OF BRAND

There is another reason Boumendil believes we should all be listening on the topic of audio branding: given the subconscious power of sound, what we think we know about its effect on behaviour, might actually be wrong. He quotes Sixieme Son's research completed for a Canadian client on how people react to the human voice:

> The research subject was vocal identity from a branding point of view. It overlapped with some of the neuro-scientific research in the field of audio perception. It was conducted in French and in English, and regardless of the language spoken, we found something surprising. It seems that people react less to those voices they prefer hearing.
>
> In other words, you are more likely to respond to a call to action, such as "click on this link", if you prefer the voice less. Now when you think about it, it stops being surprising. Voices we prefer make us feel comfortable, but it's not comfort that makes you act. Actually, what motivates us is the opposite of comfort, perhaps when something takes you a little bit out of your comfort zone.

Boumendil says this has huge significance in terms of how you cast voices in your marketing campaign. "In our study potential customers said that they preferred the female voice. And I am sure they did. But when we looked at which voice triggered better results, it was the male voice."

"Touché!", concludes Boumendil. "This takes us back to my earlier argument that when thinking about music and sound in branding, there is a view that they should be pleasant. My approach is that we should start from an understanding of what works for the brand."

Going back to Sidney Levy, we can see how his thinking evolved, just as branding itself. In his essay "Marketing and Aesthetics" published in 1974 he writes that the marketing ideal should be the Functional-Psychosocial-Aesthetic pyramid. This grandly named theoretical construct seeks to unite purpose of marketed object, with its human audience and its impact on the senses.

Similarly, as it must, Michael Boumendil's work draws on science, art and branding philosophy. It is taking an activity perhaps as old as trade itself, into the future.

In one of his last essays, co-authored with Wilson Bastos, Levy—a true believer in the power of branding—poetically wrote:

Branding is exciting and alluring, it is a challenge to creativity; its burning, fiery heart suggests its power to draw devotees, fans, co-creators, and communities rather than merely buyers and users. It implies the union of technology and aesthetics, the integration of the pragmatism of engineering and the elevation and elegance of art, addressed to the sociology and psychology of the intended audiences. A brand manager is more glamorous—that is, able to cast a magic spell—than a marketing manager.[13]

Notes

1. Raymond Carver's collection of short stories *What We Talk about When We Talk about Love* was first published in 1981, by Knopf in the United States. The title story was widely anthologised, such as in Charters, Ann, editor. *The Story and its writer: an introduction to short fiction,* Bedford Books of St. Martin's Press, 1991, pp. 210–219. The collection also gives a short essay by Carver "Creative Writing 101".
2. Gardner, Burleigh B. and Sydney J. Levy. "The Product and The Brand", *The Harvard Business Review,* March–April 1955, pp. 33–39.
3. Ibid., p. 35.
4. Levy, Sydney J. "Symbols for Sale", *The Harvard Business Review,* July–August 1959, pp. 117–124. As the author concludes: "If the manufacturer understands that he is selling symbols as well as goods, he can view his product more completely." Ibid., p. 124.
5. See the company's website sixiemeson.com, subpage "Our Work".
6. Twede, Diana. "Commercial Amphoras: The Earliest Consumer Packages?" *Journal of Macromarketing,* Vol. 22, No. 1, Jun. 2002, (doi:10.1177/027467022001009). Twede describes in detail the sophistication of the Mediterranean trade in liquid goods. Amphoras even had "tamper-proof closures" as evidence of "truth in packaging".
7. Davidson, James. *Courtesans and Fishcakes: The Consuming Passions of Classical Athens.* St. Martin's Press, 1998, p. 43.
8. Eckhardt, Gina M. and Anders Bengtsson. "A Brief History of Branding in China." *Journal of Macromarketing,* Vol. 30, No. 3, Jun. 2010, (doi:10.1177/0276146709352219). Eckhardt and Bengtsson's point is that the *White Rabbit* brand of the Song Dynasty was the first *symbolic*

brand, making it the first modern brand. *White Rabbit* was a brand of needles, and in China the story of the White Rabbit has strong feminine associations, which were a handy marketing enabler. It is very similar to how we understand that the name Apple, denoting the American electronics brand, has nothing to do with the produce trade, but has been chosen for its symbolic value.

9. Girling, Frank Aldous. *English Merchants' Marks; A Field Survey of Marks Made by Merchants and Tradesmen in England between 1400 and 1700.* Oxford University Press, 1964, p. 9.

10. Sacks, Oliver. *Musicophilia—Tales of Music and the Brain.* Knopf, 2008, p. 16. Sacks describes a number of music-related neurological cases, including a friend who could not stop hearing a song in his head for ten days straight: *"It interfered with his schoolwork, his thinking, his peace of mind, his sleep."*

11. AP: Seatlle Times News Service. "Rolling Stones Sell Microsoft Right To Use Song In Ads." *Seattle Times,* 18 Aug. 1995. archive.seattletimes.com/archive/?date=19950818&slug=2137069.

12. Perez, Sarah. "Nearly 70% of US smart speaker owners use Amazon Echo devices" *TechCrunch,* 10 Feb. 2020. techcrunch.com/2020/02/10/nearly-70-of-u-s-smart-speaker-owners-use-amazon-echo-devices/.

13. Bastos, Wilson and Sidney J. Levy, "A History of the Concept of Branding: Practice and Theory.", *Journal of Historical Research in Marketing,* Vol. 4, No. 3, Aug. 2012. pp. 347–368, (doi:10.1108/17557501211252934). With contagious enthusiasm, the great Sydney Levy and his co-author use the format of an academic article for something approaching an ode to branding. They also weave in an explanation of, among other things, Levy's tongue-twistingly titled Functional-Psychosocial-Aesthetic pyramid.

5

BRANDING IN AMERICA

MARY POWELL AND MARI MCCLURE ON BUILDING AND MAINTAINING AN AMERICAN ENERGY BRAND

There is a stream of thought on business that draws inspiration from the great writers on military and political strategy: von Clausewitz, Sun Tzu, Machiavelli . . . Sometimes, these thinkers are served up directly as business gurus, without the mediation of an author drawing on their ideas. In bookshops, for instance, I have come across "The Prince" or "The Art of War" in the business section, bundled with editions on financial management, corporate leadership and sales strategies.

I am somewhat ambivalent towards this approach, having bought into the idea of business as a consensual, rather than confrontational activity. Instead of war and strife, looking through a pair of social-science tinted binoculars I chose to see collegial contest and commonality.

In saying that, though, there is a useful maxim often attributed to von Clausewitz, the great Prussian general and military theorist, which, in fact, had been first formulated by his younger contemporary (and also a soldier), Helmuth von Moltke: "No battle plan survives first contact with the enemy." According to one book of quotations, von Moltke said that "No

DOI: 10.4324/9781003351030-6

plan of operations reaches with any certainty beyond the first encounter with the enemy's main force", which over time was condensed into the pithy expression we know today.[1]

I guess business thinkers, and businessmen in general, find strategists compelling, not because trade is normally a martial activity, but because both groups try to mitigate risk. As Udo Milkau has shown in his article "Risk Culture during the Last 2000 Years: From an Aleatory Society to the Illusion of Risk Control", it was during the Renaissance that merchants—first in Italy and then throughout Europe—started distinguishing between the concepts of risk and danger.[2] Risk, with its nautical connotations (from Greek *rhiza* meaning root, but also cliff, then by association the danger of sailing along a rocky shore)[3] "was used in the context of individual (commercial) conscious decision under uncertainty".[4] On the other hand:

> "*Periculum*" or, respectively, "*fortunam*" were used for exogenous (natural) forces, which the merchant could not be aware of and which could be covered by a contract . . . something unrelated to the individual decision making of a professional and experienced sea merchant.[5]

To put it in terms understandable to merchants old and new—storms at sea are a danger to maritime trade. But the risk of losing your cargo can be mitigated by appointing a competent captain and an able crew.

To all of this strategic thinking on risk and uncertainty, I am tempted to add my own theorem, based on more than twenty years of marketing theory and practice: "Many marketing plans don't survive first contact with the new chief executive." This book, I believe, offers much evidence to support it. The reason, I speculate, is not just because a new CEO is eager to emboss his own stamp of authority all over the new company; nor even perhaps because there was something wrong with the brand. Sometimes, prosaically, it is down to sales cycles.

In his business bestseller *What They Don't Teach You at Harvard Business School* Mark McCormack sets out his classic advice that "the best person to sell to is someone who has just arrived at a new company or is just leaving".[6] A new CEO, as an ideal sales target, will be constantly bombarded by pitches from potential suppliers.

Even if you have an unshakeable belief in the power of your company's brand (which is rarely the case), the pressure of your internal dynamism and creativity (which had won you the job in the first place), coupled with incessant prompts to do things differently, will tempt you, as the new CEO, to tinker with, or overhaul the brand. You will venture something new. And where there is a venture, or broadly speaking a transition, there is risk.

The interviews with Mary Powell and Mari McClure offered an intriguing opportunity to test all of these assumptions. I spoke to Mary Powell a number of times as she was leaving Green Mountain Power, the Vermont utility, after 12 years as CEO. I recorded our interview after she had already handed the job to her successor Mari McClure. Indicatively, a profile on the Vermontbiz.com portal bid her farewell with the headline "She was fast, fun and effective", and concluded that "she created a company culture of 'Yes!'".[7] From first-hand experience, I could not but agree with the author that "even over the phone, she bubbles with energy and enthusiasm".

Around a year after interviewing Powell, I spoke to McClure. The differences in background between the two CEOs were intriguing. Powell graduated from a specialised New York high school for the music and arts, and went on to study Liberal Arts in college. She landed a job as a receptionist for a financial start-up, and left as associate director of operations, the company having reached $3.5 billion in value. After moving to Vermont, Powell set up as consultant, and was then hired as CEO, to bring both her creative flair and financial nous to the struggling utility.

McClure, a high school and college athlete, came up through Green Mountain Power. Her prior job was to represent the company as attorney. Once she joined, she worked close to Powell. Using a sporting analogy, she said that "Mary was passing me the baton. And the most effective way for that to happen is that, as she hands me the baton, I am actually already running. It's the way to stay in the lead . . . And so that's how I felt particularly when it came to brand."

The company passed on to McClure was vastly different to the "very bureaucratic, very stuffy and very traditional" entity described by Powell. She recalls that the company was not so much concerned about the delivery of power, but on internal politics and power. Worryingly, the company was in financial distress and petitioning the regulator for a 16% rate increase. "Thankfully", says Powell, "they didn't get it". Instead she drove

BRANDING IN AMERICA

$8 million out of the operating cost structure and shrunk the workforce from 340 employees to around 190.

> I sold all the corporate offices and jammed us into a service centre. I opened it up to a sort of colourful warehouse feeling, where we moved away from any private offices. When I was CEO I ultimately ended up at a stand up table, which I shared with three other people. I was right next to where the linemen and the field staff were, going in and out during the day.

It was, Powell concludes, an opportunity for a complete cultural transformation, as much as a transformation in service quality.

McClure sees "the cultural discussion on who is Green Mountain Power" as something that needs to be "constantly revisited". "That is what, in my view, results in your brand—that cultural foundation". Applied to Green Mountain Power, this means that "you're going to have the experience that doesn't feel like a utility". She explains that "the very expression 'traditional utility' seems to stir up a set of associations . . . Male, inflexible, lacking customer focus. Those are the types of things that come to mind. It is almost as if 'traditional utility' is in itself some kind of weak brand, that needs to change."

Powell, for her part, says that as an "accidental executive" she brought to the job a disdain for that traditional approach. "I'm not one of those people that thinks 'Oh my gosh, it is my dream to be in corporate America'". It is an outlier perspective, supported by her artistic sensibility.

> You know, the offices of every utility I've visited so far in the country, seem to be painted in some version of grey or brown—or maybe blue or black. But if you came to see us, you see really vibrant primary colours. We had a yellow wall, red wall, orange wall—a bright green wall. In our first five years, if you said to an average employee "What is Mary up to, what is the company trying to do?", they would say, "Trying to become the un-utility."

But, how much of an un-utility can you be, in a heavily regulated power market such as that of the United States? How far does that regulatory environment limit what you can or can't do with your brand? This might sound like a superfluous question, as the American economy seems not just an embodiment of liberal capitalism, but also the birthplace of the world's most famous brands.

However, when it comes to energy, legislation such as the Robinson–Patman Act, and agencies such as the FERC (Federal Energy Regulatory Commission) determine and enforce, to a very significant extent, how electricity companies can brand their services. Under "brand" read here "package and sell" electricity. For instance, the Robinson Patman Act, deems it unlawful "to discriminate in price between different purchasers of commodities of like grade and quality".[8] In other words, putting consumers on different electricity tariffs, or offering rebates, could be construed as discriminatory business practice.

In 2012 Duke Energy fell foul of the legislation, with the court finding that the rebates the company offered to large customers were unlawful. But, a further determination in the same case reverberated even louder through the American energy industry—the determination that, under the Robinson–Patman Act, electricity was a commodity.

The significance of this ruling was far reaching. In a paper on Lexology. com antitrust lawyer Jeffrey S. Spigel and colleagues commented that "while the statute does not extend to services and intangible items, the court held that electricity is a commodity because it can be produced, felt, stored, and distributed in discrete quantities".[9] They also noted that "other courts have been divided on the status of electricity, with some holding that it is more akin to services such as cellular telephone service and cable television programming".[10]

If federal antitrust laws and their evolving interpretations determine how power companies brand their products and services, so does the structure of the American retail market. Beyond the façade of a diverse industry with dozens of energy companies, you will find a complicated system variously called "hybrid", "two-tier" or "regulated-deregulated". For instance, a minority of states (so-called *deregulated markets*) allow retail choice for household consumers. But, even such states might not have deregulated their entire territory. Within those states there could be service areas which do not permit consumers to switch suppliers.

Actually, the majority of states have *regulated markets*, structured akin to those in Europe pre-liberalisation. As the United States Environmental Protection Agency explains, they feature "vertically integrated utilities that own or control the total flow of electricity from generation to meter".[11] It is then clear that energy companies' attempts at branding will have to take into account state-level (regulated or deregulated) market structures, federal laws, and finally, wider consumer sentiments aligned with political and environmental concerns.

The demands of negotiating this complex equation are bound to draw out those individualistic qualities in a CEO, traditionally associated with US business culture, such as decisiveness, self-confidence, competitiveness and vision. Powell says that when she got the job felt like "I was unleashed to be just who I was".

"The backbone of what we did could never have happened if I didn't have licence to completely transform the place financially. I'm sure there are some super-bloated companies that have amazing brands but I've just never seen one." This was the start of a process Powell terms "inside-out branding":

> First you change your inside, and you build your brand. Then through the changes you've made to your inside, your brand becomes an external force through good times and bad. I'm a firm believer in that your brand is the result, not the beginning.

And that result is an emotional connection with your customers.

> My first message, right up through my last message, has always been about how do we create an organization that is doing things that make customers want to love us. I remember telling my predecessor that we needed to become the Ben & Jerry's of the utility world.

The world-famous brand of ice cream was founded in Vermont in 1978. Over the last 40 years has become synonymous with an activist attitude to corporate-social responsibility.[12] Building on this idea of an emotional connection with customers Powell says:

> I wanted everyone internally to consider, how do we become the company that people are writing to the regulators about, saying, "I want to be able to become a customer of Green Mountain Power". How do we create that much love?

She adds that "deep emotional resonance is the best way to build connectivity".

A practical corollary of this "activist" approach to branding is Powell's insistence on earning, rather than paying for media coverage: "My whole strategy, has always been 'We are going to build our brand, by getting earned media for things that earn us media.' I actually dramatically cut the traditional advertising and marketing budget, in fact, I almost completely eliminated it."

The insistence on unpaid coverage follows traditional wisdom that, as opposed to marketing content, it has more power to influence customer behaviour. Such assumptions were robustly challenged in a number of studies, with the authors claiming that people do not consider earned media more credible or efficacious than traditional advertising. But the pendulum seems now to be swinging in the opposite direction. According to "A Mixed Methods Examination of How People Assess the Credibility of Sources Used by Public Relations Practitioners"—a study by Julie O'Neil *et al.* from 2019—the simple conclusion is "Participants viewed earned media stories as the most credible."[13]

In practice, though, energy companies are notoriously sluggish marketing spenders. In the August 2016 edition of the CMO Survey—issued twice a year by Deloitte, Duke's Fuqua School of Business and the American Marketing Association—energy is in last place out of 13 industrial sectors, in terms of marketing spend as percentage of overall budget.[14] If, as a sector, "Consumer Packaged Goods" (on top of the list), spends 24% of overall budget on marketing, and "Service Consulting" (in sixth place) spends 12%, then "Energy" is at 4%. The cross-industry average is 11.6%. In other words, the energy sector spends three times less on marketing, than the industrial average.[15]

This might be relevant for brand implementation. The CMO Survey also traditionally includes a revealing question: "What marketing leads in companies?" In the Fall 2019 edition of the survey "brand" is on top of the list. In 91 per cent of the companies, brand is led by marketing, meaning that for the vast majority of companies brand policing sits squarely within the marketing department or within the company's marketing work-stream. Considering all of the above, industries with traditionally strong marketing budgets will have more money for brand implementation, and consequently stronger brands.

When talking about that bond of trust between company and consumer, McClure goes further and mentions "intimacy". She agrees that the energy companies' product is "somewhat invisible . . . Rather than a product that the customer is holding in their hands, it makes the lights come on". But, she says, "as they travel around their own community they might notice our assets—the substations, the poles and the wires. They might notice our solar or wind farm."

> And then, at a more intimate level, we are not just in the community, we are in our customers' homes and in their lives. With the advancement of smart technology this process will intensify. While electricity use will be getting more efficient, people will be using more of it, including to power their vehicles. The interaction between the various devices will be more complex. You will be using your smartphone or iPad to control your thermostat through your Wi-Fi connection. These are all electrical devices, and we, as the utility, provide a foundation.
>
> This intimate relationship will go way back into the supply chain. Customers increasingly care where power is coming from. It is important to them that their energy is clean, reliable and affordable—they tell us that much. And this is where opportunity exists in the energy industry, for utilities and other providers: to build on and access that intimacy. More and more people understand the relationship with energy in their lives.

This conceptual matrix translated into Powell's vision of an energy-progressive company. "I think we were the first utility in the country to divest our pension funds from fossil fuels, and also to announce that we will be 100% carbon free by 2025 and 100% renewable by 2030." A far-sighted energy executive, then, should be mindful of the consumer pressure bearing down both on conversations around environmental policy, and the actual workings of the energy business.

Powell says that "the main challenge with energy companies is still putting profits before people. I don't disparage profits, and I don't disparage success. But, I won't sign on financial success being the worthy value to pursue, nor one that will work over decades of time. In fact, what still astounds me is the obsession of so many energy companies on shareholder value versus title value." This could be the view many in Vermont share. It has become one of the most consistently left-leaning states in the US, electing avowed democratic socialist Bernie Sanders to the Senate since 2007.

In fact, Green Mountain Power is in many ways similar to Germany's *Stadtwerke* (city-utility) companies, which have not only survived the market deregulation of 1997, but have continued to hold on to their assets and customers. There are around 1500 such companies in Germany, on the electricity side supplying around 66 billion kilowatthours of electricity per year.[16] A report from 2015, published by Clean Energy Wire and titled *Small But Powerful*, ran a set of impressive numbers:

> [Stadtwerke] employ nearly 250,000 people, and in 2013 had com-bined sales of about 110 billion euros, and invested 8.5 billion euros overall in their assets. Their market-share in German energy retail amounts to 46 percent in electricity, 59 percent in gas and 65 percent in heat distribution. In comparison, RWE, the largest single retailer in Germany, has a market share of 16 percent in electricity and 10 percent in gas in the retail business to private households.[17]

Returning to the theme of *inside-out branding* in the context of corporate budg-ets, Powell connects it with her staff-development agenda:

> Once you start aligning your brand with the internal world of the company, then some of the things that might not strike you as obvi-ously connected to branding, such as training, development and building the company culture, become part of it. Spending money on branding is about the internal work you need to do to become the company you want to be. You need to look at things such as leadership training and communicating within and without, to your employees and to your customers.

The "people first" doctrine, applied externally as "customers first", offers an easy reckoner, says McClure, when triangulating all the different inter-ests that bear down on Green Mountain Power:

> Public utilities know three different types of stakeholders: the cus-tomer, the regulator, and investor or owner. The management would

then try to consider whether what is good for the customer would be good for the investor, all the while considering whether that is something the regulator would want you to do. At Green Mountain Power we shut all that. Always, in all of our decisions—customers first. Because, if you keep your customer happy, you will keep your regulator happy, and if you keep your regulator happy you will keep your owner or investor happy. In fact, it is a cycle, not a triangle.

Echoing Powell, McClure calls that approach "customer accession, customer love". She says that it rolls up into every decision the company makes. "It permeates the entire organisation, not just the customer care rep, but also the accountant in our finance department . . . The success of our organisation starts and ends there: customer, then regulator, then investor, then back to customer."

On the issue of brand-spend, she thinks that it is not all that different from considering how any kind of spend shows up on the company's balance sheet, or profit and loss statement. Ultimately, it is the question about how it produces value for the company, and in that sense too, it is not different from a conversation about paying your employees:

For instance, the conversation around "I've just spent a dollar on marketing—how's that showing up in my financial statement?" is not different from a conversation on how having highly talented people has helped, or how having medium performers has showed up in a medium way on our balance sheet.

But, there is an important indirect financial benefit to consistently successful branding, in the ability to attract the right human resources:

Look at Duke's men's basketball team. They continue to recruit very talented people, because of the brand that they've built. That brand is built on winning, and conversely, companies build their brand on doing the right thing. If they don't, they're not going to acquire the talent they need to keep building their business, and they're going to miss a customer base.

This chimes with Powell's belief that "branding is happening whether you focus on it or not". She says that every minute you're not focusing on your brand, you could actually be doing something wrong. "Good luck to you because every action you take, intentional or not, is building up or tearing down your brand. It is not like a choice, especially today, when we have much more of an activist society, and socially networked and engaged customers."

The way to strengthen the brand, then, might be through a handy decision-making tool, a sort of Occam's razor for the indecisive energy executive. McClure mentions it as we discuss sustainability, and the business strategies energy companies must adopt to fight climate change:

> Perhaps instead of worrying about the right decision or strategy, let's reverse our dilemma, and ask ourselves—"If I'm going to be wrong about the decision I made, which way would I rather be wrong?" For instance, if you are considering "Do I want to move quickly to address climate concerns?" or "Do I want to move slowly?", then every time it has to be "I'd rather be wrong in moving quickly".

I found this a useful guide in thinking about branding in energy companies. Traditionally, energy companies worry that branding will divert resources from core activities, such as keeping the lights on. Those resources are not just financial resources. To energy engineers, economists, accountants, researchers and technicians, to CEOs and senior management teams, resources are also "intangibles" such as time, expertise and attention.

All that notwithstanding, when it comes to your brand, which way would you rather be wrong? If you had to choose, would you rather over-commit or under-commit? Would you rather keep your focus or lose focus? Would you rather be wrong in doing more or in doing less? Handing the baton from one CEO to the other, Green Mountain Power have already decided.

Notes

1. Knowles, Elizabeth (ed.). *Oxford Dictionary of Quotations*, 8th edition. Oxford University Press, 2014, p. 539. Helmut von Moltke (also known as "Moltke the Elder") was a Prussian field-marshal, and, like von Clausewitz, a writer on strategy.

BRANDING IN AMERICA

2. Milkau, Udo. "Risk Culture during the Last 2000 years—From an Aleatory Society to the Illusion of Risk Control." *International Journal of Financial Studies*, Vol. 5, No. 31, Dec. 2017, (doi:10.3390/ijfs5040031).

3. The etymology of the word "risk" is uncertain, with the internet offering theories that it stems from Classical Greek, Latin, Byzantine Greek, Spanish, Italian and Arabic. See, for instance, Skeat, Walter. *An Etymological Dictionary of the English Language.* Clarendon Press, 1924. We have followed, as probable, the etymology offered in Ayto, John. *Oxford School Dictionary of Word Origins.* Oxford University Press, 2004, p. 383.

4. Milkau, "Risk Culture during the Last 2000 Years", p. 6.

5. Ibid.

6. McCormack, Mark H. *What They Don't Teach You at Harvard Business School.* Bantam, 1984, p. 104.

7. Marcel, Joyce. "She Was Fast, Fun and Effective: Mary Powell Leaves GMP." *Vermont Business Magazine*, 18 Jan. 2020, https://vermontbiz.com/news/2020/january/18/she-was-fast-fun-and-effective-mary-powell-leaves-gmp.

8. The text of the Robinson-Patman Act can be found on the website of the Cornell Law School/Legal Information Institute (LII), at law.cornell.edu/uscode/text/15/13. The legislation is filed as 15 US Code §13. For an overview see Calvani, Terry and Gilde Breidenbach. "An Introduction to the Robinson-Patman Act and its Enforcement by the Government." *Antitrust Law Journal*, Vol. 59, No. 3, 1990–1991, pp. 765–775, jstor.org/stable/40841343.

9. Spigel, Jeffrey S. et al. "Sixth Circuit Holds that Electricity Is a Commodity under Robinson-Patman Act and Limits Applicability of the Filed Rate Doctrine." *Lexology*, 27 Jun. 2012, lexology.com/library/detail.aspx?g=3ccb1959-79c4-4de5-80a0-bfe39b806e3d.

10. Ibid.

11. See the website of the United States Environmental Protection Agency, subpage "Policies and Regulation", heading "Understanding Electricity Market Frameworks & Policies", at epa.gov/green-power-markets/policies-and-regulations#three.

12. Information on the history of one of the world's most famous ice cream brands, Vermont's own Ben & Jerry's, can be found in the "Our History" section of company's website, at benjerry.com/about-us.

BRANDING IN AMERICA   67

13. Julie O'Neil et al. "A Mixed Methods Examination of How People Assess the Credibility of Sources Used by Public Relations Practitioners." *Journal of Promotion Management*, Vol. 26, No. 1, 2020, (doi:10.1080/10496491. 2018.1536619). O'Neil and Eismann give a detailed overview of the study on the website of the Institute for Public Relations, under the heading "Is Earned Media More Credible than Advertising?" (15 Jul. 2019). The short answer is yes.

14. Deloitte *et al.* "CMO Survey Report: Highlights and Insights." *Deloitte,* Aug. 2016, deloitte.com/content/dam/Deloitte/us/Documents/CMO/us-cmo-survey-highights-and-insights-report-aug-2016.pdf.

15. See also Deloitte. "Marketing Budgets Vary by Industry." *Wall Street Journal*, 24 Jan. 2017, deloitte.wsj.com/articles/who-has-the-biggest-marketing-budgets-1485234137.

16. Information on Germany's Stadtwerke companies can be found at vku. de. VKU stands for Verband Kommunaler Unternehmen—Association of Municipal Enterprises.

17. Schlandt, Jakob. "Small, but powerful—Germany's municipal utilities", *Clean Energy Wire*, 18 Feb. 2015, www.cleanenergywire.org/factsheets/small-powerful-germanys-municipal-utilities.

6

BLACK GOLD AND GREEN ENERGY

RAHUL MALHOTRA ON MARKETING SHELL IN THE AGE OF RENEWABLES

The Hudson Institute, formed in 1961, and currently at Pennsylvania Avenue, a 10-minute walk from the White House, was home to a special kind of social scientist—the futurist.[1] Once the staple guests of political chatshows and magazine interview columns—prognosticating what society will look like in centuries to come—the peculiar thing about the futurists is that they failed to predict their own reputational demise.

That demise followed their 1970s heyday. Today, it is reflected not so much in their banishment from serious mainstream media, but in the disinterest of the general public. Some say this disengagement is a consequence of a failure by the futurists—despite their considerable analytical firepower and intellectual heft—to predict some of the most notable developments of the last 50 years, such the rise of the internet or the disintegration of the USSR. As the phrase goes, they should have seen it coming.

It is as if straight-up fantasists and visionaries, for instance, Jules Verne, Aldous Huxley or George Orwell, were able to divine the future by intuition and imagination, where scientists failed by statistics and analysis. And

DOI: 10.4324/9781003351030-7

BLACK GOLD AND GREEN ENERGY   69

yet, going back to Herman Kahn's futurist classic *The Next 200 Years*, published by the Hudson Institute in 1976, it becomes apparent that, almost half a century after it was published (and a quarter of the way into those 200 years Kahn was trying to glimpse), the concerns of that book are still valid.[2] And not only the concerns. Kahn, who was also a game theorist, was one of the pioneers of the "scenario approach" to planning. It was an approach also adopted by Shell in 1965 when it commenced the Long-Term Studies programme at its London headquarters.[3]

First, though, it is worth noting that, compared to books by the authors I had just mentioned, which can still be read for pleasure and intellectual stimulation, *The Next 200 Years* now has mostly historical value. Much of Kahn's ruminations have been overtaken by events. His solution to the quadrupling of crude oil prices which happened during the Oil Shock of 1973—to accelerate the commercialisation of coal liquefaction and gasification (because coal is the most abundant fossil fuel)—now sounds positively outdated.

And yet, one of the chief concerns set out in the book is still live: how will future societies, one of which happens to be the society we live in, deal with the impact of fossil fuel consumption on the environment? In fact, it now seems that rather than the futurists having been beaten back by current affairs and innovation they could not foresee, they had served their purpose in turning us all into futurists. The difference being that whereas they could only speculate on likely outcomes of trends they saw unfolding, we now know, with a great deal of certainty, that unless we take action on climate change, the Earth in 2176 will look very different from how it looked in 1976. In fact, the *futurists* have turned most of us into *activists*.

We now have both the data and solid historical evidence on the consequences of environmental recklessness. As the anthropologist Jared Diamond writes in *Collapse: How Societies Choose to Fail or Succeed*, his magisterial study of human-caused environmental disasters, "the suspicion of unintended ecological suicide—ecocide—has been confirmed by discoveries made in recent years by archaeologists, climatologists, historians, palaeontologist, and palynologists (pollen scientists)".[4]

As if adding personal relevance to me and every other Icelander, Diamond writes extensively about European colonisation of Iceland and Greenland, as textbook examples of ecological mismanagement. The Icelanders, he says, "were exploiting the soil and vegetation in the way that miners exploit oil and mineral deposits, which renew themselves only infinitely slowly and are mined until they are all gone".[5] I can only hope that history will judge my generation and our custody of the land more favourably.

All of which was swirling in my mind as I approached my interview with Rahul Malhotra, head of brand strategy & stewardship at Shell. The oil business is not so much the elephant in the room of the world's energy economy, but a 100-thousand tonne oil platform right in its front garden. How do you talk about it? On the one hand, without oil the world economy would not merely grind to halt, it would cease to exist. On the other, media pundits and energy experts often talk about our societies' "addiction to oil" and "our unhealthy relationship with oil". It is more than "black gold". In the title of Dilip Hiro's book, it is the *Blood of the Earth*, with all the connotations this entails.[6]

But, is that entirely fair? On that particular point, I wonder if the perception is due to "oil" (as such) becoming the ultimate problem brand, rather than to its inherent moral badness. What is often forgotten is that the world's largest oil producer is the United States, with Canada in fourth place, China in sixth, Norway in thirteenth and the United Kingdom in nineteenth.[7] Correlating Transparency International's Corruption Perceptions Index with the list of countries ranked according to oil production produces some overlaps, but also notable exceptions.[8] The oil business is one of many industrial sectors, and its corporations more similar to other corporations, than we care to admit.

At a workday level, then, any oil company brand manager has to reckon with his employer's output being considered both essential and problematic, which is perhaps another definition of "controversial". But, actually, a large part of Shell's business is distinctly uncontroversial. It is in retail, at the petrol pump, where the famous yellow and red scallop (or Pecten) logo is most visible. It started life as a black and white design, trademarked in 1900. According to Shell's website it is "the oldest of 22,000+ trademarks owned by Shell."[9]

Of the retail business Rahul says: "We've always been one of the world's largest retailers. Today Shell has 46,000 service stations operating in more than 80 countries." He adds that getting people into Shell stores, increasing footfall, as well as basket value and the purchase of premium products is an outcome of some "very savvy marketing". As Shell diversifies into new lines of business such as becoming a home energy supplier and building solar parks and wind farms, in Rahul's view the company has become "even more conscious of the need for good quality marketing".

The word "savvy" with its etymological links to the Spanish language, seems to encapsulate not just Shell's current marketing strategies, but also its early days. In their essay "An Evolutionary Examination of the Royal Dutch Shell Logo: Semiotic Perspectives" Jonathan Matusitz and Erica Cowin say that "over the last century, [the] logo has been modified about ten times".[10] It seems to have happened through a process of iteration attuned to the emerging global oil market—a process very different in its series of decentralised increments—from the "big idea" branding strategies going around today.

The company claims that although "yellow and red have been a fairly consistent element of Shell's brand image from the earliest days", their "exact origin is uncertain":

> It may come from the company's origins in exports, as both yellow and red are used in maritime signalling. Samuel Junior [the son of Shell's founder] also chose red to make his kerosene cans stand out against Standard Oil's blue when the companies were competing back at the end of the 19th Century.

Matusitz and Cowin, following Charles Peirce's semiotic approach, say:

> People in the Far East—where Shell's founder Marcus Samuel used to ship oil—considered the shell a symbol for containing genius, like containing a unique and fine pearl . . . The interpretant of this Shell logo is that oil (or petroleum or kerosene) is precious like the unique and fine pearl contained in the shell. Another interpretation is that, just as a shell can be found anywhere on the planet, oil can be delivered to any place on the planet.[11]

Adding colour to the original black and white logo, during the construction of Shell's first service stations in California, was a key semiotic gesture. "Owing to California's early Spanish connections, the red and yellow colours of Spain were chosen. The symbolic connection was timely . . . Shell anticipated that an emotional bond would take form." Matusitz and Cowin point out that "before the advent of fax machines and the Internet, most logos included slight details that would end up being blurred at small sizes". Consequently, Raymond Loewy, the legendary industrial designer who authored logos for BP, Exxon and TWA, and packaging for Coca-Cola and Lucky Strike, simplified the Pecten in 1971.[12]

Zooming out away from the logo and the other four elements of a corporation's visual identity—name, typography, colour and slogan—we see that, as part of branding practice, their joint purpose is to reinforce that "emotional bond." In Rahul's view "emotional connection is around trust and reliability". In fact, a brand needs to be "infused with those emotional benefits, in addition to the functional benefits". The purpose of this fusion of emotional and functional benefits is differentiation. As he sums it up— "that differentiation is branding", or "you will have to be differentiated if you want to be preferred".

But, when it comes to energy branding and marketing, do we all respond in the same way to supposed emotional cues? This question is particularly pertinent to energy companies as they sell commodities, and have a limited number of differentials at their disposal, some of them not especially emphatic. However, among these *weak differentials*, price being one exception, the energy source is a clear differentiating factor. Green energy or green electricity seems to be a clear brand signal, the effectiveness of which any energy giant, including Shell, would be interested in. But, has this signalled the universal power to motivate consumer behaviour that is often ascribed to it?

My own research, as part of my PhD thesis completed in 2016, paints a surprisingly complex picture of trans-national diversity, not just in attitudes, but in basic understanding of green energy. As I wrote there, "ethos to green differs between countries. Applying a universal definition and expecting consumers of different nationalities to accept it in the same way is not possible."[13] It became clear to me that there was considerable ambiguity out there as to what green electricity is or should be: is nuclear energy green? Is combined cycle gas green, because it is less polluting than other forms of fossil fuel power? This confusion was compounded by companies resorting to "green measures" such as tree planting to prove their environmental credentials. Understandably, then, against a backdrop of low or high scepticism, country attitudes in general were arrayed on a spectrum from powerlessness and indifference to enthusiastic endorsement, with concerns around who actually profits from decarbonisation.

Rahul agrees that "as media penetrates, people are getting more aware of the importance of sustainability. This is increasing very rapidly." But, he cautions, "this varies country to country". Like many of my other interviewees in this book, Rahul sees an internal benefit to sustainability commitments: "It not only helps drive business—by driving reputation through having a clear purpose and values, it also drives customer attraction and retention, employee morale and recruitment." But, as to whether an energy brand of the future can afford not to be green Rahul offers a cautious assessment:

> It is potentially possible in some geographies as well as in some demographic segments. There are many benefit vectors in the energy sector. One of those vectors could be convenience. Another could be affordability or price leadership. You could have at any given time deals and promotions, a conviction that you should go with the brand that always gives you the best deals. Or perhaps other relevant factors of interest, such as affinity: I can relate to this brand because it speaks my language, it is a local brand.
>
> I mean, there's an energy brand advertising with the message that they are a true local brand, because they understand the people and their needs. I assume they have done their homework and found that this marketing strategy will work. Really, the message isn't even a country-wide affiliation, such as "we are a national brand". It is a purely local benefit vector, to use technical marketing speak.

Rahul suggests that some customers might choose sustainability as one brand vector. "But, with legislation and consumer expectations evolving," he adds that "in the future sustainability could become an even more important element for many industries. As marketers, we don't know yet", he concludes. However, Shell is already offering low-carbon solutions to an increasing number of customers, one of which is a 100 per cent renewable energy offering to its Shell Energy UK customers.

A further interesting branding vector has emerged as energy consumption becomes an ethical issue. In his book *A Moral Case for Fossil Fuels* Alex Epstein argues that fossil fuels are not just "absolutely good to use . . . They absolutely need to be championed." The moral case could not be put more bluntly: "Mankind's use of fossil fuels is supremely virtuous—because human life is the standard of value and because using fossil fuels transforms our environment to make it wonderful for human life."[14] If you are reading this and feel your blood boil, the point to note is that you are getting upset exactly because energy consumption has become entwined with our deepest moral values and beliefs. For many of us (and not just for the Greta Thunbergs of this world), this has become not just *any* moral issue, but the one of *the* biggest issues of our time.

To this Rahul says "it is very important that we recognise that climate change is real". As the world's energy economy is being upended by the three-pronged pitchfork of energy security, sustainable growth and climate change, Shell is holding its nerve. And that could also be the explanation behind the company's loyalty to its red and yellow Pecten.

As we have seen in Chapter 2, the rebranding wave that swept over some of Europe's biggest power companies in the mid-2010s, for the rechristened giants heralded both a new direction in energy production and a disassociation from fossil fuels, at least at reputational level. Yet despite sticking to a century-old branding solution, Shell has also invested in new renewable technologies, such as offshore wind.

I wonder whether this cautiousness, a focus on commitment and delivery rather than on grand branding gestures has been reinforced by the failed BP "Beyond Petroleum" launch. Beyond Petroleum has become a case study on how not to rebrand your company, and has encouraged any and every energy company to think carefully about ditching its name and logo in favour of something that has no connection with either your tradition or your core activities.

But it is, undeniably, also a function of assessing the long-term perspectives of the oil business. And it is a business that does way more than pump fuel at the petrol station:

> Big consumption of fossil fuels happens in some industries that you don't see on the road, and which are harder to decarbonise, for instance, shipping and aviation. Then, you have oil used in the petrochemicals industry. For example, we don't have the scale yet to make the billions of everyday items such as mobile phones and other consumer goods from sustainable plastics. So, decreasing emissions and increasing circularity is a priority, and Shell has an ambition to use one million tonnes of plastic waste a year in its chemicals sites by 2025.

In fact, the company's website details the new decarbonisation roadmap, announced in February of 2021:

> We have set targets to reduce the carbon intensity (Net Carbon Footprint) of the energy products we sell. This includes short-term targets of 3–4% by 2022, and 6–8% by 2023 (compared to 2016). It also includes medium- and long-term targets of 20% by 2030, 45% by 2035, and 100% by 2050 (compared to 2016).[15]

These carbon reduction targets, which have been adopted in one guise or another by other energy companies, rest on assumptions that oil consumption for road transport will fall, due to factors such as greater vehicle fuel-efficiency, the phasing out of diesel passenger vehicles, and the electrification of transport. However, according to the International Energy Agency (IEA), "petrochemicals—components derived from oil and gas that are used in all sorts of daily products such as plastics, fertilisers, packaging, clothing, digital devices, medical equipment, detergents and tyres—are becoming the largest drivers of global oil demand, in front of cars, planes and trucks".[16]

The IEA says:

> Petrochemicals are set to account for more than a third of the growth in world oil demand to 2030, and nearly half the growth to 2050, adding nearly 7 million barrels of oil a day by then. They are also poised to consume an additional 56 billion cubic metres (bcm) of natural gas by 2030, and 83 bcm by 2050.[17]

This shift in market focus is certain to cause a shift in marketing and branding strategies. Not just because private vehicle use is associated with traits such as individualism and independence, but also because the market for petrochemical feedstock is a business-to-business (B2B) market, as opposed to the business-to-consumer (B2C) market. Rahul explains:

> The concepts don't change across these different types of marketing. You still have the who, the what, the how . . . The question of "what is your message?" still remains. I think one of the things that changes compared to B2C is that the purchase cycle is not as long as in B2B.

For example, as a consumer, immediately after you finish your bottle of shampoo, you will need shampoo again, and the interval between two purchasing decisions might be weeks, or a couple of months.

He adds:

As an advertiser, you frequently have the opportunity to launch a different message, or reinforce an aspect of your existing message. Compared to B2B, the B2C marketing cycle sometimes works at a higher speed. The second difference, setting aside the obvious differences in channels and styles of communication (for instance, using technical or expert, versus non-expert language) is data availability. In B2B obtaining data is not easy, for instance, you are likely not aware of price or service differentiators.

Rahul is a great believer in the science, rather than the art of marketing:

I'm of the school that it is possible to measure anything. It is possible to quantitatively measure brand equity improvements over time. It is also possible to quantitatively measure how that higher brand equity translates into stronger preference, purchase intention, readiness to trial new products and customer loyalty. One can easily make a NPV (net-present value) chart to show how marketing delivers over a five-year period. But, frankly, the most important thing is that the CEO must believe in the power of building a brand.

From such numerical analysis further insights are possible on the overall business benefits of branding, and not just relating to customer relations:

The energy industry being a highly competitive market, it makes financial sense to invest in branding as it reduces your cost of acquisition, and, at a minimum, reduces the need for frequent discounting and promotion. If you have a reputational incident, strong branding translates into greater resilience, regarding both the stock price, but also in terms of customer retention. I guarantee you that the financial benefits of branding and marketing can be put on a P&L sheet.

There is a case to be made that the readjustment to new legislative frameworks in developed countries, aiming to reduce CO_2 emissions and ramp up the use of renewable sources of energy, has been handled by Shell more adroitly than by other established energy corporations. It has included an earnest and extensive push into offshore wind, where it can utilise its experience of offshore oil exploration. Shell's Perdido spar (single point anchor reservoir) floating platform is the world's deepest, anchored in water depths of 2,450 metres, in the US portion of the Gulf of Mexico. The Appomattox, a platform of similar size and ambition, in water depths of 2,195 metres, has started production in 2019, 129 kilometres off the coast of Louisiana.

Between those two projects Rahul says that the company has "invested massively" in new technologies:

> We have committed several billion dollars in the last few years to wind and solar farms, products with a lower carbon footprint, recycling, less packaging, energy saving devices and systems, low energy lighting in our retail sites, and we have also deployed carbon offsetting via nature-based solutions—and we continue to invest.

The most eye-catching of all these moves was the formation of the Shell New Energies division in 2016. Just in case there was any confusion about the kind of energies the new division was exploring, in 2021 it was renamed "Shell Renewables and Energy Solutions". In 2022 Shell aims to invest $3 billion in this area.

In 2016 the Blauwind consortium, led on the engineering and project development side by Shell New Energies, caught the headlines with its bid to supply electricity from the Borssele 3&4 offshore wind farm (in the Dutch portion of the North Sea) at just €54.5 per megawatthour (MWh). Close to wholesale electricity contracts, it was the lowest price ever offered at an offshore wind auction. The project, rated at 731 megawatts (MW), would supply close to 2.5 per cent of total Dutch annual electricity consumption.[18]

The news proved that a nineteenth-century company had much to contribute to the development and commercialisation of a twenty-first-century energy technology. By February 2021 the Borssele 3&4 offshore wind farm was fully operational. Reading about this project in the industry trade press at the time, and again recently, I was reminded of something I had found in that now almost-antiquated book by the futurist Herman Kahn.

Granted, he did not foresee how the internet will transform almost every facet of our lives, but thinking about the future of the global energy supply, and despite his support for oil exploration, he said this: "The world is at the beginning of a transition from fossil fuels as the primary energy sources to the phasing in of long-term alternatives—a transition we expect to be largely completed about 75 years from now."[19] As the book was published in 1976, it is clear Kahn was thinking of 2050. A few pages later he says: "The new technology available for generating and storing power from windmills makes this an attractive and economical power source for regions where the wind blows rather steadily or at higher than average speed . . ."[20] And then, towards the end of the book, he adds: "For example, offshore locations are now being considered seriously for large energy installations."[21]

That one of the world's largest oil companies would be at the vanguard of this transition perhaps no futurist could have foreseen.

Notes

1. Hudson Institute is a "think tank and research centre dedicated to nonpartisan analysis of US and international economic, security, and political issues". It was founded by Herman Kahn, Max Singer and Oscar Ruebhausen. See hudson.org.
2. Kahn, Herman. *The Next 200 Years: A Scenario for America and the World.* Hudson Institute, 1976.
3. In the May 2013 issue of the *Harvard Business Review* Angela Wilkinson and Roland Kupers wrote about the "futures" operation at Shell. The task of the futures team was to develop long-term outlooks, using Kahn's scenario approach. See Wilkinson, Angela and Roland Kupers. "Living in the Futures." *Harvard Business Review*, May 2013, hbr.org/2013/05/living-in-the-futures#.
4. Diamond, Jarred. *Collapse: How Societies Choose to Fail or Succeed.* Viking, 2015, p. 6.
5. Ibid, p. 199.
6. Hiro, Dilip. *Blood of the Earth: The Battle for the World's Vanishing Oil Resources.* Nation Books, 2007.
7. International oil production statistics and country rankings have been taken from the US Energy Information Agency's website, subpage titled "International", at eia.gov/international/data/world.
8. In its *Corruption Perceptions Index* the NGO Transparency International "scores 180 countries and territories by their perceived levels of public

sector corruption, according to experts and business people". See transparency.org/en/cpi/2021.

9. Information about the history of the Shell logo, as well as company history in general is taken from the company's website, subpage "Brand History", at www.shell.com/about-us/our-heritage/our-brand-history.html.

10. Matusitz, Jonathan and Erica Cowin. "An Evolutionary Examination of the Royal Dutch Shell Logo: Semiotic Perspectives." *The Journal of Creative Communications*, Vol. 9, Issue 2, July 2014, pp. 93–105, (doi.org/10.1177/0973258614528607).

11. Ibid.

12. There is ample reading material online about the French-American industrial designer Raymond Loewy. A good place to start is the official website: www.raymondloewy.com.

13. My first book continued the exploration of some of the themes in that PhD thesis—see Larsen, Fridrik. *Energy Branding: Harnessing Consumer Power*. Palgrave Macmillan, 2017.

14. Epstein, Alex. *A Moral Case for Fossil Fuels*. Portfolio, 2014, p. 209. This is a book which is unlikely to find itself on any environmentalist's Christmas wish list.

15. See web-page titled Achieving Net Zero Emissons, subheading "Shell's strategy to achieve net-zero emissions" at shell.com/powering-progress/achieving-net-zero-emissions.html.

16. International Energy Agency (IEA). "Petrochemicals set to be the largest driver of world oil demand", 5 Oct. 2018, iea.org/news/petrochemicals-set-to-be-the-largest-driver-of-world-oil-demand-latest-iea-analysis-finds.

17. Ibid.

18. See the Blauwind consortium website at blauwwind.nl.

19. Kahn, *The Next 200 Years*, p. 67.

20. Ibid, p. 69.

21. Ibid, p. 155.

7

OIL COMPANIES

HENRIK HABBERSTAD AND TOM VAN DE CRUYS ON SOVEREIGN ENERGY BRANDS IN THE SOCIAL MEDIA ERA

In January of 2014 Reuters ran a headline that said "All Norwegians become crown millionaires".[1] The news travelled the world and turned into something of an urban myth. Since then, I had encountered it many times. At industry conferences and social events, for instance, I have overheard snippets of conversation affirming that "in Norway every child is born a millionaire". Sometimes, with the corner of my eye I could see people nodding sagely in agreement, although I suspected that not many fully understood what it meant.

The Reuters article clarified that "everyone in Norway became a theoretical crown millionaire", because the nation's sovereign wealth fund has "ballooned thanks to high oil and gas prices". It explained that "a preliminary counter on the website of the central bank, which manages the fund, rose to 5.11 trillion crowns ($828.66 billion), fractionally more than a million times Norway's most recent official population estimate of 5,096,300". The fund has since 2014 appreciated in value to 11 trillion crowns.

DOI: 10.4324/9781003351030-8

The article also notes that the fund "set up in 1990 . . . owns around 1 percent of the world's stocks, as well as bonds and real estate from London to Boston". At the time of writing a million Norwegian crowns is just under 100,000 euros.

Whatever the currency fluctuations, however (and they haven't deviated more than around 10 per cent from the median exchange rate with the euro over the last 20 years), a million crowns per Norwegian tells us something about the history of the oil business. Broadly speaking, according to their origin, there are two types of oil businesses. Shell or Exxon Mobile started off as privately owned companies, in the narrow sense of initially headed by charismatic and/or controversial entrepreneurs: Shell by Marcus Samuel, and Exxon Mobile (originally Standard Oil), by John D. Rockefeller, still considered the wealthiest man of all time.[2]

Then, there are the state-owned, or sovereign oil companies. The state that founded them might, as with Equinor, still have a controlling stake, or it might not, as with Total. Regardless, it was a government decree that had midwifed an oil giant.

Equinor, then called Statoil, was formed by an act of Norwegian parliament, unanimously approved on 14 July 1972,[3] while Total dates its birth to a directive sent on 20 September 1923 by French Prime Minister Raymond Poincare to the industrialist Ernest Mercier.[4] At the very top of the page the directive stated that "The Government wants to create a tool capable of achieving a national oil policy. The Company will therefore have to be essentially French and remain completely independent."

The brands of Equinor and Total, as sovereign oil companies, contain some of that history, not just as inert layers, but as a direct force for change. It is hardly a coincidence that in the last five years three sovereign oil companies have rebranded (Statoil into Equinor, DONG into Orsted and Total into TotalEnergies), while companies such as Exxon Mobile, Shell and BP have not only stayed put, but in the case of BP have actually reversed a rebrand.

In the examples we have mentioned the rebrand is not a token customer-pleasing gesture, nowadays called "greenwash". Rather, it answers the challenge of how to serve your country (by generating profit from oil and gas extraction), while discharging a wider responsibility to the environment. For Equinor that challenge is perhaps even more pronounced as 41 per cent of Norway's exports are petroleum products, generating 14 per cent of GDP. As the Norway Petroleum Directorate says of oil and gas extraction:

> One of the overall principles of Norway's management of its petroleum resources is that . . . revenues must accrue to the Norwegian state and thus benefit society as a whole. The main reason for this is the extraordinary returns that can be obtained by producing petroleum resources.[5]

Total also rose to the challenge of returning money to the treasury. The privatisation of 1992 raised close to \$1 billion. In fact, the French government earned over \$34 billion in the decade 1985 to 1995 from selling off state owned companies—in European terms, second only to the UK.[6]

Building on this theme of social responsibility, Henrik Habberstad, Head of brand and creative at Equinor, says that for the company taking branding seriously means building "a meaningful and relevant connection with the population in Norway . . ." Yet, one population segment stands out. "It also means building a meaningful relationship with younger people. That is why branding is important—because we are developing a relationship with the next generation."

That relationship is important, as Norway is in a peculiar position when it comes to energy production. Almost 100 per cent of the country's electricity comes from renewables. To ample hydro and wind resources 160MW of solar panels have been added in recent years, which means that only around 2 per cent of Norway's electricity now comes from thermal power plants.[7] Most of Norway's oil production, and with it the associated problems of carbon emissions and air pollution, are exported. As electrification of transport gathers pace you can easily imagine a situation in which Norway itself has no direct use for its most valuable export commodity, except in the function of generating sovereign wealth. The next generation, the Greta Thunbergs of this world, however, are ready to challenge the status quo.

Henrik, a true devotee of the Equinor brand, has worked all of his career (including 5 years at Norway's multinational Telenor) in marketing and branding. He is aware of the challenge of transition, which usually amounts

OIL COMPANIES   83

to the conundrum of opening your hands to grasp a new opportunity while not letting go of something you already hold.

In my dealings with him over the years, I have found that, like many other marketing executives, Henrik had developed around him a "marketing armour" (metaphorically speaking), to fend off the constant sales-calls, and demands on his time and budget. Under that armour, however, Henrik has retained a keen sensitivity for the social implications of the energy business and is passionate about Equinor's transition from an old-school sovereign oil company to a renewable brand.

> The generation that has created Statoil and the Norwegian oil and gas industry, has perhaps not awakened yet to the need of doing things differently. But the next generation hasn't seen anything else, they take Statoil's reputation for granted. They are not concerned with how things were before the discovery of oil and gas in the North Sea. Rather, they are looking to the future. We need to gain their confidence and build a strong connection.

Part of building that confidence in the future is Equinor's sizeable investment in offshore wind farms. The company already has one of the largest offshore windfarm portfolios in Europe and has been awarded contracts to deploy the technology off the coast of New York "in one of the largest renewable energy procurements in the US to date".[8] In the UK it is part of the Dogger Bank consortium—the biggest and most daring offshore wind farm project ever to go into construction. At the nearest point, it is 130 km off the UK's shoreline and at its furthest around 290 km—right in the middle of the North Sea, between the UK and Norway.

On its part Total is also considering the basic principles of its business, which, as Tom Van de Cruys explains, is "to bring energy to people worldwide, and do that in a way that is fit for today—and for the future". He believes, as Henrik does, that "if you're realistic about the future, you accept things will change". But, although the French colossus has rebranded itself as TotalEnergies, the company has chosen a gradualist approach. In setting it out, Tom starts with a cautious double negative.

> Total is not saying that we are not going to be an oil company. Rather, we are saying that we're going to be an energy company—and all

that we do is a part of it. It's oil, it's gas and in today's world it has to be power, especially renewable power. That extension to what we do today, uses oil as our foundation, building into gas, which is a part of our future.

In Tom's view, natural gas will remain a necessary ingredient of the energy mix, until renewable energy storage solutions are available at the scale required.

But, storage or no storage, Total's turnover, amounting to $200 billion per annum, means the company doesn't have to wait at the sidelines when it comes to developing renewable power. As Tom's says, "We are a company of big investments, and renewable power is typically a business of big investments." To underline this enthusiasm Total joined other sovereign oil companies in choosing a new name, one that puts a measure of distance between its history and its aspirations. In May of 2021 Total rebranded as TotalEnergies, with the BBC reporting chief executive Patrick Pouyanné's statement, "We want to become a sort of green energy major." The story also noted that, "while several small investors opposed the company's plans at the annual general meeting, arguing they did not go far enough, the resolution was passed with more than 90% of the vote".[9]

Equinor, then known as Statoil, went through the same process in 2018 (interestingly, also concluded in May). On that occasion the company's CEO Eldar Sætre took a view echoed by Henrik. Sætre said, "Statoil has almost become a separate term, a concept in its own right. But I have to think of future generations who don't necessarily have the same relationship to the 'concept' of Statoil." He added that the new name, derived from "equi", the Latin root of words like equality and equilibrium, and "nor," which signifies a company proud of its Norwegian origins, "says something about our views on people, and on energy".

As Henrik points out "innovation was in Statoil's DNA". That hard-wired ability to overcome technological challenges of offshore oil and gas extraction, also evident in renewable energy projects such as Dogger Bank, is actually the very same ability to reinvent and rebrand the company for the "net zero" age. In Henrik's view, this is where branding, as a marketing discipline comes in:

Brand is more important than ever before, as it postulates how the company relates to the world around it. These days branding, especially in our industry, is more than advertising, it is about education. Our brand indicates how we work and how we behave, as a company. I think that the perception of branding has changed in the last few years, to take this in.

That is, at least, the theory of it. And then, as Henrik ads, there is the practice of branding at a company ranked among Europe's top 50, in terms of revenue. To be effective, the brand message needs to cut through a considerable amount of noise, much of it coming from the media. Henrik says that Equinor is easily "the most talked about company in Norway". He adds that "it could end up featuring on the front pages of the country's financial press at least once or twice every week". But, it is here that branding starts to matter.

> The next generation perceives traditional media as "old". They might not be watching the same TV programmes that we have been watching, nor reading the same newspapers. In fact, they might not be reading newspapers at all. Branding opens a new means of communication, it gives us an opportunity to create a new set of associations through media that are closer to our target audience.

Tom, a social media enthusiast, who (I noticed over the years) is very adept at harnessing it for business communications, offers a similar view on the synergy between branding and the internet, particularly in a business-to-business, or B2B environment.

> In B2B (business-to-business) a strong brand, promoted on social media, does the job that in B2C (business-to-consumer) you would need millions in spend to complete—particularly, when you take into account marketing and PR budgets. B2B is more about tactics and understanding how they work in that environment, rather than about sheer budget. In B2C you need to create customer awareness, and creating customer awareness costs serious money. On the other hand, you can get a great deal of traction with your business clients, on the back of your brand on social media.

Over the last 15 years the brand/social media dynamic has increasingly come under the magnifying lens of academics and marketing experts.

Their interest had been prompted by the proliferation of social media web-sites, an ever-increasing number of users, and the various ways such users engage with the sites, including to promote and endorse brands. An influential article, "Introducing COBRAs—Exploring Motivations for Brand-Related Social Media Use", published in the *International Journal of Advertising* in 2011, by researchers from the University of Amsterdam Daniel G. Muntinga *et al.*, introduces the concept of consumers' online brand-related activities (COBRAs) with the aim of understanding their motivation.[10]

The article starts off by offering different COBRA typologies. According to one there are "four internet user types, namely lurkers, socialisers, personal connectors and transactional community members", while another distinguishes "six types of social media users: inactives, spectators, joiners, collectors, critics and creators".

The authors, however, offer "a COBRA typology as a continuum of three usage types—consuming, contributing and creating". **Consuming** includes activities such as "viewing brand-related video, listening to brand-related audio, watching brand-related pictures and reading product reviews," all the way to "playing branded online videogames, downloading branded widgets and sending branded virtual gifts/cards". **Contributing** includes "rating products and/or brands, joining a brand profile on a social network site and engaging in branded conversations, e.g. on online brand community forums or social network sites". Finally, **creating** encompasses "publishing a brand-related weblog, uploading brand-related video, audio, pictures or images, writing brand-related articles and writing product reviews".

Each one of these usage types us driven by a specific set of motivations. For instance**, consuming** is driven by "information, entertainment and remuneration". While the first two motivations are self-explanatory the third, which the authors claim "has been found in earlier studies on consuming brand-related content on social media" includes incentives such as "a trip, a pair of the latest Adidas sneakers, or simply value for money". Motivations for **contributing** are threefold, "personal identity, integration and social interaction, and entertainment", as are those for **creating** content. The authors point out that personal identity branches into three sub-motivations "self-expression, self-presentation and self-assurance", while integration and social interaction branches into the sub-motivations of "social interaction, social identity and helping".

This elaborate taxonomy of social media user types, their activities and their motivations offers a corporate brand manager a menu of strategic options in building a brand's social media profile. It also aids the understanding of classic concepts such of brand loyalty or commitment, as it brings home the importance of brands for our own sense of social belonging.

Tom says that the biggest challenge for every energy brand is understanding its societal role, and how it "translates its business mission into something that is relevant for the environment". Solving this challenge, that he sees as the most "complicated part of the brief handed over to a branding agency" is important as environmental concerns (CO_2 emissions, air quality, protection of habitats) are both regulatory issues, and social identity drivers. A successful energy brand, then, aligns it business mission with the duty of care for the environment. This duty is an internalised expression of societal and individual values. A toxic brand, on the other hand, seems to set aside such values and concerns. As Tom sums it up, "you can do it very wrong".

It turns out that, while branding specialists have a role in advising on overall strategy, one of those things that you could do wrong is entrust your social media channels to outsiders. When asked about mistakes in branding and communications he had committed and would not repeat, Tom says:

> When social media really started taking off in 2012 or 2013, as many other companies, we hired an outside agency to create social media campaigns. The way that they did it, I felt that they had burned out social media content.

He continues:

> In any case, the outcome of this engagement was the decision not to use an agency or a consultant again, but to be authentic. I think this is a key concept in social media. Rather than have someone from the outside filming things with a fancy camera, in a staged setting, it should be me and you, or someone from the team, sat around this table, with one of us filming.

As Tom explains:

> I cannot imagine an external agency getting so close to our corporate culture that they could represent us adequately on social media. Think about the instantaneous nature of the internet: you have to be on the ball when something is happening, answer questions quickly and react in the moment. Who can do that better that your own team?

He concludes, "In the end, these are the only people you can trust as totally into your culture—you can trust they will do the right thing."

Developing the theme of company culture and how important it is to your company's public perception and to the image it projects to your business customers, Tom offers an interesting example of brand congruity from his time as CEO of independent electricity and gas retailer Lampiris:

> In Belgium there is a cult of the company car. It is a benefit in addition to your salary, so many people will try and negotiate the biggest car possible. Now, I like the BMW as much as anyone else, but this brand didn't fit with our company culture. I, for instance, drove a Prius. One of the owners drove an Audi A3 and the other an old Audi A4. Our policy was also for account managers to visit customers in modest, low-cost cars. And then we switched everybody to electric cars.

Tom concludes that "Once we're all aligned and on the same page if somebody steps out of line, the others will immediately correct it. That's what it means to get your culture right."

It is not just culture that is important to brand messaging, but also proximity to information. Henrik says that the main challenge for any company and even more so for those in the energy sector is "turning words into action, especially when it comes to climate change." With a great deal of openness, he says that although we are all in this together, in the sense that we all burn carbon in our daily lives for activities that are perhaps non-essential, he emphasises that "Equinor as a big energy company is a big part of the problem. However, on the positive side, this means that we are also thrilled to be part of the solution. Our brand signals that determination, to deal with the challenges very close to us."

Henrik gives an example of Gullfaks, one of the largest oil and gas fields on the Norwegian continental shelf. At 800,000 tonnes of CO_2 annually, it is one of the largest carbon emitters in Norway. For some years the company has been trying to reduce emissions there, and at other exploration sites, in order to realise its ambition of being a net-zero energy company by 2050. Henrik concludes:

> Because I am the creative director, in charge of producing Equinor's content I am very close to that problem. There is no other way I could write or review copy about it. But, not only am I keenly aware of the issues at Gullfaks, I am also aware of what it takes to solve it. In a sense, I am also close to the solution, and I can tell you that it's a good solution. Still, as I said, turning words into actions is a challenge.

Given that energy companies offer solutions to the problems of climate change which are highly technical and often scarcely understandable to the layperson, my question to Tom was on the role of emotions in energy branding. His answer reveals an interesting shift in the emotions versus reason debate:

> Before, you could have big branding campaigns around emotion, and that was what everybody did. If you look at Engie or GDF campaigns in the past, B2C was all about emotions and nothing rational. I think this doesn't work anymore. My issue with emotions as something emanating from a brand is that I believe you need to give it personality first. Even in a campaign, I would rather bring out authenticity, something real, then immediately appeal to emotion. That doesn't mean campaigns should be emotionless, on the contrary. Bring out the personality, make it human, and that is where your emotion is.

Tom gives an example:

> Let's say we put our CEO Patrick Pouyanne, in front of the camera. He will be prepared, as always, with the relevant facts. He is good at that. But, he will also bring something else to the screen—himself, his personality. That is very authentic, and that's your emotion right there. That is the best way to represent your brand, just

by being authentic. I don't think you should ask him to do anything else. Now, a brand consultant might want to bring out something else, but if your audience feels the authenticity, if it sees an honest and real conversation, that makes up for everything. That is also company culture.

Perhaps this view reveals something about the energy business, as it goes against the marketing gospel of emotions as motivators of consumer behaviour. Writing in the *Harvard Business Review*, Scott Magids *et al.* flag their research that "across hundreds of brands in dozens of categories . . . it's possible to rigorously measure and strategically target the feelings that drive customers' behaviour". The authors call these feeling "emotional motivators" and add that "they provide a better gauge of customers' future value to a firm than any other metric, including brand awareness and customer satisfaction, and can be an important new source of growth and profitability".[11]

Magids and colleagues give the example of a major bank introducing a credit card for Millennials that was designed to inspire emotional connection, and note that its "use among the segment increased by 70% and new account growth rose by 40%". They also write about a leading household cleaner, who within a year of launching products and messaging to maximise emotional connection, "turned market share losses into double-digit growth". Similar examples, according to the authors, abound.

On the other hand, I am not the only person to have noticed that the energy sector messaging seems particularly dry and technical. I have often thought that this is either because the is dominated by engineers and technicians, or because power companies sell a product that is difficult (some say impossible) to brand.

But, as I conducted these interviews I started thinking there could be another reason. It is hard to argue that there isn't now a special responsibility on the global energy business. Nothing less is at stake than the future of our society, and perhaps even the future of the planet. Emotion alone shouldn't be enough, or as Henrik puts it: "We need some strong, rational arguments in the conversation. Actually, we need to start with rational arguments, which you then need to present in a passionate, emotional way."

Henrik links this idea with the challenge of branding a commodity. Commodities, by themselves undifferentiated or standardised, seem particularly unresponsive to branding. If you are buying a Brent Barrel of crude, a metric tonne of iron ore or a megawatthour of electricity, you are essentially buying the same thing. But, who you are buying it from? Are all companies alike? Energy branding then turns out to be about company reputation, or as Henrik puts it about "building a meaningful relationship in the world out there". Parameters by which you measure a success of a brand, such as brand-awareness, have a point only if they measure how the brand actually fortifies the company's reputation.

This is, of course, complicated by what reputation means for an energy multinational, working across national borders. As Rahul in Chapter 6, Tom also notes that in developed or Western societies we tend to talk a lot about CO_2 and air pollution. But, he says "there are other parts of the world where Total is very active, but where that is not even an issue. There, the key issue could be finding the energy, from whichever source, to keep the economy going—to survive. If that energy can be used for social and economic development—even better."

Tom believes that the awareness of this dual perspective on energy, in developed as opposed to developing countries, differentiates oil companies from those which are purely utilities, especially Western utilities. "We are in spaces and environments where there's something else at stake." He concludes, "There is no choice about the road we are going now. We are all sustainable-future oriented. Look at investment trends, and international agreements. Let's see what companies such as Exxon will do, will they survive, will they stick to their current image? I think everybody's going that way, which is the only way in the future."

Going over Tom's interview, in preparation for writing this chapter, I realised that he might have spoken prophetically. As the New York Times and much of the world's business media reported in May 2021:

> Big Oil was dealt a stunning defeat on Wednesday when shareholders of Exxon Mobil elected at least two board candidates nominated by activist investors who pledged to steer the company toward cleaner energy and away from oil and gas . . . Analysts could not recall another time that Exxon management had lost a vote against company-picked directors.[12]

Then, a few weeks later, in June 2021 investor mutiny at Exxon Mobil secured a third seat at the board: "While the first two new dissident board members were oil company veterans, the newest member, Alexander

OIL COMPANIES

A. Karsner, has strong environmental credentials and is expected to pose more of a challenge to senior management."[13]

Could this mean that even the oil-baron, old school, head-in-the-sand petroleum companies will soon be queuing up for a rebrand? However, perhaps a more crucial question is whether such a change in direction will make up for lost time in fighting climate change.

Talking about strategies which should have been in the energy sector's communications toolkit from the start Tom is pensive:

> I'm always wondering if instead of the energy debate focusing on CO_2 emissions, it should have targeted air pollution. It sounds like a different discussion, but it comes to the same point. Yet, air pollution is much easier to connect to something very close to all of us—which is our own health and well-being . . . And that of our families. Instead of fighting global warming, a somewhat abstract and long-term problem, perhaps we should have been fighting the effects of air pollution, such as respiratory illnesses and cancer.

Henrik sees Statoil's future in oil and gas production and in renewables. But, oil and gas production, in keeping with the company's commitments, will be offset by a push towards overall decarbonisations, such as via carbon capture and storage.

He says, "it's all about producing the old product in a new way". Which, actually, could be the mantra of any energy company around today. Both electricity and oil and gas, as widely traded commodities, have been around for over 150 years. Turning them into new products is actually a similar task to turning old companies into new ones. And that is essentially the challenge of branding.

Notes

1. Doyle, Alister. "All Norwegians Become Crown Millionaires, in Oil Saving Landmark." *Reuters*, 8 Jan. 2014, www.reuters.com/article/us-norway-mill ionaires-idUSBREA0710U20140108.
2. For a brief history of Shell and its scallop logo, see previous chapter.
3. Information on the history of Equinor (Statoil), as well as information on the company's notable projects, such as Dogger Bank and Gullfaks, have been taken from the company website at equinor.com.

4. TotalEnergies.com website contains a wealth of material on the company's history, including a documentary mentioning the letter from French Prime Minister Raymond Poincare to the industrialist Ernest Mercier, instructing Mercier to form the state's oil company. See subpage titled "TotalEnergies, a Pioneering Spirit", at https://totalenergies.com/group/identity/history.

5. Facts on Norway's petroleum production can be found on the norskpetroleum.no, the site of the Norwegian Petroleum Directorate. See subpage headlined "The Government's Revenues" at norskpetroleum.no/en/economy/governments-revenues/.

6. See Wolf, Christian and Michael G. Pollitt. "Privatising National Oil Companies: Assessing the Impact on Firm Performance", 29 Feb. 2008, www.jbs.cam.ac.uk/wp-content/uploads/2020/08/wp0802-v2.pdf. A wider look at the issue of privatisation across Europe can be found in Parker, David. "Privatization in the European Union: A Critical Assessment of its Development, Rationale and Consequences." *Journal of Economic and Industrial Democracy,* Vol. 20, No. 1, February 1999, (doi.org/10.1177/0143831X99201002).

7. The website energifaktanorge.no ("energy facts Norway" in English) is the source of data on the country's energy mix. See subpage titled "Electricity Production" at https://energifaktanorge.no/en/norsk-energiforsyning/kraftproduksjon/.

8. See press release issued by Equinor on January 14, 2022, titled "Equinor and bp achieve key step in advancing offshore wind for New York". It can be found on https://www.equinor.com/news/archive/20220114-key-step-advancing-offshore-wind-new-york.

9. "French Oil Giant Total Rebrands in Shift to Renewables", BBC, 28 May 2021, www.bbc.com/news/business-57282008. The article also reported the company's aspiration to reach "net zero" by 2050.

10. Muntinga, Daniel G. et al. "Introducing COBRAs: Exploring Motivations for Brand-Related Social Media Use", *International Journal of Advertising,* Vol. 30, No. 1, pp. 13–46, (doi:10.2501/IJA-30-1-013-046). the research contained therein "was funded by a grant from the Dutch Foundation for Fundamental Research on Brands and Brand Communication (SWOCC)." SWOCC was established by Giep Franzen in 1995. One of Professor Franzen's areas of academic interest was the phenomenon of "brand personality". This personality is derived from people associated with a brand, as well as via product-related attributes such as brand name, logo, communication style and price. See also Smit, Edith G. et al.

"Brands are just like real people! The development of SWOCC's brand personality scale." Hansen, Flemming and Lars Bech Christensen, editors. Branding and Advertising. Copenhagen Business School Press, pp. 22–43.

11. Magids, Scott *et al.* "The New Science of Customer Emotions." *Harvard Business Review*, Nov. 2015, hbr.org/2015/11/the-new-science-of-customer-emotions.

12. Kraus, Clifford and Peter Eavis. "Climate Activists Defeat Exxon in Push for Clean Energy." *The New York Times*, 26 May 2021, nytimes.com/2021/05/26/business/exxon-mobil-climate-change.html.

13. Kraus, Clifford. "Exxon Board to Get a Third Activist Pushing Cleaner Energy." *The New York Times*, 2 Jun. 2021, nytimes.com/2021/06/02/business/exxon-board-clean-energy.html.

8

THE ITALIAN JOB

ANTONIO CAMMISECRA ON ENEL'S POWER DISTRIBUTION BRANDING STRATEGY

As I type this sentence I am mindful that I should put a full stop at the end of it. I also recognise the value of the comma, in separating parts of sentences, grouping words together or enumerating lists. What about the question mark? Just like the semi-colon, it is widely used; we can scarcely imagine a system of notation without it.

But, where did these useful signs come from? If your intuition tells you that they came much later than the written word, you are right. For many centuries, texts in Europe, in the Latin language, were written in something called a *scriptio continua*. Not only were there no full stops or commas, but words were joined together in continuous hand-written script. There were no standards for how sentences should be terminated, clauses separated, or direct speech quoted. And then punctuation, like so many other practical or beautiful things (such as concrete, perspective in painting, or ice cream) was invented . . . By the Italians.

Reading Malcolm Bowles, one of the world's greatest palaeographers (see here *Pause and Effect: An Introduction to the History of Punctuation in the West*[1]),

DOI: 10.4324/9781003351030-9

it becomes clear that the evolution and standardisation of such symbols contains a list of almost exclusively Italian names: from Buonocompagno of Bologna, the twelfth-century scholar who proposed a *"virgula standing upright"* (a forward slash) to indicate a pause, and the *planus* (the dash), to indicate end of sentence; via Coluccio Salutati of Florence who introduced the parentheses; culminating in the work of the Venetian printer Aldus Manutius who, among other things, published the world's first semi-colon, and compressed Buonocompagno's *virgula* into the comma we use today. Appropriately, he also developed the precursor of the *italic* typeface.[2]

Now, when I say that all these handy inventions—or perhaps conventions—were the work of Italians, I am well aware that the unification of Italy, the *Risorgimento*, was not completed until 1871. It is then perhaps more accurate to say that the cultural milieu of what is now Italy, had over the centuries, guided Europe, in art, design and, not least, business. The words *bank* and *merchant* come from Latin and Old Italian, as do *capital* and *investment*. The legacy of the renaissance is so rich, that the fact of Italy being the world's eighth largest economy in terms of GDP,[3] often gets overlooked.

I have taken punctuation as an example of good design—a perfect blend of form and function in their visual simplicity and functional versatility—as I have a professional, yet also somewhat innate interest in typography. If you work in branding or marketing, you likely have it too. Actually, you might have a talent for using fonts and other elements of graphic design to condense messages into as few words as possible.

Perhaps it was a natural affinity for such things that has brought you into this industry. But, regardless how you got here, once you start looking at brands professionally, you will also notice that a brand is more than its design. It is more than its name or logo. In my experience a successful brand is, in fact, a deliberate blend of strategy and design.

Not that names or logos are unimportant. If you are a marketing or branding practitioner, often that's where the money is. As Chekitan S. Dev and colleagues write in "What's in a Brand Name?", an article on the impacts of rebranding, "when Amoco rebranded to the BP name, the company spent £4.6 million to design the logo and invested £132 million over two years just to rebrand its stationery, van liveries and manufacturing plants".[4] The paybacks of successful branding, however, are also significant. Summing up their results, the authors claim that in the US hospitality industry "rebranding results, on average, in a 6.31% increase in (room) occupancy rates". Given that there are five million hotel rooms in the US, and that the three biggest chains alone own over 2 million, this a significant uptick.

Going back to my examples of Italian inventiveness, I wonder if it was the Italians that were particularly astute in grasping that brands, dependent on as they are on strong marketing and product design, are built on much more than that. Were they also the first to realise that the aim of branding strategy is to produce a kind of brand charisma, a condensed amalgam of positive reputation, desirability and dominance? Many Italian fashion and automotive brands have exactly this kind of aura, both romantic and timeless.

I also wonder to what extent this cultural instinct for strategy and design has contributed to Enel's becoming the world's biggest privately owned power company. According to Power Technology rankings, Enel has earned $90 billion in 2019, ahead of second placed EDF's $80 billion. Commenting on the list the portal said that "Enel's 2019 revenues increased by 6.3%, driven by infrastructure and network operations in Latin America, distribution business in Brazil, and thermal generation activities in Italy."[5]

Perhaps this growth in the Americas is a consequence of Enel daring to be different. The company was very bold in using colour, with its 2016 rebrand introducing a logo of fluid lines and nuanced shades of red, blue, grey and green.[6] It was a kind of transposition of the "United Colors of Benetton" aesthetics into the power business, as if Enel was saying: "Hey, we are not just a reliable energy company, we are also fresh and dynamic."

All of a sudden, other American brands seemed old-fashioned in comparison, and Enel was gaining market share. However, the multi-coloured logo was signalling not just youthful zest, but also an aptitude for business in different environments, and across continents. Another example of the brand as a potent blend of strategy and design.

For Antonio Cammisecra, who at the time of the interview is Head of Enel Global Infrastructure and Networks but who has also led Enel's Green Power brand during an important merge of the renewables and thermal divisions into a Global Power Generation division, the brand is the "most condensed form of communicating something . . . That can be your company's goals and values, your vision and performance. Everything is there—your history and your behaviour, and by extension, your next move." Brand is inseparable from its communication, adds Antonio. Taking this assumption on board is particularly important for power distribution businesses, as they deliver a standardised commodity to people's homes.

"In our business it's difficult to be perceived, to be differentiated, through what you are delivering. The brand is a means of differentiation, but only around the way you're doing it, around quality of service." Antonio has run the Enel grid business since October 2020. He thinks that consumer companies don't face such branding challenges. "For instance, if you have a beautiful product, and you have a fantastic brand, the product and the brand work together, by association." A distribution brand, on the other hand, conveys a sense of power, and perhaps, more importantly, a sense of possibility.

That sense of possibility, as the energy business evolves, also needs to cover adaptability. But power distribution companies seem unassailable, perhaps more so than other parts of the energy value chain, as there is simply no other way to distribute electricity except through high, medium and low-voltage networks. And each stretch of wire, with its pylons and poles, can only have one owner-operator.

It is hard to imagine the electricity system functioning otherwise, or distribution companies coming under serious pressure from alternative technologies. Yet, we have seen in recent years the rise of distributed generation and virtual power stations. Whatever the full potential of this new technology, there is a wider point here, explored by the German American economist and professor of marketing at Harvard Theodore Levitt, in his widely anthologised 1960 essay "Marketing Myopia".[7] It was this essay that introduced the now famous question, "What business are you really in?"

It starts with a powerful but often forgotten truth that "every major industry was once a growth industry", before Levitt moves to the example of the railroads: "Railroads did not stop growing because the need for passenger and freight transportation declined. That grew . . . They let others take customers away from them because they assumed themselves to be in the railroad business rather than in the transportation business."[8]

Levitt also writes with a great deal of foresight about electric utilities, asking provocatively "Who says that utilities have no competition?" He warns that, "this is another one of those supposedly "no substitute" products that has been enthroned on the pedestal of invincible growth",[9] and speculates that the end of these monopolies could be hastened by solar panels, fuel cells or other devices on the horizon—devices which might not be commercially available yet, but are developed by non-utility companies. "To survive", he concludes, "they themselves will have to plot the obsolescence of what now produces their livelihood."[10]

Levitt's message is now part of any respectable MBA course: "The view that an industry is a customer-satisfying process, not a goods producing process, is vital for all businesspeople to understand."[11] The pull out quote at the top of the 2004 reprint of the article sums it up thus: "Sustained growth depends on how broadly you define your business—and how carefully you gauge your customers' needs".[12]

Enel's response to the challenge of adaptability was to invest heavily into R&D and diversify into smart energy technologies, by creating a new brand Enel X (see also Chapter 3). In a sense, the new subsidiary's vision statement, as quoted on the company's website, answers the question "What business are you really in?" in these words: "To make the complex simple through innovative solutions . . . designed around ever-changing needs." It is almost as if, across its subsidiaries, Enel is in the business of anticipating changes in customer behaviour.

Antonio highlights the task of branding the conglomerate's distribution arm. "For us, there are a number of questions to consider as we expand into global markets. Are we a local, or national distributor, or should we think of ourselves primarily as part of a global company?" This is not a pedantic question as regulators across the world impose a variety of rules on energy companies regarding corporate structure. Antonio quotes the example of the European Union where, in certain cases, the laws prescribe a clear demarcation line, or unbundling, between generation, distribution and retail.

"We don't have a separate brand for Enel's grid activities, instead we have local companies in those countries where we are present as network operator, such as in the Brazilian states of Ceara, Rio de Janeiro, San Paolo and Goias." Thinking about what a global unified brand for the distribution business could be, Antonio says he would be fond of Enel Grids. "It is something simple and straightforward. Within Enel that brand could blend together aspects of that middle layer of operations—the layer between our local companies and the global brand."

Speaking as someone with a penchant for branding, Antonio passionately extols the advantages of creating a separate grid brand:

> Enel strategy, so to speak, stands on two big legs—decarbonisation and electrification. We now aim for complete decarbonisation by 2040, with our sustainability plan specifically promoting the electrification of consumption. Here we also aim to increase the use of second generation smart meters, hosting capacity, demand response and electric vehicle charging stations.

As Antonio explains:

> The grid brand is important as it brings all of these possibilities to the consumer. Both in the sense of individual inventions, and on the strategic level of decarbonisation and electrification. It would also enable an evolving dialogue with the consumer, which could then be used to increase the awareness of the wider public. A brand, then, should be as much about education, as it is about marketing.

For now, Enel's official position is that Enel Grids will not be developed into a separate brand (with its own logo and brand identity), but rather it will be the legal and organisational name of that particular business line.

Reaching out to regulators and the general public is essential to support and promote grid companies' investment and maintenance programmes. Grid operations are one of the most visible parts of the energy business, and the education Antonio mentions is essential both for understanding the operators land-use requirements, and their concern that they are properly funded. A credible grid brand—which raises awareness of forward maintenance programmes and fair tariff rates—will, in the final instance, increase service quality and system resilience.

Such a strong grid brand is particularly important when the infrastructure is under stress, as it ensures that the system can cope. It would have done that through scheduled maintenance, as much as by improving the regulatory environment, and increasing public acceptance. Antonio mentions the February 2021 Texas power crisis during which more than 3.3 million homes and business were left without electricity, causing state-wide shortages of food, water and heat.

A follow-on article on this catastrophe by *Bloomberg Businessweek* reminded readers that "Texas' grid is almost entirely disconnected from the rest of the country, which exempts it from federal rules but also means it's unable to pull power from neighbouring states in times of crisis. In 1999 the state went further, passing a law that deregulated its power market."[13] The article also noted that the focus of many Texans' frustration was the Electric Reliability Council of Texas (Ercot), the nonprofit company that manages the state's electricity grid. On February 23 five Ercot board members, including the chair, resigned. But, as the company pointed out, although they have the responsibility for running the grid, they can not impose regulatory penalties on plant operators who ignore extreme weather precautions.

To increase their social leverage, some grid operators have mobilised large public relations and branding campaigns, which have rolled on for years. In May 2011, United Kingdom's transmission operator, National Grid, in partnership with RIBA (Royal Institute of British Architects), launched a design competition for the next generation electricity pylon, for the construction of new power lines in England and Wales.

The government hailed the competition as an "astonishing success attracting media coverage from around the globe", and awarded the first prize to Danish architects Bystrup's. Their T-pylon bested 250 other entries, including designs with funky names such as "Totem" and "Silhouette". Proving the old journalism motto that a good story can run and run, the competition was still being mentioned four years later, with Design Week reporting in 2015 that the first six T-pylons (with their "sweeping curves") were being installed at National Grid's training academy in Eakring, England.[14]

I explored with Antonio the concept of a brand as a somewhat intangible and charismatic connection with the consumers, based on loyalty and good will. In his view, it was the advent of renewables that has changed how people relate to energy companies:

> From a niche, technical issue power generation has, in the last five years, become a top issue! Now, after the Paris Accord and with Greta Thunberg it is all around us, discussed in great detail by almost everyone. This has also made people more aware of the importance of the distributor. Renewable energy sources, which are often in remote locations, require new distribution infrastructure, in addition to existing power lines.

But, it is sometimes the regulators, who despite being vocal about the need for energy companies to build links with host communities, that hamper the establishment of strong distribution brands. As he notes, regulatory separation between parent brand and local brand, disconnects that supply of public good will, leaving distribution companies with a peculiar problem:

> We are at our most recognisable at a time of crisis, during an emergency or when disaster strikes. It is then that you see our people working hard in the field, on top of electricity poles, to connect the wires and get energy flowing again. So, really, we are at our most visible at the moment of greatest customer dissatisfaction.

That is the moment the distribution company needs to be on top of its game, both in terms of field operations, and communications. If the crisis is promptly averted and the public kept informed, Antonio says you get something stronger than customer loyalty—gratitude. It leads him to reflect on the role of emotions in getting the public engaged in the energy transition:

> There is no doubt about it, the energy transition won't work without the customer playing an active part. But, it impossible to motivate customer activity, whether in implementing energy efficiency or installing renewable devices, without reaching for emotional levers.

And there is no more powerful lever than getting the customer to understand that "they have a role in saving the world". Otherwise, he says, the relationship will revolve around the most prosaic part of the retail business—the energy bill. In which case, if you are a government owned company, at the end of each month you will be perceived simply as a government agency which levies a toll on the helpless consumer.

Antonio's assumptions on the role of emotions in driving energy-customer behaviour, or perhaps more importantly in prompting behavioural change, are borne out by studies of prosumers and their motivations. The concept of "prosumer" (a portmanteau of "producer" and "consumer"), coined by futurologist Alfin Tofler in his 1981 book The Third Wave[15] has become especially relevant to the energy sector, with the proliferation of affordable energy-generating devices.

Still, "affordable" here should be understood in the cautious sense of being cheaper to install than it once was, not necessarily as producing cheap electricity.

THE ITALIAN JOB   103

And yet, prosumers are prepared not just to pay more per kilowatt hour, but they put up large sums of money upfront to have a renewable energy system (RES) installed. Researchers studying this phenomenon have noted that "energy consumer and prosumer behaviour can not be explained solely by economic factors".[16] They talk about intrinsic and extrinsic behavioural motivators, such as values, beliefs and aspirations.

What has become clear is that socio-ecological concerns have become a key driver in RES implementation. The PROSEU project, for instance, a research coalition studying the renewable energy prosumer phenomenon, has found that for the majority of collective prosumer types (which they have classed as market, community, not-for profit, state and hybrid) socio-ecological motivators rank as "high".

On the other hand, in her thorough-going legal article on individual energy prosumers in the United States, Sharon Jacobs identified a number of motivators for prosumption. The economic motivator is key, but others, which to my ears somehow sound typically American, also get a detailed mention: greater control over electricity supply and patterns of consumption, desire for energy autonomy, libertarian ideals (in the sense of disconnecting from local utilities because they are controlled by the government), and environmental concerns.[17]

However, whether you are an American libertarian or a European socialist, what you have in common as prosumers is a sense that energy is more than just a commodity. It enables you to live independently—or perhaps, it connects you with your energy community. In either case, it opens up possibilities, which is a theme Antonio returns to as we discuss the challenge of branding a commodity:

> With electricity you can do one thing or the other. For instance, if you are a business owner, and energy is reliable and affordable, you can open a factory. You can just plug in and get to work. Rather than selling you a commodity, we are opening up a possibility. With us you can live and plan a better life.

Antonio wonders if energy companies are missing a trick in terms of how they talk about power:

> Imagine if you were a laptop manufacturer highlighting an improved screen as the chief feature of your new product. Would you talk about

all the transistors and microchips behind that screen, and how you put it all together. Or would you talk about all the wonderful people in your life that you will talk to online and see on that screen, your friends and family, your business partners and colleagues.

It again comes down to Levitt's question of "Which business are you really in?" If you are in the business of trading a commodity, than branding might not be on top of your list. But, how many energy retailers and distributors really see themselves that way? Antonio continues:

> Even if we concede that energy is a commodity, distribution companies are in a different niche. We are infrastructure providers. You could say we provide a service. To choose a parallel, we are similar to highway operators. We aim to open new traffic lanes, to take you, for instance, quickly to the airport. But we also maintain existing lanes, for when you need them.

This is analogy that is sometimes lost on the consumer. Distribution brands fail to communicate clearly either the demands of system maintenance, or the value of availability at the point of use. Antonio gives the example of customers complaining about bills to their second homes, which they use a few weeks or months a year. It is, he says, an often repeated line: why do we have to pay bills, even if we don't use any energy? Why do we have to pay just for the connection?

"This is why brand strategies need to evolve, aiming to increase customer knowledge and awareness, by focusing on their emotions. They need to support the efforts the energy system will undertake to ensure electricity for all", Antonio concludes. In the coming years, as there are more renewable power sources connected to the grid, electricity as a commodity will get cheaper. But the cost of connecting and managing this advanced grid system—with its distributed and geographically dispersed power sources, varying in output throughout the day—will be more expensive. As a consequence, energy bills will look different, and that is why distributors need to start taking branding seriously. There is much work ahead in convincing, perhaps even educating, both regulators and energy customers on the need for change.

"Enel started on this journey early on", says Antonio:

We saw what kind of future was coming down the road, and planned 20 years ahead. We started our journey and we never stopped. Then we built our brand according to our long-term plans. In a way, the brand is an exercise, a marathon: you can decide whether to go forward, accelerate or retreat. We decided to speed up, because we know that when we cross the finish line, the fatigue will disappear, and we will reap and share with our stakeholders the benefits of our effort.

Notes

1. Bowles, Malcolm. *Pause and Effect: An Introduction to the History of Punctuation in the West.* Routledge, 1994. The book has gained wider prominence since it was mentioned by Lynne Truss in her surprise bestseller *Eats, Shoots and Leaves: The Zero Tolerance Approach to Punctuation.*
2. For more information about the great mediaval Italian scholars of rhetoric and grammar, from Buonocompagno to Salutati see the standard reference work Kleinhenz, Christopher (ed.). *Medieval Italy: An Encyclopedia.* Routledge, 2004.
3. Country GDP rankings are based on International Monetary Fund data published on the organisation's website imf.org, subpage "GDP, current prices", imf.org/external/datamapper/NGDPD@WEO/OEMDC/ADVEC/ WEOWORLD. Italy has been ranked the world's 8th largest economy in 2020.
4. Dev, Chekitan S. at al. "What's in a Brand Name? Assessing the Impact of Rebranding in the Hospitality Industry", *Journal of Marketing Research,* Vol. 52, No. 6, Dec. 2015, (doi.org/10.1509/jmr.13.0221). The article offers an empirical approach to the effects of rebranding in the US lodging industry between 1994 and 2012. The authors look specifically at the branding effect and the interaction effect, between the product (hotel property) and the brands involved.
5. Internet portal Power Technology publishes annual rankings of the world's biggest energy companies at power-technology.com. In 2019 the list excluded the China State Grid company and other monopolies.
6. For more on Enel's rebrand, from a design point of view, see Dawood, Sarah. "Wolff Olins Turns to Cursors for Energy Company Identity", *Design*

Week, 27 Jan. 2016, designweek.co.uk/issues/25-31-january-2016/wolff-olins-turns-to-cursors-for-energy-company-identity/. Also, Wolff Olins, the consultancy in charge, highlighted the rebrand in a short article in the "Work" subpage of its website, here www.wolffolins.com/case-study/enel. The pull-out quote states succinctly: "53% increase of (Enel's) share price in the first two years after launch".

7. Levitt, Theodore. "Marketing Myopia." *Harvard Business Review*, Vol. 38, No. 4, Jul.–Aug. 1960, pp. 45–56.

8. Ibid, p. 45.

9. Ibid, p. 46.

10. Ibid, p. 47.

11. Ibid. p. 55.

12. Levitt, Theodore. "Marketing Myopia." *Harvard Business Review, Best of HBR*, Jul.–Aug. 2004, hbr.org/2004/07/marketing-myopia.

13. Heard-Adams, Rachel. "Why Texas Broke: The Crisis That Sank the State Has No Easy Fix." *Bloomberg*, 25 Feb. 2021, bloomberg.com/news/features/2021-02-25/texas-blackouts-what-went-wrong-with-ercot-and-state-power-grids.

14. Montgomery, Angus. "Britain Gets First New Pylon Designs for 85 years." *Design Week*, 9 April 2015, designweek.co.uk/issues/6-12-april-2015/britain-gets-first-new-pylon-designs-for-85-years/. The competition in 2011 for the next-generation UK pylon design was backed by the UK government, and is generally considered an example of a successful public awareness campaign, going by the criteria of media buy in, positive coverage and public backing.

15. See Tofler, Alvin. *Third Wave*. William Morrow and Company, 1980. The word "prosumer" appears for the first time on page 27. Tofler says "Third Wave civilazation begins to heal the historic breach between producer and consumer giving rise to the 'prosumer' economics of tomorrow."

16. The PROSEU project, wound up at the time of writing, published it's findings in Wittmayer, J.M et al. "A multi-dimensional typology of collective RES prosumers across Europe." PROSEU—Prosumers for the Energy Union, 2019, proseu.eu/resource/multi-dimensional-typology-collective-res-prosumers-across-europe.

17. Jacobs, Sharon B. "The Energy Prosumer." *Ecology Law Quarterly*, Vol. 43, 2016, pp. 519–580 (2016), (doi: 10.15779/Z38XS02), also available at scholar.law.colorado.edu/articles/709. This is an immensely informative look at the legal implications of individual prosumption in the United States.

9

A SOLAR COLLABORATION

ANTHONY AINSWORTH ON TURNING E.ON INTO A POP BRAND

Gorillaz is a pop band that defies categorisation. Some call it a virtual music group. Its members are four animated characters—2-D, Murdoc Niccals, Noodle and Russel Hobbs—designed by artist Jamie Hewlett. These avatars appear in the band's music videos, live performances and short films (of which later). The chief contributor to Gorillaz' musical output is Damon Albarn, leader of the Brit-pop sensation Blur. The songs cover a range of styles—dance, hip-hop, soul and rock, with guest appearances from some of the best known musicians of today. On YouTube their videos have notched up around 3 billion views, and their concerts have been seen by millions of people around the world.

E.ON, on the other hand, does not quite defy categorisation. It is an energy brand. Granted, one of the world's largest, but still in many ways a typical utility. Like other utilities in Europe, it sprung from state-owned enterprises.

It was formed when two large industrial conglomerates merged in 2000. One of the conglomerates, VIAG (from the German for United Industrial

DOI: 10.4324/9781003351030-10

Enterprises Joint Stock Company), was formed by the German Reich in 1922 and privatised in 1986. The other, VEBA (from United Electricity and Mining Corporation) was formed by Prussia in 1929, and privatised in 1965.[1]

As the Wall Street Journal reported at the point when the two companies announced their merger, they were "a combined enterprise with annual sales of 76 billion euros, net profit of 1.8 billion euros and a market capitalization of 41.2 billion euros".[2]

Now, anyone would be excused in thinking that Gorillaz and E.ON are unlikely bedfellows. Perhaps the studio where Gorillaz record is subscribed to one of E.ON energy tariffs, and perhaps some of E.ON's staff listen to the Gorillaz, but that would seem to be the limit of the crossover. They inhabit distinct worlds, one of pop-music glamour, and the other of power-industry level-headedness.

As it turned out, however, one of those E.ON staffers listening to the Gorillaz was Anthony Ainsworth, Senior Vice-President of Global Marketing. His backing for the idea of a creative partnership between the two would lead to one of the most memorable and effective energy-industry marketing campaigns of recent years.

Summarising it in a 2018 article, *Marketing Week*, the UK industry bible, started off by saying that "as one of the big six energy companies, E.ON faces the challenge of marketing its business and brand in a category that many consumers are at best ambivalent about and at worst actively dislike". It added that it is a "notoriously low-interest sector", but then it added that "the [Gorillaz] campaign led to E.ON standing out from the crowd. The online film (created by the campaign) was viewed more than 100 million times . . . leading to an 8.1% increase in website traffic".[3]

In fact, the campaign was a success by any metric. "It resulted in a 146% increase in brand interest and a 97% increase in creative interest in the UK. There were even higher spikes in other markets, such as Italy—where brand interest rose 443% and creative by 243%."

"Perhaps most importantly", concluded the article, "the campaign shifted people's perceptions of E.ON from being a 'boring utility company' to an 'enabler of amazing energy solutions' by 94%". And it was exactly this enabling of amazing solutions, that Anthony wanted the campaign to focus on. The idea, developed with marketing agency WCRS, was that Gorillaz should record a music video overnight in a studio powered entirely by stored solar energy—coming from E.ON's battery storage system, introduced to customers in 2016.

The campaign went on to produce that rarest and most valuable of all marketing content, the one that lives beyond the campaign. The song went on to be played on the radio, while the video featuring Gorillaz' animated characters trended on its own merit, its views driven by fans and music lovers around the world. In October 2018 the campaign was awarded *Marketing Week*'s Branded Experiences and Event award.[4]

Now, to someone unfamiliar with the dynamics of corporate marketing departments, this link up might have sounded like an easy sell to E.ON's senior executives. A match made in heaven, between an exciting, creative and wildly popular music group, and an energy brand with immense marketing budgets—one seeking to dispel that "low-interest" miasma. But that's rear-view mirror perspective. As the saying goes, success has many fathers while failure is an orphan.

Corporations, and by extension, their marketing departments are painfully risk averse. All sorts of questions get asked at meetings, which in many cases paralyse progress, and revert strategy to successful examples of yesterday. Because, things *can* go wrong.

Brand ambassadors, even if thus far model citizens, can suddenly go off the rails. They can say and do things that compromise the brand. The link between brand and ambassador might be lost on your target audience. Or, the endorser will simply choose to do things their own way. In a famous example, Oprah Winfrey, the world-famous TV host, was engaged by Microsoft to plug the Surface tablet, Microsoft's answer to the iPad. She tweeted an endorsement saying that she loved the Surface so much she bought twelve for Christmas gifts. Unfortunately, she tweeted it from an iPad.[5]

These marketing 'fails'—a great source of amusement to the general public—are usually followed by the executive in charge having to look for a new job. (As another saying goes, comedy is tragedy happening to other people.)

This is why I was somewhat surprised at meeting Anthony in person. He didn't strike me as a risk taker, on the contrary, a sturdy fellow, he is of a reliable and well-judged appearance. Seeing him at industry conferences, in his business suit, I could not imagine anyone less likely to cross paths with Noodle and 2-D. In fact, he seems a man you would entrust with managing your pension fund.

It turned out this was not just a hunch as, prior to joining E.ON Anthony had worked at Lloyds and Santander, two of the UK's biggest banks. He had also worked in leisure and hospitality before being asked by E.ON to strengthen the company's global marketing function:

> I took on the challenge of helping E.ON reposition itself for the changing energy world. Essentially, I really wanted to enable the organisation to be more focused on its customers—to start standing for something different. I knew that to do this both E.ON and I had to be bold and take some risks.

Asked what experience from his previous employment he brought to the energy sector, Anthony explains that in those industries the customer isn't just an account number.

> The customer is a real person. I insisted that we needed a good understanding of all of their needs, wants and desires. Only then we could understand how our products and services match those. This sounds a bit textbooky, but having worked in the past for Avis, Lloyds TSB, and for Universal Studios in Florida, I knew that the focus on customers in such businesses goes far higher and deeper than in energy companies—especially in the past.

One of the ways E.ON has sought to strengthen customer focus within the organisation was with an "annual pulse check" of all the employees:

> There we look at how we are bringing our vision and values to life, and one of those values is putting our customer first. In the November 2018 iteration of the survey, "putting our customer first" was our highest scoring value internally. The brand has started to change our organisation.

Back in 2015, says Anthony, the E.ON brand was seen simply as a set of words, a set of colours. But, once the traditional generation businesses were spun off into a different company (now called Uniper) "there was a real opportunity to restate and reposition what we wanted our brand to stand for".
He continues:

> We did a huge amount of research with all our customers, and all our segments across the different markets, to gage what was important

to them, and we then built that into our brand. Our brand promise became "create a better tomorrow", resting on two pillars, that of "brilliant experience" and "more and smarter sustainable solutions". Our brand personality shifted to being collaborative and authentic.

In addition to his experience in the financial and hospitality sectors, Anthony credits his approach to marketing, which could be summed up as thinking globally, yet retaining a firm focus on the customer, on having professionally matured in his native Britain. He says that the United Kingdom is a complex market, but also advanced from a "customer and marketing perspective", and that he was able to transpose the knowledge gained there into his global role.

Indeed, there is a case to be made for London being the advertising hub of Europe, at least until Brexit. Writing in 2017 on the LinkedIn blog Tom Pepper, the platform's EMEA and Latin America Director, highlighted an interesting statistic: "London has more advertising and marketing professionals per 10,000 LinkedIn members than any other major advertising hub that we analysed: more than New York, Sydney, Paris and Amsterdam."[6] According to the UK's Advertising Association, one in eighteen people in London work in the advertising sector.[7]

In fact, further to Anthony's assessment that the UK is a complex and advanced energy market, it could be said that it is also a sophisticated marketing environment, with the sector supporting around one million direct and indirect jobs.[8]

I wonder whether that marketing sophistication is actually an essential requirement for E.ON as a German energy company, for the reason that the nation's energy policy is riven with a deep and thus far intractable contradiction, that can only be solved through full customer engagement.

On the one hand, Germany is the European Union's biggest electricity producer. In 2018 it produced close to 22 per cent of all EU electricity, and in 2019 consumed as much as 18 EU members put together. On the other, Germany has been at the forefront of Europe's energy decarbonisation programme. Its strong grass-roots environmental movement, whose demands are articulated in the German parliament by the influential Greens and other left-of-centre parties, has pressured decision-makers to shut down all coal power stations in the country by 2038.

The problem, though, is that coal-powered stations still supply over 35 per cent of Germany's electricity. To put it in perspective, those power stations produce more than the 11 countries at the lower end of EU's electricity usage-table consume. Added to this generating capacity going on the scrap-heap are Germany's nuclear power stations. They currently produce around 12 per cent of the nation's electricity.[9]

Even before the 2010 earthquake in Japan government policy was to cancel nuclear power. A brief "phase out of the phase out" (introduced when the pro-nuclear coalition led by Angela Merkel came to power) was reversed as the scale of the Fukushima disaster became obvious.[10]

This energy has to be replaced by new sources, and in a country as densely populated as Germany, there is an ever-narrowing scope for the development of either traditional or new renewables. Thus smart energy has become the new frontier in power development. Virtual power stations, home energy storage systems, distributed generation, local energy networks, should fill in some of the shortfalls left by the retiring coal and nuclear generators.

However, the installation and operation of these news sources requires a much tighter relationship with the customer, a relationship which treats customers as partners—as active participants in the energy transition. Energy companies will require greater access to people's homes, customers will be required to host new hardware, and the data generated by all these devices will raise privacy issues. It is not hyperbole to claim that the renewable energy era calls for a new type of marketing executive: one who will be able to not just recruit customers, but get them to open their front doors.

In this energy paradigm, Anthony says, "the brand is a catalyst for change". He adds that internally the biggest hurdle was explaining that the brand was about more than PowerPoint templates, business cards, logos and advertisements. "In other words, the biggest hurdle is explaining what a brand is and how it touches everything that we do, and then getting everyone to influence and shape that." Asked what advice he would share with another energy company going down the brand repositioning route, Anthony concludes, "really making sure that you're linking the brand to commercial outcomes—you need to be talking a language that the business will understand. If I had my time again I would be much firmer on linking branding and marketing to a commercial performance matrix, as early as possible."

A SOLAR COLLABORATION   113

His view is that marketing buzzwords and hot branding concepts such as "equity", "personality" and "leverage" are very seldom understood outside the marketing community:

> People can be somewhat sceptical towards branding experts when they use this kind of language. It sounds impenetrable, and seems like it clouds reality. We made a very conscious effort to use everyday language and standard commercial terms when we spoke about marketing and branding to colleagues outside our department.

Anthony explains that a particular challenge in talking to senior energy sector executives about branding is that it is perceived a soft subject:

> Energy is a business that revolves around long asset cycles, politics and regulation, risk management, NPVs (net present value) and IRRs (internal rate of return) . . . Investments could run into hundreds of millions, or even billions. I really needed to hand-hold colleagues on the senior management team, almost explain one-on-one what branding and marketing is all about, so that they could support the journey. There was a lot of individual coaching of key stakeholders.

Anthony's observation on how professionals respond to marketing-speak, and how the subject is viewed in general, reminded me of the gloomy predictions of Malcolm McDonald, currently one of the world's most influential thinkers on marketing. McDonald wrote in a 2009 article that "the discipline of marketing is destined to become increasingly less influential, unless there is some kind of revolution, or at the very least a new beginning".[11]

In "The Future of Marketing and Sales", a 2016 paper published on his website, McDonald continues in a doom-laden tone. "The reputation of marketing as a discipline is at an all-time low . . . Not much progress has been made since the Deloitte report in 2007 which was a damming expose of the deeply-held belief by CFOs and CEOs that marketing has lost its place in the boardroom because of its unaccountability."[12]

Among the reasons for this sorry state of affairs, he identifies "the widely held belief that marketing is mainly a communications function, leading to the decline of marketing's influence in the boardroom", and "the deliberate organisational and professional separation of marketing and sales as business disciplines".

Could Anthony's proselytising, hand-holding mission, be marketing's ticket back into the boardroom? In the summary to "The Future of Marketing and Sales", McDonald talks of "major contribution to corporate wealth" made by successful marketers. That contribution "goes beyond understanding markets, doing proper needs-based segmentation, developing quantified value propositions, competitive analysis, portfolio analysis and managing marketplace risk".[13]

It is, essentially, the ability to convert brand equity into "real" equity, the skill to negotiate the "show-us-the-money" mentality at the top of most companies, and tap into the 80 per cent of the company's value that does not appear on the traditional balance sheet.

As a way forward to restoring the effectiveness of marketing and boosting sales, McDonald advises integrating marketing and sales under one director, which, strikingly, is a route Anthony's career has followed at E.ON. Could this be the lesson of the British school of marketing, as opposed to the Nordic school, which McDonalds (a Professor of Marketing at Cranfield University) blames for reducing the discipline to a "promotional function"?

More importantly, how do you justify spending money on branding? What do you say in those one-on-one conversations with the chief executive? Anthony says:

> The energy markets are becoming much more competitive, and that is the accepted reason to continue investing in your brand. But there is something else. This new, competitive environment is producing a host of new technologies. If you want to help your customers capitalise on all these innovations, in this new energy world, you need to create a market.

Solving customers' cost and sustainability issues is your mission whether your market is B2B (business-to-business) or B2C (business-to-consumer). They also have in common the requirement that you position yourself— you need to think about your value proposition and market segmentation. As Anthony puts it, "In both markets you need to decide what you stand for." The main difference is in how you reach your audiences.

> With B2C you tend to use mass communications. Social media helps you reach both mass and niche audiences, but B2C still relies on above

the line advertising such as TV, display ads and billboards. In B2B you need to be thinking how do you reach smaller, and very selective audiences. Selective in the sense that such audiences will quickly discard or block marketing communications that are of no relevance.

As an example of what falls under modern B2B marketing Anthony lists one-on-one outreach, podcasts, webcasts and other media which might only be seen by 50 or a 100 people:

> You are actually only trying to reach the decision makers, so you have to be far more precise and surgical with B2B than B2C marketing. Having said that, however, there is a strong halo effect from B2C to B2B, so you need overall positive associations and positive messages that work together.

Anthony adds that part of that market-creation strategy is "to capture those early adopters and innovators within the segment, as the market builds out". His conclusion is:

> If you don't invest in your brand and your marketing, then you won't make the transition into these new areas. So branding's is strategically essential for energy companies—this is not an industry that is standing still. Of course, there is uncertainty which technologies will win out and what the adoption rates will be, but you have to be playing in those markets.

It is a technical answer, Anthony concedes, one a bet-hedging economist might offer. But, he continues, "there is something more emotional that we are trying to flow through our brand, that makes it more personal and relevant. In marketing everyone is trying to be distinctive, but it has to be relevant and authentic. There's no point in being gimmicky"

He concludes, "All of this is the at the strategic level. At the operational performance level, marketers and brand leaders need to demonstrate the impact of what they do on commercial and not just brand performance indicators."

Those brand performance indicators have been meticulously analysed and quantified by academics in a field of study which has been flourishing over the last few decades. The purpose is to understand the effectiveness of marketing and branding initiatives. Generally, approaches examine the dynamic between *brand equity* and *consumer-based brand equity*.

Brand equity, in the simplest terms, is the price-premium consumers are prepared to pay for a branded product, as opposed to its generic equivalent. If you reach for a can of Heinz baked beans on a supermarket shelf, rather than the generic and cheaper can of beans sitting next to it, the difference in price is the Heinz' brand equity.

Brand equity can easily be linked to financial performance indicators and is commonly taken to signify a brand's financial strength and its commercial advantage over other brands. Consumer-based brand equity (CBBE), on the other hand, examines customers' attitudes towards the brand, and operates with 'softer' concepts such as brand loyalty, reputation and consumer satisfaction.

In applied measurements of brand performance researchers often look at both. For example, they would examine loyalty, satisfaction and reputation, but also financial indicators such as market share, sales growth, margin and return on investment. This is in keeping with studies which shows that, despite brand equity showing how much your brand is worth (as a brand), CBBE could be a more emphatic predictor of financial performance.[14]

Such brand performance metrics are becoming more important to the sector as energy companies are moving, in Anthony's words, "beyond pure commodity supply of power and gas". In terms of retail, energy companies are getting closer to sales models existing in mobile telephony: different tariffs and bundles, targeted levels of service, with friends and family coming into play as a billing factor (or neighbours if you are part of an energy community). The important thing to remember, continues Anthony, is that these models create more contact with customers, than just selling a commodity:

> In fact, new entrants into the market, that come in without that legacy of electricity being a commodity, or the legacy of ever having been a utility, advertise fast plug-and-play systems and tightly focused offerings for particular market segments. The challenge for the more established players is to be proactive, not just react to the competition, but get ahead of these new entrants.

His conclusion is that "if you are in a 100 per cent regulated market where customers never move and you never want to sell a customer a single new thing, then don't worry about branding".

The dilemma, then, for energy companies is not whether to invest time and money in branding. Rather, strategic decisions need to focus on aligning commercial and marketing goals, and getting your marketing and branding mix right. "Now within that, there can be timing challenges, but if you've got the marketing and the branding mix right, then every tactical sales campaign that you do is a brand builder."

Antony offers some words of caution:

> Just be mindful that if you're doing, for instance, purely brand-building TV campaigns without a clear call to action, and an online way of capturing customer and information flow, then your brand is missing the digital age. Don't fall into the trap of saying "the payoff will be in two or three years' time".

He adds that no opportunity should be missed to increase your brand's reach:

> Every piece of communication to your customers should be aiming to retain them, to migrate them to a better tariff, to tell them about a new product or solution, to help them monitor their energy use or give them tips on saving energy . . . All of those things can have a really positive short-term impact, as well as build out your brand.

Now, if you remember, the creative partnership between E.ON and Gorillaz produced a song and a music video. Maybe you heard the song on the radio, maybe you've seen the video online. How did it go? It went: "We got the power to be loving each other/No matter what happens/We've got the power to do that . . . I got my heart full of hope/I will change everything/No matter what I'm told/How impossible it seems (we got the power)".[15]

Notes

1. For the history of E.ON see the website referenceforbusiness.com, particularly the subpages "History of VEBA A.G." (referenceforbusiness.com/history2/19/VEBA-A-G.html), "History of E.On AG" (referenceforbusiness.com/history2/2/E-On-AG.html) and "History of VIAG AKTIENGESELLS-CHAFT" (referenceforbusiness.com/history2/98/VIAG-AKTIENGESELLS CHAFT.html).

2. Boston, William. "Veba and Viag Agree to Merge In $14 Billion Stock-Swap Deal." *Wall Street Journal*, 28 Sep. 1999, wsj.com/articles/SB938411000976891267.

3. "How E.ON Repositioned as the 'Un-utility' Energy Company." *Marketing Week*, 29 Nov. 2018, marketingweek.com/how-e-on-repositioned-as-the-un-utility-energy-company/. In addition to this article, the E.ON and Gorillaz link up was reported by other advertising industry's portals, such as The Drum and Campaign.

4. See "Marketing Week Masters Awards 2018: The Channel Winners", *Marketing Week*, 9 Oct. 2019. marketingweek.com/marketing-week-masters-awards-2018-channel-winners/.

5. See Griggs, Brandon. "Oprah Plugs Surface Tablet—from Her iPad", CNN, 21 Nov. 2012, edition.cnn.com/2012/11/20/tech/social-media/oprah-surface-tweet/index.html. The article also said: "So maybe there's room in Oprah's heart for two tablets? Apple fans may remember the original iPad made Oprah's 'Ultimate Favorite Things' list back in 2010. 'Words cannot describe what I feel for this magnificent device,' she said at the time. 'I really think it's the best invention of the century so far.'"

6. The blog post by Tom Pepper, LinkedIn's Senior Director, EMEA & LATAM, titled "The Secret to the UK's Creative Success" was published on 18 October 2017, on the platform's blog-pages. The claim that "London has more advertising and marketing professionals per 10,000 LinkedIn members than any other major advertising hub . . ." can also be found on page 6 of the report quoted below (see note 7).

7. Credos. "Advertising Pays 6: World Class Talent, World Class Advertising." *Advertising Association*, 2015, pp. 6 publitas.com/p222-15108/advertising-pays-6-world-class-talent-world-class-advertising/page/6–7.

8. Ibid, p. 9.

9. Statistics on Germany's electricity production are from the web-sites of Destatis, the German federal statistics office (Statistisches Bundesamt) at destatis.de/DE/Home/_inhalt.html, while the EU statistics are from Eurostat at *Energy, Transport and Environment Statistics—2020 Edition*. Publications Office of the European Union, 2020, (PDF edition), (doi:10.2785/522192).

10. For Germany's coal and nuclear exit strategies see Appunn, Kerstine. "The History Behind Germany's Nuclear Phase-out." *Clean Energy Wire,* 9 Mar. 2021, cleanenergywire.org/factsheets/history-behind-germanys-nuclear-phase-out. Also, Wettengel, Julian. "Spelling out the coal exit—Germany's

phase-out plan." 3 Jul. 2020, cleanenergywire.org/factsheets/spelling-out-coal-phase-out-germanys-exit-law-draft.

11. McDonald, Malcolm. "The Future of Marketing: Brightest Star in the Firmament, or a Fading Meteor? Some Hypotheses and a Research Agenda." *Journal of Marketing Management*, Vol. 25, No. 5–6, pp. 431–450. A discussion on some of the issues McDonald has raised over the years can be found in Davey, Janet et al. "Marketing's Great Identity Crisis: A Revised Definition and an Urgent Research Agenda", *World Journal of Management*, Vol. 2, No. 1, March 2010.

12. McDonald, Malcolm. "The Future of Marketing and Sales." (PDF) *Malcolm-McDonald Consulting Ltd*, 2016, malcolm-mcdonald.com/perch/resources/mmcarticlefuturemarketingsales-1.pdf.

13. Ibid., p. 12.

14. In the past few years there has been a plethora of approaches to classifying, analysing, quantifying and rating brand performance indicators. A good overview can be found in the introduction to Molinillo, Sebastian et al. "A Consumer-Based Brand Performance Model for Assessing Brand Success." *International Journal of Market Research*, Vol. 61, No. 1, March 2018, (doi:10.1177/1470785318762990). An interesting empirical comparison of brand equity vs. consumer-based brand equity, in terms of financial performance over time, can be found in Johansson, Johny et al. "The Performance of Global Brands in the 2008 Financial Crisis: A Test of Two Brand Value Measures." *International Journal of Research in Marketing*, Vol. 29, No. 3, 2012, (doi:10.1016/j.ijresmar.2012.01.002). Of course, for an overview of basic concepts we recommend Kevin Keller's foundational book *Strategic Brand Management*, published by Pearson and currently in its fifth edition.

15. Berthomier, Camille and Damon Albarn, lyricists. "Gorillaz—We Got the Power (Official Audio)", *YouTube*, 23 Mar. 2017, youtube.com/watch?v=HSivlaSVk1k.

10

IN THE BIG COUNTRY

PAULA GOLD WILLIAMS ON LEADING
AMERICA'S LARGEST MUNICIPAL UTILITY

It had been noted many times before, and, finally, as a student at the University of Louisiana I could vouch for it myself: to someone from Europe (let alone an Icelander) the sheer vastness of America is mind-boggling. Take, for instance, Louisiana's neighbour Texas. Not only is it roughly the area of France, Belgium and the Netherlands put together, or around seven times that of Iceland, but at around 35 people per km^2 its population density is less than half of the European average.[1]

Driving home the point about these wide empty spaces, a region of Texas—covering the North Central Plains—is even called the Big Country. But, when it comes to the rugged terrains and vast solitudes I feel Iceland can hold its own. Our version of the Big Country, the Highland (or *Hálendið* in Icelandic) covers 40,000 km^2. Virtually nobody lives there.

Sparse though its population may be, on an individual basis Texans are prolific electricity users. Yearly per capita electricity consumption is around 14 megawatthours (MWh)—around three times that of Denmark. An interesting fact if you consider that average monthly temperatures in Texas vary

DOI: 10.4324/9781003351030-11

between 10°C and 30°C. On the whole, the United States have one of the highest per capita rates of electricity usage in the world, and Texas is only slightly above the US national average.[2]

In the interest of full disclosure, however, and continuing the comparisons between Texas and Iceland, the nation with the highest per capita consumption of electricity in the world is actually Iceland. To offer an explanation, if not an outright excuse, in relation to population numbers our geothermal resources are so plentiful—while the climate is so harsh—that it makes sense to electrify as much of our total energy consumption as possible.

Texas, on the other hand, is fossil fuel reliant. But, if under "reliant" you think "needful", you would be mistaken. It produces more natural gas than Iran and double as much as Qatar. If Texas were a country, in terms of production it would be ranked second only to Russia.[3] Conversely, when it comes to renewable energy the state is also a powerhouse. It has over 35 gigawatts of wind and solar generating capacity, which produce one fifth of its electricity.[4]

Finally, the main electrical grid in Texas, serving around 75 per cent of the state, is notable for being independent from the other two grids in the contiguous United States—the Eastern and the Western Interconnections. This independence is politically motivated as it circumvents federal regulatory oversight. There are five interconnector cables, or ties, linking the Texas with Mexico and the Eastern Interconnection, but even at full throttle they can only provide a fraction of the state's electricity. In fact, it is claimed one of them had been switched on only once in its history, during hurricane Ike in 2011.[5]

On the face of it then, the power sector in Texas should work like a dream: bountiful local resources, an independent grid overseen at state level and a strong economy keeping demand steady. The electricity market deregulation, started in 2002, was meant to be the final piece of the jigsaw the icing on the cake for energy consumers. Not only would the state be energy secure, but competition between suppliers would reduce retail prices.

In practice, however, the set-up has creaked on a number of occasions. Grid independence, an embodiment of the Lone Star State's "Don't mess with Texas" attitude, for all its advantages in terms of light federal supervision, means diminished resilience. When things go wrong, as they did in February of 2021 (see Chapter 8) there is not much the Electricity Reliability Council of Texas (ERCOT)—the state's network operator—can do. Total interconnection capacity, according to estimates, barely covers 4 per cent of the state's average demand.

Furthermore, it seems that deregulation has actually raised energy prices. As the "Texas Coalition for Affordable Power" stated in its 2014 report *Deregulated electricity in Texas—a history of retail competition*, "Texans in deregulated areas have consistently paid more for power than Texans outside deregulation". The report goes on to claim that "Texans living in deregulated areas would have saved more than $22 billion dollars in lower residential electricity bills since 2002 had they paid the same average prices as Texans living outside deregulation". In the interest of balance though, the report also says that "average electricity prices in areas of Texas both inside and outside of deregulation have declined in recent years. For the first time in a decade, average prices in deregulated areas of Texas have dipped below the national average."[6]

During supply crunches, such as that in February 2021, the combination of deregulation and independence (read "low interconnection") can cause some freaky problems for energy consumers, on top of catastrophic power shortages. For instance, customers of an especially enterprising retail supplier, who sold on electricity at wholesale prices (prices without a retail mark-up), found to their consternation that—as spot-market prices hit $9,000 per MWh—their bills went up by tens of thousands of dollars.[7] But, even companies with more conservative sales models were caught out, and had to pass the storm's cost to the consumer.

My interview with Paula Gold Williams, former president and CEO of CPS energy, the USA's largest municipally owned energy utility, was an opportunity to revisit the complexities of the Texan power sector. It is one of the world's richest and most developed energy markets, and yet, it is still developing. From a European perspective it is fascinating that, whereas in Europe legislation leads deployment, especially when it comes to renewable energy, in Texas (which prides itself on its title as a "state that is best for business") it is deployment that surpasses legislation.

As the US Energy Information Agency points out "the Public Utility Commission of Texas first adopted rules for the state's renewable energy mandate in 1999 and amended them in 2005. The mandate required 10,000 megawatts of renewable capacity by 2025, including 500 megawatts from resources other than wind. Texas surpassed the overall 2025 goal in 2009."[8] If I was a betting man, I would wager that by 2025 the state will have at least three times what was mandated by law merely 15 years ago, a situation highly unusual in Europe, where meeting targets, rather than overshooting them is considered the height of achievement.

Paula Gold Williams has been at CPS Energy for 17 years, climbing the ladder from Controller & Assistant Treasurer, to the company's top position. A native of San Antonio, she worked at Time Warner and Luby's, the chain of cafeterias and restaurants founded in San Antonio in 1947. CPS Energy, which Paula joined in 2004, employs over 3100 people, while, according to the company's website it is "serving 840,750 electric and 352,585 gas customers".

Born on the Lackland Air Force Base, Paula says she had a "military upbringing". Speaking of her childhood she recalls being raised with discipline and encouraged to treat people right. Her first few years at CPS Energy coincided with the final few terms of an MBA course at Regis University. Of that time she says, "I was just super hungry for information and super hungry to contribute. Somehow that manifested in a couple of promotions. I have never, ever grown tired of this company."

San Antonio's first light bulb went on in 1860. Texans are quick to point out that this was six months before Thomas Edison opened his first New York City generating plant. In 1942 the City of San Antonio acquired the San Antonio Public Service Company. The utility was later to be named City Public Service before being rebranded as CPS Energy around the time Paula joined. The utility owns and co-owns a number of power stations including the nuclear South Texas Project, and over one gigawatt of wind farms. Most of its generating capacity (around 45 per cent) runs on natural gas.

As a vertically integrated utility CPS manages over 7 gigawatts of plant, worth around $11 billion. It is guided by the motto "People First", introduced by Paula to reflect the company's municipal history and its commitment to the community. It is also an expression of the company's morale:

We are fortunate that we own all these assets. We don't take for granted our license to operate in our designated area. For example, every two years there is a discussion on whether we should retain our right to be sole proprietor and these conversations have a powerful influence on our strategy.

As Paula explains it, "we have to make sure that people are certain we're giving them all the benefits of being in an open competitive market, certain that our service is equally good to anything they would be getting anywhere else in America."

Whether your company has to compete outright, or it's in a tightly regulated market there is now a near universal belief that market competition drives improvements in service quality. Instead of thinking you market is protected, you should take these assumptions on board. "People expect their banking to be better, they expect their entertainment to be better. Why should they not expect their utility to do better?"

To improve as a utility Paula believes you need to understand your relationship with technology:

> When you don't think about technology you get blown away by smaller companies, that are more in tune with the emerging technological environment. They are more willing to change and evolve, and respond to new trends. But, in our case, we are very clear that although everything we do as a utility is tech enabled, we're not a tech company.

For an electrical utility technology and innovation are important for all the obvious reasons, but in the context of brand building they also serve the purpose of converting customer satisfaction into brand loyalty. Expanding on the model offered by Claudio Alvarez and Susan Fournier in their article "Consumers' Relationships with Brands", it becomes clear that technologically savvy utilities, offering customers the latest devices and tech-enabled services, foster a sense of interdependence, where customers feel they need a brand and rely on its benefits, and accept the brand as an integral part of daily life.[9] Such interdependence has a partner quality, where the customer feels the brand takes care and listens to them.

As the authors point out, such experiences culminate in the feelings of brand love. It is a "consumer–brand relationship prototype that goes beyond self-brand connection and attachment". Characterised by passion driven behaviours, such as "passionate desire to use, willingness to invest resources, and involvement" it even manifests as "anticipated separation distress".[10]

The findings of Fournier and other academics in the field of brand relationship theory, lean on the seminal work of Richard Oliver. As a researcher in consumer psychology and a professor at Vanderbilt University, Oliver's academic preoccupations resulted in the book *Satisfaction: A Behavioural Perspective on the Consumer*, published in 1997.[11] It offers an understanding of the process by which "repeated episodes of positive affect toward a brand" develop into brand loyalty, a phenomenon which in a later article Oliver comprehensively and somewhat technically describes as "a deeply held commitment to rebuy or repatronize a preferred product/service consistently in the future, thereby causing repetitive same-brand or same brand-set purchasing, despite situational influences and marketing efforts having the potential to cause switching behavior".[12] In other words, brand loyalty should be understood as a resistance to switching.

According to Oliver loyalty develops over four incremental steps. At the stage of cognitive loyalty customer prefers a brand. Affective loyalty means that the customer likes the brand, while at the conative stage the customer is motivated, and intends to buy the branded product or service. Finally, action loyalty is brand loyalty in the full sense of the term, because the customer, having moved through all the stages, repurchases the product again and again. A customer at the stage of action loyalty is extremely reluctant to change behaviour, despite incentives.

Of action loyalty Oliver writes, "The motivated intention in the previous loyalty state is transformed into readiness to act . . . This readiness is accompanied by an additional desire to overcome obstacles that might prevent the act."[13] For Oliver, the final stage of loyalty is equivalent to "action inertia". It is this action inertia which facilitates repurchase. Loyal customers will not usually change their purchasing behaviour. They are not just impervious to rival brands' marketing content or promotional offers, but they are ready to overcome situational obstacles to purchase favourite products.

But, how do you get to action loyalty? Paula mentions recognition, which rests on a connection with customers:

> When it comes to positive expectations, my belief is that we gotta give them more. For instance, our customers have to feel valued, and they have to feel that we are willing to listen. Going beyond simply listening, in some cases customers want to tell you a story. They might have a problem that takes longer to explain and resolve, and

you need to build a customer-service culture that has the capacity to handle such cases. Make sure you understand when your customer is getting stressed.

Paula continues:

> You should be embracing your customer. Meaning, the contact with us, although we are a large utility, should feel personal. If your customer service representative starts the conversation with "How we can help you today?", then they should end it with "Feel free to call us back". There has to be a sense that you are interested.

Paula's point on customer-care reminded me of something I had noticed in working with energy companies. Regardless of whether they are customer-facing businesses, such as electricity suppliers and retailers, or they incorporate this function in a wider, vertically-integrated structure, they are dominated by engineers. Meaning, engineers are heavily represented on the senior management team, and even if there are influential voices with other occupational backgrounds high up in the organisation, an engineering legacy and spirit permeates the firm's activities.

This is good, of course, when it comes to solving technical problems, which any energy business faces almost daily. But, extending that engineering, problem-solving approach to customer relations risks alienating people. Clearly, your customers are calling you because they have a problem—but they are not the problem. They are your customers. To state the obvious, a customer is not a problem to be solved.

Asked on the role of emotions in communicating with the world outside your utility, Paula has a number or practical recommendations, aimed at strengthening the emotional bond between customer and company:

> When people come to us, if we're not careful, things can get unnecessarily complicated. Yes, energy is a complicated industry, there is a lot of jargon, but this should challenge us not to be on autopilot.
>
> When we do presentations, we don't read. I have told everybody that I want to eradicate that kind of automatic reading. You shouldn't read a speech—you have to look at your audience. You have to listen

to them and confirm that you understand each other. In fact, we will
be doing more training with employees on emotional intelligence
and active listening. We'll try to take it to the next level, really.

In Paula's view respect towards the customer, a kind of warm, personal regard
should be part of your brand culture regardless of whether you're a business-
to-business (B2B) or business-to-consumer (B2C) company. "Branding is
important no matter what. If you are a B2B company, you might have a ten-
dency to prioritise major accounts. But, no one likes getting dismissed because
they're not your biggest customer. We all want to feel special."

These notions chime with what has been termed "American customer
service culture". As Micah Solomon, one of the foremost experts on the
subject—also the author of the book *Ignore Your Customers (And They'll Go
Away)*—wrote in his *Forbes* column, customer service culture is "an atmos-
phere in which employees, management, and leadership serve their customers eagerly and effectively".[14] I find that word "eagerly" the essential
American ingredient to the definition.

Solomon claims that across companies, "each culture, on the surface, [is]
quite distinct". Nevertheless, there are eight characteristics "that are shared,
and consciously nurtured, by all of them". Some of these are pride, humility, empowerment and no "not my job" attitudes. Other characteristics
are conceptually or practically more complex. They include the ability to
formulate "legendary stories" ("Tales of over-the-top customer service . . .
valuable in making a point to prospective, incoming, and even veteran
employees about what is valued in the culture") and "culturally consonant
HR practices" ("starting out with employees who possess the right personality traits for customer service").[15]

Finally, nurturing a customer service culture is synergic with building a
powerful brand. As one of the characteristics, Solomon mentions a "common language" that helps bring a company together. Whether internal
branding guidelines specify the use of creative spelling, or prescribe how
customers and employees should be addressed ("Employees at the Ritz-
Carlton Hotel Company are not 'associates', they are Ladies and Gentlemen.
It sounds anachronistic to an outsider, but it makes a difference to the
employees"[16]), such language conventions build a common identity, while
strengthening the brand.

Paula insists that this kind of strong internal customer service culture is a particular asset in a B2B context:

> You could have staff who are members of business associations. For instance, they could belong to a manufacturing association, a real-estate council or a council within the oil and gas industry. When they join those meetings or conventions they have the opportunity to tell colleagues how we could help them improve margins and save them money on energy costs.
>
> In our case, by getting you on the right tariff or service, we can help you expand your business. But, this kind of business outreach, the drive to make these connections, won't necessarily happen if there isn't an internal culture. There has to be an understanding that we are serving customers.

Paula concludes that managers and frontline employees' passion for the brand, translates into trust. In B2B transactions this goes beyond the value of goods or services:

> If, as a utility, you're proactive in rolling out energy saving initiatives, then it is clear that within your organisation people are passionate not just about selling, but also about conservation and environmental protection. Business leaders, those who authorise purchasing decisions, will then come to trust you beyond service delivery. They will conclude that trading with you will improve their organisation and have a positive effect on their employees.

On a community level, Paula believes in old fashioned talking to people. Despite the communication opportunities offered by social media, CPS energy has an outreach team, whose members turn up in person to community meetings or public gatherings, and visit local businesses. "We will tell them about our latest journey," says Paula.

The company also runs programs such as Critical Care and the Residential Energy Assistance Partnership (REAP), to which it contributes around $1 million per year. REAP offers assistance with energy bill payments to vulnerable groups such as those experiencing financial hardship, the elderly, handicapped or those having small children in the household.

Critical Care gives additional time for paying bills to those using electrical medical equipment at home.[17]

Looking at these programmes from a European perspective, it seems that CPS as a municipal utility has actually taken on some of the functions of that very municipality, or its host state. Normally, social care aimed at alleviating energy poverty in European countries would be discharged by the government, through its agencies at state and local level. This understanding of the state's responsibility to its citizens, the ideology of the "big state", stands in contrast with the American preference for a "small state". A question meriting further attention would be whether energy brands in "small state" political environments will actually have a bigger community role, as they take on various social care and support functions.

However, hearing Paula outline CPS Energy's development plans towards the end of our interview, I realised that such comparisons might be concealing wider, common trends on either side of the Atlantic. Like any utility the world over CPS is pushing for more renewable energy and storage capacity. Recent plans include 900 MW of solar and 50 MW of battery storage, with a further 500 MW of firming capacity in the pipeline. Paula talks about the potential for micro-grids and a number of technologies that will save customers money. She mentions her "excitement at doing the right thing".

"It's going to take time", Paula says, "But we are already a good way down the road." This being Texas, it might take a lot less time than people expect.

Notes

1. Texas population statistics have been taken from the website of the United States Census Bureau, subpage "Quick Facts—Texas", at www.census. gov/quickfacts/TX. European statistics have been taken from Eurostat, subpage titled "A Growing Population until 2020", at https://ec.europa. eu/eurostat/cache/digpub/demography/bloc-1a.html?lang=en.

2. The information on Texas energy production and consumption is from the website of the US Energy Information Administration, subpage "Texas Profile—State Profile and Energy Estimates", at www.eia.gov/ state/analysis.php?sid=TX.

3. A good source of data on Texas's oil and gas industry is the state's Railroad Commission (RRC), the regulatory agency with "primary regulatory jurisdiction over the oil and natural gas industry, pipeline transporters, natural gas and hazardous liquid pipeline industry, natural gas utilities, the LP-gas industry, and coal and uranium surface mining operations". The website of the RRC is www.rrc.texas.gov.

4. See above, note 2, subheading "Renewable Energy" and "Electricity".

5. There are three electricity grids covering the "contiguous US", or the lower 48 states: the Eastern Interconnection, the Western Interconnection and the Texas grid, which covers most of the state. These three grids are independent of each other, save for a few interconnector cables. Texas, for instance, has no links to the Western Interconnection. In the aftermath of February 2021 storm the state's grid has been the subject of a number of articles, mined for information used in this chapter. See Frazin, Rachel and Rebecca Beitsch. "Five Things to Know about Texas's Strained Electric Grid", *The Hill*, 17 Feb. 2021, thehill.com/policy/energy-environment/539300-five-things-to-know-about-texass-electric-grid/. Also, "Texplainer: Why Does Texas Have its Own Power Grid?" *Texas Tribune*, 8 Feb. 2011, texastribune.org/2011/02/08/texplainer-why-does-texas-have-its-own-power-grid/.

6. Dyer, R. A. Jake. "Deregulated Electricity in Texas—a History of Retail Competition." *Texas Coalition for Affordable Power*, 2014, http://tcaptx.com/wp-content/uploads/2014/02/TCP-793-Deregulation2014-A-1.7.pdf.

7. Heard-Adams, Rachel. "Why Texas Broke: The Crisis That Sank the State Has No Easy Fix." *Bloomberg*, 25 Feb. 2021, bloomberg.com/news/features/2021-02-25/texas-blackouts-what-went-wrong-with-ercot-and-state-power-grids. We have also quoted from this article in Chapter 8.

8. See above, note 2, subheadings "Renewable Energy".

9. Alvarez, Claudio and Susan Fournier. "Consumers Relationships with Brands." *Current Opinion in Psychology*, Vol. 10, Aug. 2016, pp. 129–135, (doi:10.1016/j.copsyc.2015.12.017).

10. Ibid, p. 130. For further reading on the topic of consumer/brand relationships see Fournier, Susan. "Lessons Learned about Consumers' Relationships with Their Brands." Chapter 1, *Handbook of Brand Relationships*, MacInnis, Deborah J. et al. editors, Routledge, 2009, pp. 5–23.

11. Oliver, Richard. *Satisfaction: A Behavioural Perspective on the Consumer*. Routledge, 1997 (1st ed.). The book is now considered one of the definitive texts on the subject.

IN THE BIG COUNTRY   131

12. Oliver, Richard. "Whence Customer Loyalty?" *Journal of Marketing*, Vol. 63, 1999, p. 34, (doi:10.2307/125209). Oliver notes that consumer psychology is shifting in focus from the exploration of satisfaction to that of loyalty. Quoting management consultant Fred Reichheld, Oliver agrees that "satisfaction isn't enough".

13. Ibid, p. 36.

14. Solomon, Micah. "All Great Customer Service Cultures Share These 8 Elements. How Does Your Company Measure Up?" *Forbes*, 5 Jun. 2017, forbes.com/sites/micahsolomon/2017/06/05/all-great-customer-service-cultures-share-these-8-elements-how-does-your-company-measure-up/?sh=6006e3c249af. His book *Ignore Your Customers (and They'll Go Away)* was published by HarperCollins Leadership in 2020.

15. Ibid.

16. Ibid.

17. Information on REAP and Critical Care programs has been taken from the CPS Energy website, see cpsenergy.com/en/my-home/savenow/customer-assist-programs/reap.html and cpsenergy.com/en/my-home/savenow/customer-assist-programs/critical-care.html. Note that the company also runs a "newsroom" website at https://newsroom.cpsenergy.com.

11

A MODEL ISLAND

HORDUR ARNARSON ON GOING BEYOND FULL SUSTAINABILITY

The story of mining in Iceland is a short one. Sparse mineral resources and a small local market have traditionally rendered the business moribund. The expansion of coal mining in the first half of the twentieth century should be seen in perspective: up to the start of the First World War most of Iceland's coal was imported from Great Britain, and importation would have certainly continued were it not for the outbreak of the First World War.

As Richard Pokorny *et al.* explain in their book *Mineral Resources in Iceland—Coal Mining*, during the winter of 1914/1915 "'a chilly' problem arises: Great Britain radically restricts the export of coal. Moreover, the North Sea is cruised by marine and submarine fleets . . ."[1] Thousands of naval mines are deployed and navigation becomes extremely hazardous. "As a result, the price of imported coal rapidly increases. The Icelanders are facing the threat that they will soon have nothing but peat to feed their fireplaces and heat their dwellings with."[2]

The authors credit "the strong Icelandic sense of survival and national pride" with inspiring "several visionaries, mostly entrepreneurs, builders

DOI: 10.4324/9781003351030-12

A MODEL ISLAND   133

and engineers (to) come up with a revolutionary idea: "Let's mine the surtarbrandur (coal)".[3] Within a few years, however, the Icelandic mining boom was over. As the authors explain: "The war in Europe comes to an end, international trade is slowly re-established, and imported coal from Great Britain . . . induces bankruptcy and closure of all Icelandic coal mines."

Another boom-and-bust cycle, however, began with the onset of the Second World War. Iceland's Parliament decreed that excavation should restart at Botn and at Tindar, where the nation's first vertical shaft mine was dug. Both of the enterprises went bust before the end of the war. Thomas Denk's summary in the book's introduction is succinct and to the point: "In Iceland, the extraction of coal never became a success story because of the small size of the coal reserves, the high mining costs and the low calorific value of the coal."[4]

But, to the lacklustre history of mineral exploration in Iceland there is a notable exception. The demand for sulphur, abundant around the island's volcanoes, rocketed with the introduction of gunpowder to Europe. The profitable trade in this strategic commodity was contested by the Norwegian kings, English merchants and the Hanseatic League, until Danish king Frederick II imposed a monopoly in 1561, excluding foreign profiteers from the business.[5]

A notable exception—and a modern coda . . . For all of its dearth of mineral resources Iceland has emerged as one of the hubs of cryptocurrency mining. In one of those fortunate and somewhat paradoxical historical reversals, all the factors that worked against us when it came to conventional mining, such as geology, population density and product cost-effectiveness, are now the very factors that work in favour of Bitcoin mining.

Iceland's geology means that all the electricity the country requires on an annual basis, a total of around 20 terawatthours (TWh), can be generated inexpensively from geothermal and hydro-power sources; low population density means that there is more than enough energy to go around (however, the upshot is that Icelanders are the world's most prolific energy users); and finally, compared to coal, Bitcoin is valuable enough to make all the expended effort worthwhile. In fact, according to an estimate by Deutsche Welle, eight per cent of all the Bitcoins have been mined in Iceland.[6] If this cryptocurrency was oil, Iceland would not quite be Russia (which produces around 11 per cent of the global supply), but it would be ahead of Canada (which produces 6 per cent).[7]

Around three quarters of the electricity in Iceland is generated by Landsvirkjun. The company is state owned, and it is in turn the majority owner of the Landsnet, Iceland's transmission system operator. In English the name means "land dam", harking to its chief asset class, the 15 hydro power stations, in addition to which the company operates three geothermal plants and one wind farm.[8]

This network of energy ownership and production places Hordur Arnarson, CEO of Landsvirkjun at the centre of Iceland's power sector. His responsibility for keeping the nation's lights on is magnified by the fact that the nearest neighbouring power grid is around 1,000 kilometres away, and there is no interconnection. The system has to provide not just generous amounts of electricity to each Icelander (yearly, we consume around 55,000 kilowatthours (kWh) per capita, which is 10 times more per capita than in Denmark, or 20 times more than in Turkey), but be resilient enough to stand on its own when things go wrong.[9]

But, as I hinted with my story of mining in the introduction above, and conveyed to some extent, hopefully, in the other chapters of this book, more is expected of a modern power-sector executive then just being a capable engineer. To a social and environmental consciousness should now be added strategic foresight, or at least an awareness that new technologies will put unexpected demands on the energy system—and that these shifts in energy usage patterns, could be an opportunity as much as a challenge.

Who would have thought 15 years ago, that something called cryptocurrency would eventually command amounts of energy equal to that of a medium-sized country? And that there would be money to be made not just in trading this mysterious new commodity, but in supplying the required energy. For, according to some estimates, in 2019 global cryptocurrency mining has used up more electricity than Spain.[10]

It was as if Hordur's educational background was to prepare him exactly for the challenge posed by emerging technologies. He graduated in engineering at the University of Iceland and four years later gained a PhD in artificial intelligence from the Technical University of Denmark.

His first job, at food-processing technology company Marel was to take him all the way to the top:

> I joined in 1985, when Marel had 30 employees, and focused solely on developing equipment for the fish processing industry. When I left the company 24 years later, having served the last 10 as CEO, we were a market leader. The company currently employs 4,000 people in 30 countries, with an annual turnover of €650 million.

It was this entrepreneurial spirit which prompted Landsvirkjun to get in touch:

> I was planning to go on vacation, but when they called I found it a very interesting proposition. Transition times lay ahead, and they wanted someone from the private sector to bring customer and business focus to the company. Before I was hired top executives came from the public sector, usually government ministries.

It was made clear to him at these preliminary stages, says Hordur, that there was an expectation he would put more emphasis on marketing and business development. "Was there a strong business culture at Landsvirkjun before I joined? I am not sure, it was not a black or white type of situation, but I realised there was still a long way to go." He continues:

> When I came into the company, I saw that there was no marketing department, nor any proactive marketing or market analysis. The sales side of the business was this one guy taking orders. So I established an organized group, a department within the company, focusing on marketing and business development.

Contrary to popular opinion that introducing private business practices to public utilities translates to price hikes, cost of electricity in Iceland has remained comparatively low. As the national statistical office notes: "The price of electricity in Iceland is lower than in all the other Nordic countries when prices are converted to price power parity (PPP)." In fact, price per kWh for domestic consumers is

A MODEL ISLAND

half of Sweden's, and around 50 per cent less than in Norway, Denmark or Finland. Compared also to EU countries, Iceland's tariffs are competitive. Out of 27 EU member states, only four have cheaper domestic electricity.[11]

When Hordur began staffing his new department there were questions around the viability of the jobs advertised:

> Many people were asking me "What are we going to work on?", or "Do we need a full time position for that?". I knew that we had to understand the market, and, ultimately, approach different industries encouraging them to relocate to Iceland. In a way, this was the start of building the Landsvirkjun brand, or perhaps even the start of branding Iceland as a destination for energy intensive industries.

He concludes, however, that convincing people this was the right way forward took quite a while:

> For several years many thought this was just a waste of money. But, our results showed both a more diverse customer base and a better value for our products. This led to the growth of our marketing department from two people to ten.

How successful was the initiative to promote Iceland as an industrial base on the back of cheap electricity is perhaps best gleaned from Fraunhofer ISI's 2020 report *Electricity Costs of Energy Intensive Industries in Iceland—A Comparison with Energy Intensive Industries in Selected Countries*. The report points out that 84 per cent of electricity in Iceland is consumed by the industrial sector, compared to 45 per cent in Germany, or 41 per cent in Norway.[12]

These numbers further explain the local boom in bitcoin mining, as much as the expansion in the number of data centres, and Iceland's place in the top ten of aluminium producing countries (manufacture of which uses 14,500 kWh of electricity for each metric tonne, or what 6 households in Italy use in a year); they also put pay to the assumption that Icelanders are not just prolific, but also somewhat reckless energy users. For there is an acerbic local saying that an Icelander would rather open the window than turn down the heating. However, only around five per

A MODEL ISLAND   137

cent of total electricity in Iceland is used by households. All the per capita surpluses of electricity go towards industrial development, the agenda Hordur was hired to promote:

> Before we set on this course, we made a decision where we wanted to be. In discussions between the management team and the board, we then converged on a strategy. You have to identify how you can create value for the owner of the company and for society.

All of these considerations would normally help define the brand. But then, Landsvirkjun is a specific case, as brand owner and brand audience mostly overlap:

> People in Iceland feel very strong ties to Landsvirkjun. It's the nation's biggest company. Secondly, it has been given the natural resources of Iceland to work with, so it's very important to us, that we are doing this properly—that we are taking care of the interest of the country. In terms of how we handled our responsibilities to the owner, the people of Iceland, I think we made a success of the brand.

Not only is Landsvirkjun owned by the people (nominally, the owner is the government of Iceland), but most Icelanders are its customers. This means that there is hardly a feedback loop between brand owners and its audience. It is generally the same group—particularly as Iceland's population is just over 350,000 people.

There are two prominent reasons, Hordur says, why public support is important to Landsvirkjun. Obviously, the company's licence to operate is dependent on it. The other reason is the long term strategic orientation of the company:

> Our plan is to continue to develop and maintain a generating capacity that provides five times more electricity than we need as a country. We are aiming for an 80 per cent surplus, with all the future growth sold to international companies. We want our energy to capture value. However, this requires long term investment and that is why we need support across the board.

Such plans have grabbed the attention of foreign energy-intensive industries, and also of countries along the North Atlantic rim. Among the most industrially advanced nations on Earth, they also have ambitious targets on reducing carbon emissions. Recent explosive growth in North Sea offshore wind installations should be seen as opening a new energy frontier, that circumvents land-resource constraints.

To these power-hungry regions Iceland must seem like a giant battery, which, once plugged in, could as much help balance the grid, as provide a perpetual source of renewable electricity. The IceLink project, for instance, proposed a 1,000 km electricity cable connecting Iceland and the UK. It was backed by the two governments' joint study in 2015. Hordur was reported to have said that the 1 gigawatt (GW) capacity cable could supply 5–6 TWh of electricity per year, enough to meet the demand of 1.6 million British homes. The interconnector deal "would be like a power plant in Iceland, producing for the UK".[13]

Locally such plans have met with mixed reactions. There are concerns that exporting large amounts of electricity will increase prices to Icelandic consumers. Others think that it would be better for Iceland to use that energy in upgrading its "green" industrial base. The country could become an exclusive investment destination for companies looking to manufacture or provide zero-carbon products and services. Why sell renewable energy abroad, when you can maximise its value at home—by using it as the chief commodity of the emerging low-carbon economy?

Hordur is sympathetic to that point of view:

> In the future renewable energy will become especially important because of the increased awareness of consumers about the environment. We know that some of our silicon metal and data centre customers use in their marketing the fact that their energy is 100 per cent renewable.

He gives the example of silicon metal manufacturers:

> They supply the raw material for solar panels. If they can show that their production process is fossil-fuel free they can command a price premium. The problem for the power company is how do we capture this value. In my opinion, this is why you should pay attention to your brand in a business to business (B2B) context. Your brand will capture these important attributes and they will become your brand equity.

The challenge for a company selling renewable energy is maximising returns on that brand equity:

> A company which uses our energy would market its products as sustainable or "zero-carbon". Ultimately, the consumer pays a premium, which they might do quite willingly, because they are ready to pay more for climate-friendly products. But, as we are the end of that value chain, it becomes a big fight to get a fair slice of that money. The companies higher up in the chain might argue they deserve a larger chunk of it.

Regardless, in B2B trading your brand expands your negotiating options. "It will get you a better price," concludes Hordur.

Listening back to the interview I was struck by our matter-of-fact discussion around branding energy. As I mention elsewhere in this book, my PhD thesis at Birmingham's Aston Business School hit a snag at the very start—actually, at the point I proposed the title. I wanted to complete a doctorate on energy branding, but my tutors were adamant: marketing orthodoxy says you can't brand a commodity. My intuition both then and now told me differently, and working with energy companies from around the world in the years that followed, I have found that many energy practitioners felt the same.

Branding comes from differentiation, and commodity, by its very nature, is a standardised, or undifferentiated product. It is traded in bulk, with little prior processing. Amongst other things, this means that equal commodity batches are indistinguishable from one another. Traded on open markets and across national borders they are of the same specification and price. Brands, on the other hand, distinguish themselves in consumers' minds through six main factors: product quality, positioning, pricing and packaging, communications and promotions, placement and availability, and origin and ethics. That, at least, is marketing theory.

Yet, as Chris Docherty argues in his 2012 paper "Branding Agricultural Commodities: The Development Case for Adding Value through Branding", there have been some interesting exceptions, one of which is bottled water.[14] As he reminds us:

> In 1974, the Financial Times surveyed the new market for UK bottled mineral water and concluded that "cranks and foreigners" were its

only possible customers . . . They generously conceded their mistake ten years later, calling Perrier "one of the great icons of the day".

Docherty concludes:

> Given that there is no obvious physical difference between bottled water products, the impact of brands in the water industry suggests traditional agricultural commodities are equally ripe for branding.

Perhaps certification schemes offer a way forward here—a sort of "halfway house" between branding a product and branding a commodity. Fairtrade Foundation labels agricultural products such as cocoa, tea, coffee and, beyond agriculture, even gold. Farmers in developing countries are paid a Fairtrade premium for their products, which is reclaimed as a portion of the finished article.

This "hybrid branding" approach, which differentiates the commodity as to its origin and alerts the consumer to the ethical standards of its procurement and manufacture, has also been accepted in the diamond trade. The Kimberley Diamonds Process Certification ensures buyers that their stone is not a so called "blood diamond" or "conflict diamond", meaning "used by rebel movements to finance military action opposed to legitimate and internationally recognized governments".[15]

My conversation with Hordur, on Iceland's ambition to become a sustainable energy hub, and not just a supplier of cheap electricity suggested, yet again, that whether you talk to consumers or energy-sector professionals, energy branding is moving beyond "proof of concept". If we accept that this could indeed be the case, should we not perhaps move beyond marketing theory and consider the consumer?

Concurring with Hordur's assessment that customers are willing to pay more for products manufactured by using renewable energy, estimates put the number of "ethical consumers" in the UK alone at around 15 million. These are "consumers who would prefer to choose positively "ethical" products and companies as against those which are not". But, some say these are "armchair ethicals" who are "radicals in the surveys but reactionaries at the checkout".[16] How do we motivate this constituency to be more demanding of their favourite brands when it comes to using renewable energy? And how do we get them to take energy branding seriously? Should we appeal to emotion or intellect?

A MODEL ISLAND   141

"This is a one million dollar question", says Hordur. "In Iceland it should be linked to the future of our society and the future of our children. We should appeal to a sense of responsibility, and that should be the main driving factor." Linked to this topic is his sense that, if he could do one thing differently, he would have put more work to align stakeholders:

> It was a big disappointment to realise that for many environmental groups in Iceland a credibility test is to be against renewable energy. They are on a mission to stop projects, which is a big contradiction, as renewable energy is really the solution to the biggest environmental crisis facing the world today.

He adds:

> Some people will just want to return nature, and that is fine. Many others, however, want a society like we have today, but without the drawbacks such as environmental pollution or climate change. They want a high standard of living, free healthcare and economic growth. Looking back, we should have spent more time in aligning these disparate interests and formulating a strategy to get support from both directions.
>
> The fact is we are working in remote areas where we have a big impact on the local environment. We always try to reduce our footprint as much as possible. In parallel, we work with local communities, to create value. We spend a lot of money on this, while at the same time trying to maximise project returns for our owners, the people of Iceland. It is not always an easy balancing act.

Landsvirkjun might be one of those rare companies whose business role overlaps more or less completely with its corporate social responsibility (CSR) role. What Bianca Grohmann and H. Onur Bodur describe as an exception in their article "Brand Social Responsibility: Conceptualization, Measurement, and Outcomes" is actually the norm here. They talk about "instances in which consumers' social responsibility perceptions of the firm's product brands differ from social responsibility perceptions with regard to the firm".[17] But, if you are owned by the people and those same people are you customers, and your product or service has no obvious drawbacks, then you

A MODEL ISLAND

can focus your strategy on the long game—which is how Hordur thinks of marketing:

> Our budget for branding and marketing as percentage of total budget is actually very low. Still some people might question the logic of spending money on it. The main argument is that the benefits are far in the future, while you are committing money now. But, to me that really is an argument in favour of branding and marketing. You *should* be investing in the future.
>
> In some ways, that kind of long-term investment in your brand is not all that different from investing in energy projects. If you are developing a power plant, you are spending on feasibility studies, public consultations, legal advice and many other things. The plant itself could go on-stream in 20 years. In the worst possible case, the project could get scrapped. It is simply a long-term thing, and we have to accept that.

Thinking of Hordurs worldview I sense that the Landsvirkjun brand is built on the concept of social acceptance. That acceptance is not identical to consumer loyalty, rather, it is based on the acceptance of the outsized role the company will continue to have in the economic life of Iceland. Indeed, Hordur talks about the economic, environmental and societal benefits, which have to be in harmony if a business is to be called truly sustainable:

> This harmony is important to the new generation which is seeing the world in a different way from the old generation.
>
> We have to stop using fossil fuels. The good news is that this is possible—whereas only 10 years ago people did not see how could it be possible. There were alternatives but there were also many questions on reliability and cost. Now, one thing is certain, renewable energy is getting more competitive year after year. It is getting more important.

Now, maybe it is because as an Icelander I am slightly biased; maybe it is because I recognise the potentials of this volcanic island in the middle of the North Atlantic; maybe it is because, as a marketing and branding practitioner I see something especially valuable, perhaps even endemic in Landsvirkjun's brand.

Whatever the case may be, to me something else is certain as well: whether through interconnectors or by becoming a sustainable energy hub, or even by some other means, Iceland and its largest energy company will continue to play an outsized role in the world's energy economy.

Notes

1. Pokorny, Richard et al. *Mineral Resources in Iceland—Coal Mining*. Cambridge Scholars Publishing, 2021, p. 1.

2. Ibid.

3. Ibid. p. 2.

4. Ibid. Newspaper job ads, printed at the time (and reprinted in the book) offer perhaps the best illustration of Iceland's coal industry at its peak. One printed in 1918 says: "Two skilled men can get a job with the coal mine at Dufansdalur" (ibid., p. 54) Another, from a year earlier, offers employment to 20 hard working men at Tjornes, one of Iceland's richest deposits (ibid., p. 118) Even at the best of times, it was a cottage industry, which produced coal at costs three to seven times greater than that on the world's commodities markets.

5. See Mehler, Natascha. "The Sulphur Trade of Iceland from the Viking Age to the End of the Hanseatic Period." *Nordic Middle Ages—Artefacts, Landscapes and Society, Essays in Honour of Ingvild Øye on her 70th Birthday.* Irene Baug et al. (eds). University of Bergen, 2015, pp. 193–212, bora.uib. no/bora-xmlui/handle/1956/15435. Eventually, Iceland's exports of around 320 tons per year were made obsolete, as was the whole sulphur mining business, by modern production methods, which generate sulphur as a by-product of oil and petroleum refining.

6. Walter, Jan D. "Bitcoin Mining: Is Scandinavia's Cryptoboom Coming to an End?" *Deutsche Welle*, 6 May 2021, dw.com/en/bitcoin-mining-is-scandinavias-cryptoboom-coming-to-an-end/a-57443905. The article offers some interesting statistics, including this: "Bitcoin is a real electricity guzzler. Depending on the estimate, the global energy required for mining the most successful cryptocurrency is between 67 and 121 terawatt-hours

a year. That is about half of what all data centres — for the internet, cloud computing, the entire financial sector and all other cryptocurrencies — consume. Germany's entire annual power consumption is just over 500 terawatt-hours."

7. Data on national oil production rankings can be found on the website of the US Energy Information Administration, on the subpage Frequently Asked Questions (FAQs), under the heading "What Countries Are the Top Producers and Consumers of Oil?", here eia.gov/tools/faqs/faq.php?id=709&t=6.

8. Information on Landsvirkjun and its subsidiaries is taken from the company's websites landsvirkjun.com, as well as from lvpower.com.

9. Statistics on electricity consumption per capita have been taken from the website of the World Bank at data.worldbank.org, subpage "Electric power consumption (kWh per capita)", here data.worldbank.org/indicator/EG.USE.ELEC.KH.PC?end=2014&start=1960.

10. Huang, Jon et al. "Bitcoin Uses More Electricity Than Many Countries. How Is That Possible?" *The New York Times*, 3 Sep. 2021, https://www.nytimes.com/interactive/2021/09/03/climate/bitcoin-carbon-footprint-electricity.html. The article carries a number of striking infographics about the sector's electricity use, and a sort of beginner's guide to cryptocurrency.

11. Comparative electricity price data for Iceland and Nordic countries is available on statice.is, the Islandic government's statistics bureau, subpage titled "Electricity Prices to Households and Industry Lowest in the Nordic Countries", published 21 Feb. 2019, here statice.is/publications/news-archive/energy/electricity-prices-in-iceland-and-in-the-nordic-countries. Electricity price data for the EU was taken from Eurostat's website at ec.europa.eu, the source data set was Electricity prices (including taxes) for household consumers, second half 2021, at ec.europa.eu/eurostat/statistics-explained/index.php?title=Electricity_price_statistics.

12. Zheng, Lin and Barbara Breitschopf. "Electricity Costs of Energy Intensive Industries in Iceland—a Comparison with Energy Intensive Industries in Selected Countries." *Fraunhofer Institute for Systems and Innovation Research ISI*, December 2020, publica.fraunhofer.de/handle/publica/300575.

13. Kelly, Jemima and Nerijus Adomaitis. "Giant Iceland-UK Power Cable Plan Seen Facing Brexit delay." *Reuters*, 21 Oct. 2016, reuters.com/article/uk-britain-iceland-power-idUKKCN12L1O5.

14. Docherty, Chris. "Branding Agricultural Commodities: The Development Case for Adding Value through Branding." *International Institute for Environment and Development*, 2012, https://pubs.iied.org/sites/default/files/pdfs/migrate/16509IIED.pdf?

15. An explanation of the Kimberley Diamonds Process Certification can be found on the website of the US Customs and Border Protection agency at cbp.gov/trade/programs-administration/kimberley-diamonds-process-certification.

16. "The power of ethical branding", *Marketing Week*, 22 May 1997, marketingweek.com/the-power-of-ethical-branding. The estimate of the number of "ethical consumers" as well as the quip about radicals who might be reactionaries at the checkout is attributed to Richard Adams, managing director of the fair trading retail organisation Out of this World.

17. Grohmann, Bianca and H. Onur Bodur. "Brand Social Responsibility: Conceptualization, Measurement, and Outcomes." *Journal of Business Ethics*, No. 131, 2015, p. 375, (doi:10.1007/s10551-014-2279-4).

12

FINDING THE RIGHT BALANCE

JACOB BENBUNAN ON BRANDING BETWEEN IQ AND EQ

Even the most casual researcher on the history of marketing and branding will soon enough come across academic articles and books with titles such as *Rise and Fall of Marketing in Mesopotamia: A Conundrum in the Cradle of Civilization*, or *The Birth of the Brand: 4000 years of Branding*,[1] or perhaps *A Brief History of Branding in China*. The last we have mentioned in Chapter 4, together with Diana Tweed's often quoted *Commercial Amphoras: The Earliest Consumer Packages?*

These fascinating articles, combining archaeological and historical evidence, seem to push back the birth of marketing into the distant past. Even if challenge their conclusions, by pointing out that ancient marketing was, at an operational level, vastly different from marketing today, we cannot but suspect that the very nature of business and trade precipitates such an activity. In other words, marketing and branding are not (as some see it) modern, nefarious inventions, characteristic of a consumerist economy seeking new ways to force unwanted products on wary consumers; rather, marketing and branding have been adjunct to production and trade from the start.

DOI: 10.4324/9781003351030-13

FINDING THE RIGHT BALANCE   147

And not simply adjunct, but perhaps essential. After all, what Tweed and other authors imply is that, historically, trade and advertising go together. This seems logical: if you are holding something that you intend to trade, you will, at some point, want to tell others about it. Similarly, if you are producing something of quality and distinction, intended for the purposes of exchange, you will not just want to tell others about it, but you will want to single out and protect your element of distinctive workmanship, as a stake in further transactions. Hence, there is branding.

Of course, there is one form of barter, that eliminates the need for advertising, or even communication. Known as *silent trade*, its first account was given by Herodotus in 440 BCE, in that part of *Histories* describing how Carthaginians traded with people beyond Gibraltar.

> The Carthaginians tell us that they trade with a race of men who live in a part of Libya beyond the Pillars of Herakles. On reaching this country, they unload their goods, arrange them tidily along the beach, and then, returning to their boats, raise a smoke. Seeing the smoke, the natives come down to the beach, place on the ground a certain quantity of gold in exchange for the goods, and go off again to a distance. The Carthaginians then come ashore and take a look at the gold; and if they think it presents a fair price for their wares, they collect it and go away; if, on the other hand, it seems too little, they go back aboard and wait, and the natives come and add to the gold until they are satisfied.[2]

Every form of trade, then, requiring interpersonal contact necessarily gives rise to the essential enablers of marketing and branding. And perhaps we can venture a step further and find here not just a historical or functional explanation for their emergence, but also a psychological one. It seems to me that a wholesome pride in good workmanship, as much as an element of satisfaction in producing merchandise of distinction, finds its expression in enthusiastic advertising. After all, why hide your light under a bushel?

Whether you are a practitioner or an interested observer, these considerations raise stimulating yet speculative questions: if marketing and branding are rooted in antiquity, co-evolving with trade, business and social mores (see also our discussion in Chapter 4 on the Nordic rune-based origins of trade-marks in England), then what about their future? Is our focus on *energy branding* an indicator of marketing splintering into various niches, each with its own methodology? Will sector-specific approaches, or culturally profiled marketing practices eventually require of marketeers non-transferable levels of specialisation? And what about technology—how will its evolution impact our business?

Talking to Jacob Benbunan of the branding agency Saffron is an opportunity to quiz someone who talks the same language, gets the common academic references and shares a very similar conceptual framework. But, if I'm a branding specialist, immersed in my energy branding niche, Jacob is what I would call a branding generalist. His agency's website states, under the heading of "Natively Global", that Saffron is "from everywhere and at home anywhere" and Saffron's roster of clients certainly proves it, including companies and institutions as diverse as YouTube, The Victoria and Albert Museum, Fujitsu, Siemens and The City of Vienna.[3]

Yet, together with all our colleagues, we share the same lineage. Setting aside ancient precedents, the modern marketing and branding business took shape around the turn of the nineteenth century. As Richard Hawkins explains in his essay "The Origins of Marketing Practice in Britain", it was a time when "the number of newspaper titles increased from 25 to 258", while newspaper publication "was no longer centred in London".[4] This was to prove decisive for the emergence of a new profession, because there was now a need for agents who could sell page-space and co-ordinate the printing of advertisements.

According to Terence Nevett's *Advertising in Britain: A History*, William Tayler was the world's first agency boss, having opened his office in London's Warwick Square in 1786. Tayler was not a "creative", but a sales representative for printers. However, in 1800 James White started his own agency, which wrote advertisements, making him the world's first professional copywriter. The agency changed names a number of times, but survived until 1982.[5]

On the industrial, client-side of the newly emerging marketing business, the eighteenth-century pottery entrepreneur Josiah Wedgwood is considered the first advertising guru. The view "that there was almost no facet of present day marketing that was not anticipated by Wedgwood"[6] is evidenced, for instance, by his correspondence to his partner Thomas Bentley. In one letter Wedgwood insisted "that it was 'absolutely necessary' that they mark their goods and they 'advertise the mark'".[7] Or, as Wedgwood's company website says "many common sales techniques such as direct mail, money-back guarantees, free delivery, celebrity endorsements, illustrated catalogues and buy one get one free came from Josiah Wedgwood".

Jacob's academic background is in engineering. But, although he enjoyed studying it ("it structured my brain in a particular way") he was unhappy working as an engineer. After four months at Hewlett Packard, he moved to KPMG where he worked for six years as a management consultant. A call from a head-hunter in 1991 on behalf of branding agency Wolff Olins ("it was then called corporate identity and I had never heard of corporate identity") lead to a new career:

> What the head-hunter said in those initial calls about corporate strategy and making strategy visual really resonated. My final interview prior to joining the company was with Wally Olins. I had over the nine years there, built a very close relationship with him. Working there was fascinating, it was super interesting.

When Wolff Olins was sold to Omnicom in 2001—according to media reports at the time, the deal was worth around £30 million—Olins and Jacob started their own branding consultancy:[8]

> I told him I was planning to start a branding company and he said "Well Jaco, it's a fantastic idea, and even more, I'll join you. Wally invested his own money in what was from the start going to be an unconventional business. For starters, it wasn't an Anglo-Saxon firm, but rather, with offices in London and Madrid it was a mix of the Anglo-Saxon and Mediterranean worlds.

The breadth of perspective shaped the new agency's approach to branding assignments:

> We were humble enough to understand that the world is not uniform, and that people have different cultures, and an anthropology, sociology, psychology, ethnography . . . that needed to be covered if you wanted to really be successful in branding.

Saffron grew to a staff of 70, and continued after Wally Olson passed away in 2015.

FINDING THE RIGHT BALANCE

Along the way Jacob has co-authored the book *Disruptive Branding*, with Saffron colleagues Gabor Schreier and Robert Knapp. In the introduction the writers reminds us that, "Disruption is not something to be hidden from, to protect against or wait out. It is not a wave that only start-ups can ride to fame and fortune and established businesses are forbidden or unable to capitalise upon. Disruption as a principle is much older than any of the descriptions given above." [9] Those descriptions include the Austrian economist Joseph Schumpeter's famous phrase "gale of creative destruction", as well as Jean-Marie Dru's concept of "rupture strategies" and Clayton Christensen's "disruptive innovation".

I start off by asking Jacob what career-experience prior to branding he brought to Saffron. He parries by saying that what makes Saffron interesting is how the agency combines strategy and design. He continues:

What I learned in KPMG helped me bring strategic input to everything that we do. That was very much also the legacy I got from Wally. This doesn't ignore the fact that design enhances the power of that brand. That is paramount.

And the reason it is paramount is because "a brand is about belonging . . . so by using visual elements you have to combine what does it mean to belong with how do you project your belonging."

These notions on the importance of the concept of belonging—not just for modern branding practice, but also in general psychology—are rooted in the work of Abraham Maslow. His famous "hierarchy of needs" motivational theory assumes a five-tier model, often depicted as levels within a pyramid. At the bottom of the hierarchy are the physiological needs, such as the need for food and clothing. Then comes safety, expressed, for instance, as a yearning for job security; after which comes the need for love and belonging, motivating us to seek friendships and romantic relationship. Finally, the top two layers of the pyramid are esteem and self-actualisation.[10]

Now whether you subscribe to Maslow's model or his assertion—which has since the 1943 publication of his article "A Theory of Human Motivation" gained enormous popular traction—that needs "lower down" in the hierarchy must be satisfied before individuals can attend to needs "higher up", there is no escaping the "belonging deficit" buzz-phrase in modern marketing practice. Perhaps such a deficit can be explained as a process of weakening of traditional modes of belonging, and an ever-greater degree of freedom in choosing our allegiances:

> The concept of branding has evolved dramatically over the last 10 years. Obviously, the interpretation of brand varies from industry to industry and from country to country, in the sense that the more sophisticated the market is, the approach to branding will be more holistic.

In Jacob's view the least sophisticated approach is thinking of the brand as simply logo and name:

> It's only very recently that people understood a brand stands for something deeper. I was once asked by a journalist to define brand and I said brand is a promise, it is the effect of what an organization evokes in its different audiences.

Jacob reminds me that in today's business a brand audience comprises not only customers and consumers, but also the brand's employees, shareholders, stakeholders and the society at large. That audience expects a *brand-experience*, and no matter how deeply we digitalise our economy that experience will always entail something physical. There will always be a physical point of contact between brand and user, or perhaps a convergence of the biological human faculties on the one side, and a digital interface, on the other. Jacob gives the example of the Google Glass device, a sort of enhanced pair of eye-glasses which incorporate both a camera and a display.

Zooming out from that individual point of interface between brand and consumer, we find that successful modern brands are not just global, in the sense of trans-national, but also universal. They touch the lives of almost everyone, user or not:

> We have been working for Facebook for the last year and it is a fascinating client. I mean, it has 2.7 billion users! It is such a number that I couldn't at first fully understand the power of touching 2.7 billion souls on a daily basis. We are 7 billion people on earth—even if you

leave out kids too young to use the internet, those over 80 that log on casually, plus those that don't have access, you are still left with 4 billion plus users—70 per cent of whom use Facebook. You are dealing with a forum that touches the soul of almost everyone on Earth.[11]

However, in Jacob's view, energy companies have taken longer than others to understand the power of brand. In fact, the whole of the business-to business (B2B) world has woken up late to the concept. The reason might be a delay in processing a fundamental shift both in how corporations are expected to communicate, and how they are perceived by the public:

> A fascinating analogy introduced a few years back said that, thanks to technology and social media, organisations have moved from being black boxes to glass boxes. Ten or fifteen years ago a company could say whatever wonderful thing about themselves, with the help of a good PR agency. Only an *enormous* crisis, involving outside authorities or regulators, would allow you a peek inside the black box. Suddenly, with the advent of technology and social media companies have realized that they are, in fact, glass boxes. Anyone inside or outside the organization can tweet about it.

Increased transparency (although in some cases that glass box is still somewhat opaque) has had a powerful effect on modern corporate culture, particularly regarding issues provoking a strong societal reaction. These issues are as diverse as gender, human rights and the environment. Writing in the *Harvard Business Review* in 2013, Jen Boynton gave a few examples of businesses which "moved into more sustainable practices by a social media backlash". These include H&M, Zara and Abercrombie & Fitch, who banded together "to create a safety plan to improve conditions in Bangladeshi factories", following a factory collapse disaster. Boynton also quotes the example of how "the Internet cried foul when the Susan G Komen foundation decided to yank funding for Planned Parenthood". The reaction caused the non-profit to reverse its decision within days.[12]

Greenpeace also attacked Nestlé in 2010 with a viral video over its use of unsustainable palm oil. "After 3 months of holding its ground against vocal naysayers on Facebook, the company finally agreed to cancel contracts with vendors who clear cut rainforests to make room for palm oil plantations. (Nestlé is now much more proactive about CSR.)"[13] As Jacob puts it:

> If you want to walk the talk, you have to really build a brand that stands for your organization. You have to have a purpose, and articulate that purpose to your audience. Yes, you should have a beautiful website, and a beautiful physical interface, and a global presence, but what about your purpose?

Where energy companies are concerned, it seems that they have found their purpose ("They are now realizing that something has to be done and they're doing it"), but in articulating it, they should take on board the theories of Jacob's two favourite economists, the Nobel Prize laureates Daniel Kahneman and Richard Thaler:

> I have always been fascinated by the work that Daniel Kahneman has spearheaded in the science of behavioural economics. And I've also been fascinated by Thaler because he blended psychology and economics, confirming that many of the decisions we take in a life are not rational, but emotional. The world of behavioural economics is a wonderful example of how emotions and reason have to work hand in hand.

Kahneman's 2011 bestseller *Thinking Fast and Slow* posits two ways in which we form thoughts. These two systems (the *fast*, which is automatic, effortless and seemingly involuntary, and the *slow*, which is deliberate, effortful and requires concentration) are influenced, for better or worse, by our emotions. "Mood evidently affects the operation of System 1: when we are uncomfortable and unhappy, we lose touch with our intuition". He continues that, "good mood, intuition, creativity, gullibility and increased reliance on System 1 form a cluster", while at the other pole "sadness, vigilance, suspicion, an analytic approach and increased effort also go together."[14] Kanehman offers a droll assessment of how we like to perceive our mental faculties: "In the unlikely event of this book being made into a film, System 2 would be a supporting character who believes herself to be a hero."[15]

To branding and marketing practitioners these findings offer valuable insights into mood activation of cognitive faculties. Once you think of the

FINDING THE RIGHT BALANCE

brand holistically—beyond its name and logo—as purpose driven, then you start to accept the role of both emotions and reason in brand building:

> At Saffron we always say that to build the brand you have to find the right balance between IQ and EQ. This is absolutely necessary. If you believe, for instance, that brands and branding are about belonging, and that the fundamental purpose of a brand connects with your employees, your customers, or your society, then you can't do without one or the other.

This view also encompasses companies that deal purely in commodities. In such cases, although you don't have a business-to-consumer (B2C) base, and might not be known at household level, you have your employees and stakeholders:

> Think about Codelco, Chile's national copper mining company. They are the world's largest copper producer with a workforce of around 15,000 people. When you add their dependants there could be 50,000 people very closely connected to this one company. In addition, there are further thousands of people working as contractors, or servicing various aspects of the company's activities—as well as regulators and officials following Codelco's operations. This means that although Codelco is a company producing a commodity, in Chile you are never far from meeting someone connected with it. After all, it produces in revenue something like $700 dollars per year for every citizen of Chile.

Although such a company is oriented solely towards its business customers, producing a commodity which reaches end-users only after multiple stages of refinement, production and manufacturing, it still needs to *articulate* a purpose for society. Otherwise it will be perceived as lacking values or direction, and an easy target for both regulators and rivals.

For energy companies, regardless of whether they are at the production, distribution or retail end, that purpose has been almost been articulated for them:

> I was going through an article today that spoke about the carbon footprint per capita in countries around the world. With a few exceptions,

the countries that have the largest carbon footprint happen to be the countries that have the largest energy companies.

Jacob says that these companies have the responsibility to tell us about fossil fuel alternatives, and the dangers of business as usual, but even more than that—they need to get on with doing things:

> The easy way out for them would be simply to rebrand, or try to own a certain kind of green or sustainable discourse. But, they also need to understand that investing in corporate social responsibility (CSR) rather than sustainability would be a step backwards.
>
> In the early days of corporate social responsibility, there was a sense that every company should be doing it, but nobody knew what it meant and nobody knew what to do. Some companies created a CSR line in the budget and they put there whatever they thought was socially nice, like Christmas parties for the poor. The common thread, however, was that they had no CSR strategy.

Jacob thinks that just as these companies found, in time, that their corporate social mission had to align with their purpose, energy companies will discover that sustainability should align with theirs. Rather than being detrimental to the consumer, through restrictive practices or higher prices, it could lead to decarbonisation in an intelligent, practical and pragmatic way:

> We need to get it out of our heads that OPEC will stop producing oil—because they're not. And as long as they produce it, such organisations will have a significant role in the conversation around energy.

That conversation seems to be going round in circles: every time there is a significant drop in the price of oil and gas, industry lobbyists can be heard urging the public to take the foot of the sustainability accelerator.

On the other hand, says Jacob, once power companies really start owning their purpose, they have "a wonderful opportunity" to lead the conversation:

> Of course, you need to have scientists as part of the solution, and lawmakers in Washington, Brussels and all the other places. But, really at

the forefront of this conversation you need to have private and public energy companies. They will be rolling out the technologies required to combat climate change. If they are behind the curve, if they are dragging their feet, then we are in trouble. The way our capitalist economy is set up, solutions need to come from the private sector.

The concept of branding, then, with its roots in the distant past, and co-evolving with the fundamentally human activity of trade, has over the past decades expanded to include such abstract concepts as "mission", "promise" and "purpose". This conceptual development coincides with a social transformation on an unprecedented scale: not only are modern democratic societies attempting to right ancient wrongs of gender or racial inequality, but we are also shifting away from fossil fuels, the basic energy source of the global economy.

The link between the evolution of branding and changing social mores is private enterprise. We expect modern companies to do better than just abide by the rules of fair trade. We expect them to have values, and that those values correspond with pervasive ethical norms. Or perhaps, it is that the very concept of trade has now expanded to include an expectation of progressive change.

For all these considerations, I somehow feel that those ancient traders, carrying their precious cargoes across the Mediterranean in specially designed amphoras, would not have a problem in grasping the concept of the brand as a promise. Perhaps because they understood it, they sought to differentiate their goods with seals, trademarks and exclusive packaging. And if we are merely following in their footsteps then what about the future of branding?

Rather than end our conversation by idly speculating on what lay ahead for our industry, Jacob chooses to reflect on why each company should invest in its own future. In branding the payoff is delayed and uncertain, while the outlay could be immediate and significant. You are committing to a process that might yield results long way down the line. But there is a handy parallel:

Investing in brand is like investing in education for your children. If your child is five, and you have committed to invest in their education, you won't expect them to have a PhD in physics from Princeton when they are seven. It's something that goes little by little.

FINDING THE RIGHT BALANCE   157

Now think about this: if you want your children, or your nephews, or people that you love to have a future, that future is built on the education they get. Education gives them freedom, the freedom to choose, the freedom to move, the freedom to think, but you can not attain either that education or that freedom in 15 minutes, nor in one year, nor even in two years.

This is percolating little by little. And when you look at the value that brand can give your organization, whatever money you spend on it, it is nothing compared to the value both tangible and intangible.

Notes

1. See Demirdjian, Zorah S. "Rise and Fall of Marketing in Mesopotamia: A Conundrum in the Cradle of Civilization", *The Future of Marketing's Past: Proceedings of the 12th Biennial Conference on Historical Analysis and Research in Marketing*. Neilson, Leighton (ed.). 2005. ojs.library.carleton.ca/index.php/pcharm/article/download/1610/1454. Also, Moore, Karland Susan Reid. "The Birth of Brand: 4000 Years of Branding." *Journal Business History*, Vol. 50, No. 4, February 2008, (doi:10.1080/00076790802106299).

2. A quick overview of silent trade can be found in Encyclopaedia Britannica's entry on the subject, at britannica.com/topic/silent-trade. The passage from Herodotus was quoted according to Henrich, Joseph. *The WEIRDest People in the World: How the West Became Psychologically Peculiar and Particularly Prosperous*. Farrar, Straus and Giroux, 2020 (ebook), p. 306, archive.org. In *The Histories* this passage is in Book IV, §196.

3. Information on Saffron, where not separately referenced, was taken from the company's website at saffron-consultants.com.

4. Hawkins, Richard. "The Origins of Marketing Practice in Britain: From the Ancient to the Early Twentieth Century." *Journal of Historical Research in Marketing*, Vol. 9, No. 4, 2017, pp. 467–487, (doi:10.1108/JHRM-06-2017-0024).

5. Nevett, Terence R. *Advertising in Britain: A History*. Harper & Collins, 1982.

6. Jones, D. G. Brian and Mark Tadajewski (eds). *The Routledge Companion to Marketing History*. Routledge, 2016, p. 92.

7. Ibid, p. 99.

8. Day, Julia. "Omnicom Snaps up Wolff Olins". *The Guardian*, 31 May 2001, theguardian.com/media/2001/may/31/marketingandpr2.

9. Benbunan, Jacob et al. *Disruptive Branding: How to win in times of change.* Kogan Page, 2019, p. 2. Mentioned in this excerpt are Jean-Marie Dru, Chairman of advertising group TBWA, while Clayton Christensen is the American academic and business consultant whose work offered an early contribution to the understanding of how start-ups displace established businesses.
10. Maslow, Abraham H. "A Theory of Human Motivation." *Psychological Review*, Vol. 50, No. 4, July 1943, pp. 370–396, (doi:10.1037/h0054346).
11. Jacob's back of the envelope calculation on the number of internet users world-wide tallies with World Bank data, stating that around of 56 per cent of the global population is online. Graph can be found under the heading "Individuals using the Internet (% of population)", at data.worldbank.org/indicator/IT.NET.USER.ZS.
12. Boynton, Jen. "How the Voice of the People Is Driving Corporate Social Responsibility." *Harvard Business Review*, 17 Jul. 2013, hbr.org/2013/07/how-the-voice-of-the-people-is.
13. Ibid.
14. Kahneman, Daniel. *Thinking, Fast and Slow*. Anchor Canada, 2013, p. 69.
15. Ibid, p. 31.

13

VIRTUAL POWER

NIC KENNEDY ON THE MEETING OF ENERGY AND IT

Bell Labs—official name, Bell Telephone Laboratories—one of the foremost research institutions of the twentieth century, was officially founded as a stand-alone company in 1925. It was jointly owned by AT&T, the US telecommunications monopoly of its time, and Western Electric, the electrical equipment manufacturer (whose majority owner was also AT&T).

The research and development activities at AT&T followed the expansion of the US telecommunications business. By the 1920s close to 40 per cent of US households owned a telephone.[1] But, American Telephone and Telegraph also had a corporate vision beyond servicing its customers.

As Jon Gertner writes in his book *The Idea Factory: Bell Labs and the Great Age of American Innovation*:

> AT&T's dream of "universal" connectivity was set down in the early 1900s . . . [the company] was seeking to create and maintain a system—the word "network wasn't yet common—that could connect any person on the globe to any other at any time.[2]

DOI: 10.4324/9781003351030-14

Gathering some of America's top scientists and engineers under one roof and allowing them to broadly define project scopes, guided by a distant and perhaps even utopian goal, was bound to yield surprising high-tech inventions. Over time, scientists working at Bell Labs won nine Nobel prizes and invented devices, such as the transistor, the telecommunications satellite and the laser, which have shaped the modern world.

However, as energy historian John Perlin claims, "few inventions in the history of Bell Laboratories evoked as much media attention and public excitement as the unveiling of the silicon solar cell, referred to as the Bell Solar Battery".[3]

Constructed by Daryl Chapin, Calvin Fuller and Gerald Pearson, the cell utilised the photovoltaic (PV) effect, observed on solid materials in the 1870s. This research was followed by the first working solar PV module, constructed by Charles Fritts from selenium and gold leaf. In 1885 he sent it to Werner von Siemens who presented the device to the Royal Academy of Prussia. "Siemens judged photoelectricity to be 'scientifically of the most far-reaching importance'", writes Perlin.

For over half a century, however, the efficiency of photovoltaic (PV) cells—which are made of materials that give off an electric charge when exposed to sunlight—barely topped 0.5 per cent. By the time Chapin and his colleagues unveiled their first commercial cell in 1954, its efficiency was 6 per cent. Within 18 months it doubled. But one thing that wouldn't budge was the cost. One-watt cell costing $286, "Chapin calculated that in 1956 a homeowner would have to pay $1,430,000 for an array of sufficient size to power an average house." It seemed that solar PV panels would remain an expensive novelty, and that once out of Bell Labs renewable energy and telecoms would part ways, not to meet again.

But, as Perlin contends, the space race of the 1960s revived the interest in the technology. It was deemed ideal for powering satellites, modules and orbiting space stations, and from 1958 to 1969 the American government poured $50 million in solar cell research and development. Still, by 1971 the cost was around $100 per watt. It was not until Dr Eliot Berman, working for the oil-giant Exxon, simplified the process of silicon panel manufacture, that the cost to the consumer dropped significantly. With financial backing from Exxon, Dr Berman went on to form the Solar Power Corporation which by 1973 retailed panels for around $20 dollar a watt.

At the time of writing, solar panels cost 25 cents a watt, more than one thousand times less than the first solar cell in 1954.[4] Similarly, the price of utility-scale solar electricity per megawatthour (MWh) has now dropped to around a quarter of the wholesale price, and in many countries around the world is the cheapest form of electricity delivered to the grid.

As over the last 30 years PV solar cells became part of everyday life, so did AT&T's "universal connectivity". And this is where companies like the Flux Federation come in. They are surveying the vast new land beyond the confluence of renewable energy and information technology. Or, perhaps from a traditionalist point of view, an Alice in Wonderland realm, where everything you know about the energy sector has evolved into unusual shapes.

If traditional energy companies are often led by electrical engineers, these companies are led by software engineers; if traditional energy companies run "conventional" power plants, "new energy" companies connect virtual power plants; if old-school energy companies offer a daytime and a night-time tariff, these start-ups offer dozens of ultra-niche, lifestyle tariffs.

Instead of a centralised grid, the Young Turks talk about decentralised energy resources, threatening to replace the electricity meter, the *medulla oblongata* of the energy system, with something called block-chain validation. They promise an anarchic world where data will be as valuable as energy, and communities will trade home-made, carbon-free electricity.

As a marketing and branding practitioner I notice the difference between old and new companies at the semantic level. In conducting the interviews for this book I had not heard the words "fun", "playful" and "delightful" in the context of energy branding until I had spoken to Nic Kennedy, the CEO of Flux Federation. It is as if the ebullient and enthusiastic language springs as much as from a sense opportunity, stoked by the fusion of energy and IT, as from the very tenets of modern software design, which has to be simple, engaging and user-friendly.

True to type, Nic says that she has written software "for too many years". Her personal interest is "in the intersection between great growth and great software engineering". She describes her company as a "platform for energy retailers" at the core of which is "Powershop, a very powerful piece of software that other energy retailers around the world could use". To begin with, the Powershop brand name, owned by the New Zealand energy company Meridian, covered both the software and the energy retail

162 VIRTUAL POWER

operation based on it. As the concept proved scalable, and Meridian started a Powershop company in Australia, there was a sense that the software platform on its own could be a viable business:

> When we split the platform off, we retained the brand assets at Flux, so that in the future we could roll out the entire retailer-in-the-box concept in any territory where we have a client. We now license our platform to other retailers.

In popular parlance, and even among many marketing practitioners, the need for a rebrand is often justified by saying that the brand "looks tired"—that it should be "spruced up" or "refreshed".[5] Actually, one of the most common reasons companies decide to rebrand is diversification. Others include change of ownership, asset divestment or reputational problems. Diversification can entail launching variations of the same product, or entering a new geographic or sectoral market. Regardless, it has been described as "one of the most challenging decision a company can confront", and "an unpredictable high-stakes game".[6] "We looked at it from a holistic point of view," Nic says:

> Where do we think the governments are going, where do we think the residential customers are going? What are the problems going to be? When we look at our clients, how do we see their businesses shaping up over time? If they don't have any problems today, will they face challenges in the future. Where are the opportunities?

She adds:

> As CEO I have encouraged the team to speak with a lot of people— to understand where this emerging market is going. Having had input, we had to look really deep within ourselves to decide who we are and where we want to be. That exercise cannot but touch your brand, because I want to make sure that we are able to enter a market in a way that makes complete sense to our clients. They should be able to understand immediately how we can help them in their business.
>
> When I say brand, I don't just mean what we look like. it's the whole picture: how we communicate, how we think, and most

importantly, how other people feel when they interact with us. This whole thing goes deep into our software as well—how do operators feel when they're using our software.

Whereas much of branding practice is influenced by psychology and social science—as this is the academic background of many branding practitioners—I find Nic's approach in keeping with her engineering background. This is not to say that as an engineer she considers it of secondary importance to the business—on the contrary. What is fascinating to hear is the language of software project management, transposed to branding:

> In our minds, the building blocks of our brand are quite structured. So, we just move them around. That is the thinking when we design and build software. We gather information and discuss features. Then we test little pieces out. Does that work, or does it not work? What are the ripple effects? Then we start to home in and really invest in aligning groups of people to get something done. Now that we've got a great business and a great piece of software, let's see how we can make it attractive for people to buy and use as much as possible, so it makes everyone's lives better.

Nic explains that her definition of brand might not match the "official" one, but, essentially, "it goes down to the cellular level. Meaning, the values the professionals at the organisation hold, and how they think and act, then transfers through the system, right through to the cellular level of everybody who uses the product. When I think of the concept of brand it's a touchy-feely thing, it's soft, it doesn't have hard edges."

The emotional and tactile aspects of the brand are embodied in the product, which, from a software designers point of view, should evoke certain feelings during use. Ultimately, if you want the customers to feel safe, if you want to engender a sense of trust "you should go all the way back to that voice that you use in your company when you talk to each other":

> When you talk to clients, or use words at the interface level of your software, or produce information around it—what words are you using? That language and style of communication should be the same language you use internally. It's all about creating harmony and trust.

In "Selling the Brand Inside", an article published in 2002, Colin Mitchel, at the time group planning director at Ogilvy and Mather, and later vice president of global brand at McDonalds, says something that initially might seem obvious, but upon reflection explains why some marketing and branding campaigns run into trouble. When executives think of marketing, they are naturally more likely to focus on marketing to customers. "But another 'market' is just as important: your employees, the very people who can make the brand come alive for your customers . . . Companies very often ignore this critical constituency."[7]

According to Mitchel, internal marketing and branding is important because "it's the best way to help employees make a powerful emotional connection to the products and services you sell. Without that connection, employees are likely to undermine the expectations set by your advertising."[8] Employees might simply not understand what the company has promised the public, and could end up working at cross-purposes. In other cases, they might feel disengaged, or worse—hostile towards the company.

If you are planning an internal branding campaign Mitchel advises three principles: *choose your moment, link internal and external marketing,* and *bring the brand alive for employees.* The generic reasons for branding (noted above) such as corporate restructure or change of ownership, for Mitchel are *good* reasons. "At certain turning points, times when the company is experiencing some fundamental challenge or change, employees are seeking direction and are relatively receptive to these initiatives."[9]

And while linking external and internal marketing is self-explanatory, bringing the brand alive for employees requires "a professional branding campaign, to introduce and explain the messages and then reinforce them by weaving the brand into the fabric of the company. The messages should be directed at employee 'touch-points', the day-to-day interactions that influence the way people experience the workplace."[10] This campaign should be structured into stages, just like an external branding campaign, starting with research and continuing through the planning and execution of a communications strategy. The strategy has to be designed "to convince your employees of the merits and credibility of your brand".[11]

Mitchel's parting advice is that in bringing the brand alive to employees you have to be as creative and eye-catching in your presentation as if you were addressing an external audience. "To overcome people's natural cynicism . . . the campaign must ring true for employees and must draw on the company's very soul . . . You need to surprise and charm your audience."

And don't be tempted to rely solely on memos, videos or information packages. "There's no substitute for personal contact from the organization's highest levels."[12]

How does this heavily procedural approach to branding apply to start-ups, in particular those working at the point of intersection between energy and IT? As a rule, these are smaller, business-to-business (B2B) companies which service energy retailers, and as such are at a few degrees remove from retail consumers. Nic goes back to product design and user experience:

> The most important part of your presentation is your product. It used to be that the B2B user experience could be slow and clunky. If behind the scenes, your staff were working on something, the look and feel of the platform they used was considered less important than something seen by customers. But, if you were a supplier of that platform, what does it say about you, about your brand, that you consider business customers less discerning than retail customers.

Nic says that there is a tectonic shift in software design for B2B audiences. Enterprises are starting to expect the same experience as in business-to-consumer (B2C) software, not just because it tends to look smarter, but because better designed software means more efficient work-flows and savings. "Every time we show our software the response is 'Wow, that's so easy to use . . . It's really nice . . . It's so fast and intuitive.' To me this is the sort of feedback you want to get about your brand."

An illustration of how, and perhaps why, people think differently of products aimed at a B2B market than those aimed at a B2C market, are the well-known words "No one ever got fired for buying IBM". It was never IBM's official slogan, but its meaning in the popular imagination is clear. when something as important as your job is at stake, you tend to be cautious about your purchasing decisions. You would perhaps even sacrifice some of the funkier features of a consumer product, such as design-appeal, for the reliability of a business product.[13]

Nic thinks that business purchases are decided in a fundamentally different way from consumer purchases:

> In general, it's a small committee of people, looking through some kind of a proposal or a comparison table with features and prices.

166 VIRTUAL POWER

Whereas, a consumer quite often makes a decision with their heart based on how they fell and what they like about the product.

But, in her view, it doesn't need to be like that anymore:

I hear lots of energy companies complaining that they are stuck with a clunky old billing system. Usually, it is because they have made their purchasing decision purely from an engineering perspective, rather than thinking about optionality, to be able to move as the market moves. At some point, the client will inevitably want agility, and the flexibility to improve their business.

This is where, Nic thinks, being brand-focused helps B2B companies:

If you write a piece of software and don't think about user-experience or the design, the result will be something that is intuitive for the designer, but not for the person using it. That was the gist of the point I made earlier about the brand being embedded at the cellular level of the company. It is like having the end-user sitting on your shoulder, as you're designing and building it for them. That attitude needs to go into your brand-space.

Investing in branding in such a paradigm, should not be considered as separate from business, or even product development. Nic offers a colourful example:

Design, whether at brand or product level, is putting things together. But, how do you do it? Well, think about making hot cross buns. They have raisins, but you don't put those in after the buns are baked. You knead them in with the dough. Branding shouldn't be some secret thing sitting in marketing, that you sprinkle on top, so to speak, once the bun is out of the oven.

All too often, Nic explains, as a consequence of marketing being stuck in its department, the rest of the company thinks that it should not worry about it. That it is something you add later. But, expanding on her metaphor, she says that branding and marketing have to be "baked in". From the job interview and the induction, to everyday workflows, the culture of the company

VIRTUAL POWER   167

has to prioritise it. Otherwise, one of the dangers of compartmentalising marketing is that the department may "run away with it". This happens often when it comes to balancing the emotional and rational dimensions of brand-messaging:

> The marketing team could be locked away working on a new campaign and then, all of a sudden, after a couple months, there's a new suite of photos that show people running through the grass, with the sun out, and all sorts of other wonderful things. But, making something pretty, without connecting it with true emotion, does not look real. People can smell that. The challenge for energy brands is that the topic of energy is commonly perceived as boring, and that nobody loves interacting with the energy company. So, how do you make it interesting?

In advertising (and especially for power companies which deal in the somewhat abstract commodity of electricity) the common dilemma is whether to execute your campaign around concrete product attributes or around lifestyle expressions and abstract benefits. In an article, "Can Your Advertisement Go Abstract Without Affecting Willingness to Pay? Product-Centered versus Lifestyle Content In Luxury Brand Print Advertisements", the authors Francesco Massara *et al.* remind us that the trend "whereby brands build remarkable stories of life and convey meanings that enrich their image beyond the valence of the product offered, is known as lifestyle branding . . . Through lifestyle advertising, brands become detached from the tangible characteristics of their products to become a means of self-expression."[14]

But, does it pay? Not always, say Massara and colleagues, at least not in print:

> Jumping on the bandwagon of lifestyle advertising may not be advisable always for brands. Lifestyle print advertising sometimes may be weaker than product-centered print advertising, may hinder the opportunity to impose a premium price, and may curb the overall development of brand equity.[15]

The reason is that it is perceived as more abstract than product-centred advertising. The authors, however, also offer "an easy yet effective way" to manipulate a print advertisement's "abstractness". The method, "based on established linguistic models" relies on adjusting the adjective-to-noun ratios in the ad's copy. In a nutshell, the more nouns to adjectives, the less a print advertisement is perceived as abstract.

But online and software design is a whole different game—sometimes literally. To begin with, it offers opportunities for non-verbal interaction. Nic credits the "gamification model" of purchasing your energy as playing a large part in the success of Powershop (the retailer):

> We created something playful and colourful that has delighted the customers. It has also made large industrial clients think "Hey, I would rather hook my wagon up to that particular horse". Instead of accepting that energy is boring we have created something fun, that makes people feel good—and everyone wants to feel good.

Out of all the feelgood factors influencing energy-consumer purchasing decisions, though, one is turning out to be more important than most:

> When it comes to the environment, consumers buy with their heart. Not everyone, of course, but as these problems get bigger, we will see a greater role for emotions in energy purchasing decisions. This means that consumers will still consider cost, but it might not be of primary importance.

But should energy companies then go one step further, and use this opportunity to seize the moral high ground? Should they not try to be greener than airlines, fast-food chains or other types of businesses? Perhaps go above and beyond the call of duty?

My interview with Nic convinced me not just that the evolution of our energy system is far from over, and that the future might bring an energy/IT hybrid that looks only remotely like the system of today; but, also that some of the expectations we harbour when it comes to interacting with software, we might bring to energy brands. We might expect energy to be fun. Why shouldn't it? We might even come to expect energy brands to delight us. And perhaps the most delightful thing of all would be to know that energy companies are leading by example, and that every unit of electricity we use in our daily lives is green.

Notes

1. The data on the number of telephones in the United States in the 1920s has been taken from the US Census Bureau. It is part of the series "20th Century Statistics" under the heading "No. 1440. Selected Communications Media: 1920 to 1998", at census.gov/history/pdf/radioownership1920-1998.pdf.
2. Gertner, Jon. *The Idea Factory: Bell Labs and the Great Age of American Innovation*. Penguin Press, 2012, p. 2. A passage in the book describes how the Bell Labs director of research Harold Arnold understood the institution's remit. "As Arnold explained, his department would include "the fields of physical and organic chemistry, of metallurgy, of magnetism, of electrical conduction, of radiation, of electronics, of acoustics, of phonetics, of optics, of mathematics, of mechanics, and even of physiology, of psychology, and of meteorology." Gertner adds that "from the start Jewett (president of Bell Labs) and Arnold seemed to agree that at West Street there could be an indistinctness about goals. Who could know in advance exactly what practical applications Arnold's men would devise" (ibid., p. 32).
3. Perlin, John. *From Space to Earth—The Story of Solar Electricity*. University Press, 2002, pp. 35. Leading up to the first commercial solar cell part of the book are two chapters which summarise the history of solar energy utilisation from ancient times to the nineteenth century.
4. For the current cost of solar panels, we have turned to online trading platform SecondSol, "the photovoltaic marketplace", at secondsol.com.
5. For a light-hearted, yet apposite view on motivations to rebrand see Lischer, Brian. "Six Reasons Your Company May Need To Rebrand Itself." *Forbes*, 21 Oct. 2016, forbes.com/sites/theyec/2016/10/21/six-reasons-your-company-may-need-to-rebrand-itself/?sh=9c8747c770e1.
6. Markides, Constantinos C. "To Diversify or Not To Diversify." *Harvard Business Review*, Nov.–Dec. 1997, hbr.org/1997/11/to-diversify-or-not-to-diversify.
7. Mitchell, Colin. "Selling the Brand Inside" *Harvard Business Review*, January 2002, https://hbr.org/2002/01/selling-the-brand-inside.
8. Ibid.
9. Ibid.
10. Ibid.
11. Ibid.

12. Ibid.
13. The origins of "No one ever got fired for buying IBM equipment" are not clear. Barry Popik, lexicographer and editor of the Big Apple website (barrypopik.com), which gives the etymology of many popular American words and phrases, traces the first mention to 1978, as published in trade magazine Mini-micro systems. See barrypopik.com/index.php/new_york_city/entry/no_one_ever_got_fired_for_buying_ibm_microsoft_gold/.
14. Massara, Francesco et al. "Can Your Advertisement Go Abstract Without Affecting Willingness to Pay? Product-Centered versus Lifestyle Content In Luxury Brand Print Advertisements." *Journal of Advertising Research*, Vol. 60, No. 1, March 2020, (doi:10.2501/JAR-2019-005).
15. Ibid.

14

WHO YOU ARE AND WHO YOU WANT TO BE

HANDO SUTTER ON BRAND AS THE TIP OF THE CORPORATE STRATEGY ICEBERG

If like me you are an academic, and also a business practitioner in your area of scholarly expertise there is a word for us. We are *pracademics*. I was reminded of it recently, when "pracademic" popped up in an email from my publisher. This portmanteau, perhaps best defined as "practitioner and academic", was popularised by Professor Paul L. Posner, the American political science maven. In his 2009 essay *The Pracademic: An Agenda for Re-Engaging Practitioners and Academics* he notes that the synergy between theory and practice is "a much sought after, but sometimes elusive, touchstone . . ."[1]

You could see why Posner was hung up on the concept. He was managing director of federal budget at the US Government Accountability Office for 13 years and inevitably noticed that it was "difficult to study budgeting as an academic without either a practitioner background or mind-set".[2] Public policy, thought Posner, needs "boundary spanners"—people whose careers are rooted in both academic and public service camps. They would be able not just to draw on their own bi-faceted knowledge and experience, but also to "broker academic-practitioner interactions".[3]

DOI: 10.4324/9781003351030-15

Setting aside, for the moment, to what degree all of this applies to the practice and study of marketing and branding, I am also aware that on reading the above some miffed academic might think: "I have dozens of students and dozens of assignments to grade. Secondly, every year I need to be churning out a regular stream of books and articles to keep my tenure. Finally, I'm a professor of philosophy. I apologise for not having a side-job!"

Even here Posner has a few soothing words. He is not insisting that everyone of us should hold two jobs; that right out of the lecture theatre, we should step into an office; or that, God forbid, we should drop our laser-pointers, and akin to our unfortunate colleagues during Chairman Mao's Cultural Revolution, grab a spade or hoe. Instead, Posner talks about "a shared community of thoughtful practitioners and academics, each contributing unique perspectives but learning from each other through meetings, conferences, exercises and informal discussions".[4]

Posner's pracademic—the boundary spanner, the public administration expert, the relationship broker—seems to be welcome everywhere. All doors, whether to boardroom or classroom, are open to him, and everyone wants to be his friend. The marketing and branding pracademic, on the other hand, is not as fortunate. As soon as he descends from his academic ivory tower, he is challenged. (And no, I am not just talking about myself here). In the warm and comfortable environs of his university he is needed and respected. Outside, he is often told that marketing is fundamentally redundant, and branding unimportant. He is wistfully asked to imagine a world where there is none of either.

As it happens, it is not hard to imagine such a world at all. The Soviet Union implemented a command economy, that allowed for hardly any market competition. Company budgeting and business planning was neither by practitioners or academics, but bureaucrats and politicians. Consequently, there was very little advertising (as we know it), and almost none of the marketing ecosystem, which had in other industrial nations evolved to support such an activity. By "ecosystem" I mean the network of both competing agencies and professionals, *and* collaborating institutions, all working within a regulated, yet subsidy-free industry. As Irina Yuzhakova and colleagues note "The ads dealt almost exclusively with propaganda and public service announcements . . . the volume of advertising during this period was insignificant."[5]

However, we should also note a contrary view. In her research study *Western Concepts, Russian Perspectives: Meanings of Advertising in the Former Soviet Union*, Ludmilla Gricenko Wells enumerates "common misconceptions" about Soviet advertising, two of which are that "the Soviets had not created, produced or used advertising to promote goods and services (and that) prior to 1988 there were no advertising agencies in the Soviet Union".[6] In a later article she contends that such misconceptions arose because "western advertisers and agencies did not consider Soviet advertising to be 'real' advertising".[7]

And yet there are two telling details in *Western Concepts, Russian Perspectives*. A Russian marketing professional and a participant in the study says "I've heard that people say there is no advertising in the USSR. There is, and there was, but perhaps it wasn't so obvious." To which the author ads that "the key point is not whether advertising in the Soviet Union was or was not adhering to 'Socialist ideology', but that advertising provided information about goods and services rather than brands."[8]

Whoever might be in the right on the nature of Soviet advertising there is broad agreement on fact. For instance, that the nation's biggest and most influential newspaper, the legendary *Pravda*—with a circulation 11 million at its peak—did not start printing advertisements until 1990 (except for a short time during the liberal economic reforms of the 1920s);[9] or that the viewers in the USSR got their first blast of US commercials on national television in 1987 (of the kind that interrupt the programme),[10] more than 45 years after the first-ever TV commercial was broadcast on a local station in New York.[11]

During those four decades the Soviet marketing industry produced a large number of advertising curios, such as TV ads for products that either did not exist or where unavailable to the general public, ads that resembled social documentaries and often, ads that were produced but instantly shelved (the explanation is that the bureaucrats directing the economy had stipulated how each company should spend 1 per cent of its revenue on advertising, but there was no rule saying that the ads should actually be broadcast or printed).

As a pracademic, however, I find the coda to the history of Soviet advertising as interesting as the debate on whether it existed or not.[12] No sooner had the USSR dissolved, the advertising industry in Russia (organised along the Western model) took off. Yuzhakova *et al.*: "In 1991 advertising in Russia amounted to only $3m, grew to $51m in 1992 and further to $220m in 1993. By 1994 this amount was up to $1.2b, and in 1995 exceeded the $2b mark."[13]

Hando Sutter, the CEO of Enefit, entered Tallinn University in 1988, to study Mechanical Engineering. He graduated in 1992, a year after Estonia declared independence from the Soviet Union. His career started and developed under the post-Communist paradigm of competition and private business ownership; where branding and marketing were accepted as essential enablers of free enterprise—as essential as product development or customer service. It was Sutter's generation, largely unencumbered by old commercial practices and beliefs, that has pushed through the modernisation of Estonia's business culture. Hence, his views on branding are progressive and activist, perhaps even more so than those of some practitioners in supposedly advanced advertising environments.

In parallel to completing the final two years of his degree in Mechanical Engineering, Hando enrolled in Estonian Business School:

> I wanted to understand business, and have a better grasp of everything that goes into running a company, including marketing and branding. Still, I never dreamt of being a manager. I wanted to be an engineer, to create value in the world with my inventions. But somehow life has been taking me to the top management positions in big companies, all of them over a thousand people strong.

Prior to joining Enefit, which within Estonia is known as Eesti Energia, Hando was regional manager for Baltics and Russia at Nord Pool, the Norwegian-based European power exchange:

> I started in 2006 to educate myself on power markets. I contacted people at Nord Pool. I saw that power trading was the future. At the time, power was a regulated commodity in Eastern Europe and wasn't yet market-traded, like in the Nordic countries.

Three years later, in 2009, Nord Pool called back and asked Hando to lead on market expansion in the Baltics:

> I was opening the power markets in Estonia, Latvia and Lithuania. Part of the job was training and educating stakeholders: regulators,

TSOs, and market participants. I had no plans to move from Nord Pool but then Enefit contacted me in 2014.

The Enefit board, Hando says, "wanted to accelerate the speed of innovation at the company, implement market principles and introduce new ways of thinking". One of the reasons for this sense of urgency is a shift in attitude both at home and abroad towards shale oil, Estonia's chief energy source. It supplies over 70 per cent of the country's primary energy (and has provided, as recently as 2007, around 90 per cent of its electricity), which, on the positive side, has promoted Estonia into the EU nation least dependent on energy imports.[14]

As Enefit's website claims, "The oil shale industry contributes 4–5 per cent of the Estonian GDP and contributes 300 million euros annually to the state budget."[15] In fact, Estonia is the world's largest per capita producer of the commodity and its companies (Enefit included) are global leaders in shale oil technology development. In addition to stewarding the nations reserves, the total of which was around six billion tonnes at the turn of the century, Enefit has acquired an additional six billion tonnes of reserves in the US state of Utah.

However, the large-scale use of shale oil has turned Estonia into "the second largest emitter of CO2 per capita in the European Union after Luxembourg and by far the most carbon-intensive economy among the OECD countries".[16] Used in electricity generation, the fuel is currently estimated to produce a higher level of harmful atmospheric emissions than coal (but the introduction of new energy-generation methods is expected to reduce this to the same level as coal or biomass). Also, the production of a barrel of shale oil can generate up to 1.5 tons of spent shale, which may occupy a 25 per cent greater volume than the original shale. Where this waste cannot be used as, for instance, a material in the construction industry, it has to be disposed above ground.[17]

To demands that the company cleans up its power supply, Enefit has, under Hando's leadership, responded with an ambitious set of targets. A series of public pledges published on the company's website starts with "We will increase our renewable energy production fourfold by 2026", continues with, "We will cease electricity production from oil shale by 2030 at the latest", and culminates in the promise that "All Enefit's production will be carbon neutral by 2045."

WHO YOU ARE AND WHO YOU WANT TO BE

But how can branding help you get there? Hando thinks that you need to open up the discussion:

> Branding is the tip of the iceberg. Before you brand you need to answer the question of who you are. Who you are today and who you want to be. In Enefit neither of those things was clear. It wasn't clear who we were at this moment, nor who we wanted to be in the future. We didn't have a common internal agreement on those issues. Any company should be brave enough to answer those questions internally before it starts branding.

I could not help but notice at this stage of the interview, how Hando emphasised that the internal consultation process needs to concentrate on "who you are and who you want to be". Who you want to be, rather than "where you want to be". In my view, building a brand is more of a *transformation* than a *journey*. I find that thinking about developing your brand as a journey—a progress-metaphor that could still be effective in delivering results—is a slightly more passive and fuzzy approach, than thinking about it as a transformation. The concept of a journey has almost a ring of mechanical inevitability, as if you are bound to reach your destination—or as if you are hurtling towards it like a cannonball, regardless of process.

Perhaps, a way to reconcile these concepts is an acceptance that your journey to becoming a better brand will get you to your destination, if you transform yourself as a company. Looking at Enefit's list of pledges I noticed that leading up to the final promise of carbon neutrality, there was an intermediate step, "We will transform our production of liquid fuels into a chemical industry based on the circular economy."

These kind of concrete steps are essential not just in reinforcing your credibility, but for the survival of your brand. If you are rebranding as a "net-zero" company, while thus far almost all of your revenue was derived from fossil fuel exploration and combustion, your enthusiasm for your new public image needs to be matched by a plan on how you intend to generate future revenue. Hence, Enefit's heralded transformation of its shale oil division into a petrochemical business.

Hando thinks that many CEO are afraid to ask these kinds of questions:

> Branding for me is a kind of commitment. By saying who you are you commit to your brand, while also describing the nature of your

WHO YOU ARE AND WHO YOU WANT TO BE

commitment to your customers, stakeholders and staff members. Once you make that commitment, you make it transparent and you have to follow it through. Now, some CEOs will be afraid to answer those questions, because—and I am sure many will disagree at this point—they think that the world is changing so fast that business don't have the luxury to stop and define who they are and who they want to be. They feel that they just need to keep going.

But the danger here, notes Hando, is that if you don't go through this exercise, if you don't set aside the time to refine your corporate strategy; to build that consensus inside your organisation before you move to the practical business of branding, your brand won't be strong enough to attract the best talent. Your company will languish. "Our competitiveness, meaning our efficiency, depends on who we are able to hire and if we are not very clear on our commitment, then the talent we choose will not work with us."

In business literature, experts often talk about the importance of "embedding" your corporate strategy—of ensuring that it is understood and accepted by employees. As Charles Galunic and Immanuel Hermreck explain, "This helps ensure that workers' daily decisions and behaviours support the firm's competitive intentions." But, they continue, "we know very little about why some employees get it and others don't".[18]

To better understand what facilitates embeddedness Galunic and Hermreck analysed more than 60,000 confidential responses to an employee-satisfaction survey, conducted by a global corporation consisting of more than 300 operating companies. As anticipated, they found that higher-level employees, who are happy with their compensation and work-life balance, and employees with a positive view of the company are more likely to understand and support the company's strategy. But, surprisingly, it transpired that supervisors don't play a direct role in the process. "Most significant, we found that top management has a profound impact on how well employees grasp and support strategy—far greater than any other variable we examined, and far greater than we'd expected."[19]

It is a mistake to rely on the "cascade effect". "Employees need to hear from senior managers themselves—through straight talk, and ideally in reciprocal exchanges, so that workers feel their own views are heard." This is because senior leaders have a direct understanding of their company's strategy. Their position at the top is powerful, giving them more credibility and authority than others have. "With these considerations in mind", conclude the authors, "companies need to find ways to bring senior management closer to the workforce".[20]

Hando believes that his career prior to Enefit was useful as much for gaining a technical knowledge of the power market, as for understanding how to connect people:

> When I was at Nord Pool I noticed that many of the people working in the sector were isolated. They didn't co-operate well between themselves, nor did their tiny community, let's say that of thermal generators, co-operate with other energy generating communities. When I held meetings or seminars, it turned out that people knew each other, but were not very open. I decided to change that.

Hando also decided not to be content with energy industry benchmarking. All too often, in his view, energy companies benchmark against other energy companies, when they should consider how they measure up against world-class companies, regardless of sector:

> Instead of an energy company looking at what technologies its direct competitors are introducing, let's say, in energy retail, why not go a step further and look at the best technologies out there and introduce it to your customers. Why not benchmark yourself against the world's most successful companies, those that lead on innovation and customer service?
>
> If you look at Enefit, you could ask—are we a utility? Personally, I don't like that word. It's a dinosaur-word, especially because Enefit is also one of Estonia's biggest IT companies. So are we an energy service company? Actually, the important thing to remember about Enefit is that we want to give our customers the latest technologies from around the world. And also that we want to generate our energy in a cleaner way. We benchmark our brand against those aspirations— how useful we are to our customers and how much we contribute to making the world a better place.

Hando concludes that if you want to be useful to your customers, and use the latest technologies then you need to learn from the best players in the market. "But, those are not from the energy sector." This approach blows out of the water an often repeated mantra that for business-to-business (B2B) companies branding shouldn't be as important as for business-to-consumer (B2C) companies:

> This is an outdated view. If you are happy enough with the brand to use it in your business, then you should be also happy to use it at home, and vice versa. The values we promote with our brand are equally important to corporate customers and to households. And we see that a growing number of young entrepreneurs are absolutely insisting on sustainability, both at home in business. Definitions of what is acceptable in B2B and B2C are changing very fast.

And then, as if to disapprove those who claim Estonians have no sense of humour, Hando offers a dry and defiant sound bite, "If you think branding is unimportant I would say good luck to you. You can stay where you are and we will come to your market. We will have more time before you figure out what to do."

There is no other way to develop your brand, he continues, but through long term investment. This should not be an excuse to deprioritise branding, by saying that it takes as long as five years to yield results. As Hando notes, energy companies have investment cycles which stretch over 20 to 30 years. But, it is perfectly sensible to expect a branding return on investment (ROI). The company deploys metrics once or twice a year, and sometimes every quarter, to assess the impact of its brand on perception, recognition or impact in different markets. "We have targets, and if don't reach them, we immediately think what we have to change."

On the subject of reason versus emotion in energy branding, Hando thinks that rather than focus on the dichotomy, we should be careful not to be irrational in our communication, by either raising unrealistic expectations or failing to communicate achievements:

> I hear very often in the energy sector people talking about things that they are not ready to deliver. This we need to avoid. But also, I often hear of something great, that we are not mentioning to our customers. You need to find a compromise on how much you say before something happens, versus how much you communicate on something useful that is already there. Timing is essential.

But, perhaps, the most common mistake when it comes to branding is to think of the energy sector as a special case:

> It took me too long to understand that when it comes to branding and communication, the energy sector speaks to the same people, like all the other sectors. It is the same audience. When I joined the industry there were many people who tried to convince me to the contrary, and today I can say that perhaps I was listening to them a little too much. As a newcomer to this sector should have reacted faster, to what my intuition was telling me.

Perhaps the convergence in marketing and branding practices is a consequence of energy shifting from commodity to service:

> The consumer today has a choice of buying energy from a utility, or doing things themselves. They can install solar panels and storage batteries, and they can run it off-grid or together with our service. Our business is not to hide such opportunities, but to offer them to customers. You can't call what we are doing "selling a commodity", when we are actually servicing customers. We are bringing them latest technologies and value propositions.

To illustrate how Enefit's business has changed not just from Soviet times, but in the last 3 to 4 years, Hando reminds me of something he had mentioned earlier in the interview:

> I said that have one of the biggest IT companies in Estonia, but, really, that is only half the story. We are not simply a thermal power generator any more. We sell more power than we generate, and in January our green generation exceeds our thermal generation. Who would have thought that this was possible, only a few years ago?

Hando takes the time to stress once more that "the business model is entirely changing". He says that it was

> A pretty simple and pretty solid business model for those old utilities, having a fleet of power stations and consumers who had no choice but to buy that power. But, all of this is fading fast. Those CEOs who

WHO YOU ARE AND WHO YOU WANT TO BE   181

are not acting already will be out of the game. Around the world, those utilities which are suffering huge losses have probably been too slow to react to change.

These parting words have reminded me of the value of branding in a free-market environment, even to those energy companies which, like Enefit are government owned. Perhaps they don't have business competitors, but technology is not standing still. A vibrant marketing industry signifies that those vital juices of innovation are flowing through the xylem of a nation's economy. And that the offshoots will be green and healthy.

Notes

1. Various internet resources date the origin of the word *pracademic* before Paul L. Posner's article (Posner, Paul L. "The Pracademic: An Agenda for Re-Engaging Practitioners and Academics." *Budgeting and Finance,* Vol. 29, No. 1, spring 2009, pp. 12–26, Wiley, (doi:10.1111/j.1540-5850.2009.00921.x). Be that as it may, the article offers a finely wrought concept of what a pracademic is and does, to the extent that it can be used as a reference text on the subject.
2. Ibid.
3. Ibid.
4. Ibid.
5. A number of books and articles, scholarly and journalistic, have been used in the story of Soviet advertising. To begin with, Yuzhakova, Irina et al. "A Content Analysis of Prime Time Television Commercials Reflecting Advertising Appeals Used in Russia." *Global Perspectives in Marketing for the 21st Century: Proceedings of the 1999 World Marketing Congress.* Edited by Ajay K. Manrai and H. Lee Meadow, Academy of Marketing Science, pp. 125–130. Springer, link.springer.com/chapter/10.1007/978-3-319-17356-6_39.
6. Gricenko Wells, Ludmila. "Western Concepts, Russian Perspectives: Meanings of Advertising in the Former Soviet Union", *Journal of Advertising,* Vol. 23, No. 1, Mar., 1994, pp. 83–95. JSTOR, jstor.org/stable/4188917.
7. Gricenko Wells, Ludmila. "The Emergence of Advertising in Russia." *International Advertising: Realities and Myths.* Edited by John Philip Jones, Sage Publications, 2012, Sage, (doi:10.4135/9781452231334.n12).

8. Ibid.

9. Kolesnik, Svetlana. "Advertising and Cultural Politics." *Journal of Communication*, Vol. 41, No. 2, 1991, pp. 46–54, (doi:10.1111/j.1460-2466.1991.tb02307.x). The article tells of the ad printed in Pravda in 1990 and some of the more curious Soviet advertising practices.

10. Minbaev, Alexander. "The Semiotics of Advertising in Post-Socialist Russia: Culturally Significant Meanings in Television Commercials During the Period of Transition and Globalization." Master's thesis, Central European University, 2013, etd.ceu.edu/2013/minbaev_alexander.pdf. Both Minbaev and Kolesnik (see above) date the first US (or "western-style" commercial) on USSR national television to 1987.

11. Reisinger, Don. "The First 'Legal' TV Commercial Aired 75 Years Ago Today." *Fortune*, 1 Jul. 2016, https://fortune.com/2016/07/01/bulova-tv-commercial/.

12. For those interested in reading more on the history of advertising in the Soviet Union, there are a number of intriguing articles on the portal Russia Beyond at rbth.com; see also, Specter, Michael. "Russia's Purveyor of 'Truth', Pravda, Dies After 84 Years." *New York Times*, 31 Jul. 1996, www.nytimes.com/1996/07/31/world/russia-s-purveyor-of-truth-pravda-dies-after-84-years.html; as well as "Newspaper Ad Makes A Soviet Pitch For Economic Partners." *New York Times*, 9 Nov. 1996, timesmachine.nytimes.com/timesmachine/1986/11/09/555386.html?pageNumber=15.

13. Yuzhakova et al., "A Content Analysis of Prime Time Television Commercials Reflecting Advertising Appeals Used in Russia".

14. For Estonia's shale oil gas statistics see the Estonia subpage on the website of the U.S. Energy Information Administration at eia.gov, headings "Overview" and "Analysis", eia.gov/international/overview/country/EST; also, report by the International Energy Agency (IEA) *Energy Policies of IEA Countries—Estonia 2019 Review*, available at iea.blob.core.windows.net/assets/21965e0d-c9a9-4617-b1ad-5b4539d91ad7/Estonia_2019_Review.pdf. It says that by 2018 the contribution of shale oil to Estonia's electricity mix was 75.9 per cent (p. 61).

15. See Enefit's webpage "Shale Oil Production" at www.enefit.com/technology/shale-oil-production.

16. Radma, Teet. "Estonia Needs a Plan—and Support—to Get Rid of its Dirty Oil Shale." *EnergyPost*, 3 Sep. 2018, energypost.eu/estonia-needs-a-plan-and-support-to-get-rid-of-its-dirty-oil-shale/.

17. "A Study on the EU Oil Shale Industry—Viewed in the Light of the Estonian Experience." (Report), European Academies Science Advisory Council, May 2007, easac.eu/fileadmin/PDF_s/reports_statements/Study.pdf.
18. Galunic, Charles and Immanuel Hermreck. "How to Help Employees 'Get' Strategy", *Harvard Business Review*, Dec. 2012, https://hbr.org/2012/12/how-to-help-employees-get-strategy.
19. Ibid.
20. Ibid.

15

LIBERALISATION BONANZA

STEPHEN FITZPATRICK AND KEVIN MCMINN ON "ENERGY MINNOWS" BECOMING BIG FISH— OR ONE OF THE "BIG SIX"

Many books and articles were written about energy market liberalisation, and many still remain to be written. But, whether you are just reviewing literature on the subject or planning your own contribution, you would be committing an serious oversight in neglecting Eva Barrett's article "Market Liberalization: Five Seductively Simple Steps to Making it Work". To the first and fundamental question of "what is liberalisation", Barrett gives this answer: "An easy way to think about market liberalization is as the love-child of regulation and deregulation, with some characteristics of both parents."[1] By way of explanation she adds:

> Like advocates of regulation, market liberalists accept the idea that some intervention (from the state or other external agents) is necessary for the achievement of "benign results". Like deregulists, market liberalists advocate the removal of direct state control from potentially competitive markets.[2]

DOI: 10.4324/9781003351030-16

But, although in this sense liberalisation seems a happy compromise, the love-child itself does not seem universally loved. In fact, pick two articles at random (out of the great many we had referred to in our opening sentence) and you are likely to get two radically different takes on the matter.

For example, writing in "Energy Liberalisation, Privatisation and Public Ownership" David Hall *et al.*, from Greenwich University's Public Services International Research Unit (PSIRU) claim that, "The pressures to . . . unbundle and liberalise electricity systems have faced strong resistance everywhere", and—as the authors claim—for perfectly good reasons:

> Private electricity companies are not more efficient than public sector companies . . . Privatisation and liberalisation do not decrease the price of electricity—they increase it . . . The privatisation of distribution companies has created many problems . . . A World Bank report concluded that experience shows that a centralised public sector utility delivers much better results in rural electrification than fragmented or privatised approaches . . .

And so on.[3]

On the other hand, writing in the *Energy Journal*, Paul L. Joskow (looking at pretty much the same evidence as PSIRU) concludes:

> Structural, regulatory and market reforms have been applied to electricity sectors in many countries around the world. Significant performance improvements have been observed in some of these countries as a result of these reforms, especially in countries where the performance of state-owned monopolies was especially poor. Privatization . . . has generally yielded significant cost reductions without reducing service quality Wholesale markets have also stimulated improved performance from existing generators and helped to mobilize significant investments in new generating capacity in several countries.[4]

This theoretical morass reminds one of the famous request by US President Harry Truman. Exasperated by being given conflicting advice on economic policy measures (along the lines of "on the one hand—but on the other"), he is reported to have asked for a "one-armed economist".[5]

To be fair, despite the controversies, there doesn't seem to be a huge countervailing push for renationalisation, at least not for the time being. As Barrett rightly points out:

> A return to traditional cost-of-service market regulation is not feasible. To quote John Rowe (former chairman and CEO of Exelon Corporation, a utility holding company headquartered in Chicago), "There is not going to be any putting of the genie back in the bottle . . . [we] discredited the utility monopoly a long time ago."[6]

Rather, the question is how enthusiastically have the various national energy markets welcomed liberalisation. Looking at developed countries, it might seem that countries following the Anglo-Saxon economic model have been more bullish about it than countries such as Germany. The PSIRU report points out that in the period from 2007 to 2012— supposedly the height of EU-wide energy market liberalisation— 63 municipal companies (*Stadtwerke*) were created; 192 communities have remunicipalised distribution concessions (taken it back from private operators), while a further 57 companies have remunicipalised for other reasons.[7] What this and other examples seem to prove, however, is not so much that Germany is reversing the privatisation of its utilities, but that some links in the power production, distribution and sales chain are easier to privatise than others.

For example, justifying the privatisation of a nation's electricity grid, whether as a whole or in parts is trickier than promoting the privatisation of energy retail. By the nature of things, there can't be two national grids. Therefore, in such cases, there can't be competition, nor any customer choice. And when there is neither, there is often a perception that the only reason a grid is being sold off is for private gain. Hence, ahead of the 2019 general election the UK's left-wing Labour Party had pledged to renationalise National Grid, the country's transmission system operator. In response, the company opened offshore holding companies in Hong Kong and Luxembourg, prompting Labour to say, "The idea that private owners, who have been ripping off the public, would move offshore in an attempt to prolong the rip-off illustrates just why we need the grid back in public hands."[8]

And yet, while there has been criticism of deregulating transmission, there has been little debate on reversing liberalisation at the either end of it—in generation or in retail. Stephen Fitzpatrick, founder and CEO of the UK electricity supplier OVO Energy (currently, the nation's third largest in terms of customer numbers) and Kevin McMinn, CEO of Houston-based Spark Energy have both come of age as energy entrepreneurs post-liberalisation.[9]

OVO Energy started in 2009, when Fitzpatrick was 32, and the UK market had been deregulated for nearly 20 years (the start of privatisation in Britain was the December 1990 sale of the 12 government-owned regional electricity companies). McMinn's first job in energy was in 1999 managing gas and electricity procurement for large industrial clients—a position made possible by a number of states opening up their markets to competition. From there he built up his consultancy business, advising companies including Shell and Entergy, before being drafted in to lead a number of retail energy suppliers.

If I had to resort to cliché I would say that both of these executives are children of liberalisation. The interviews, then, were an opportunity to examine a worldview unencumbered, at a workaday level, by the legacy of monopolism and stateism in the energy industry; especially, in the Anglo-Saxon economic model, which if social scientists are to be believed, is robustly pro private enterprise and light on regulation (the economist Michel Albert contrasts it with the "Rhine" model, typical of continental Europe).[10] As an aside, though, it is worth noting that things are never black and white, and that even in a free-market bastion that is the US (and as we have seen in previous chapters) around half the states are still to fully liberalise.

How does taking for granted competition in the energy market influence your marketing strategy? How does never having experienced a captive meter-end audience shape your brand? Intriguingly, as some of the other younger executives interviewed, who have had little or no experience with regulated markets, McMinn talks about fighting for each customer:

> When I was appointed chief operating officer at US Gas and Electric in 2014 I began a full-scale cultural transition of the company. I wanted to create a customer-focused environment, which I knew would lead to both to increased profits and greater customer satisfaction. It was actually an opportunity to take a brand with no recognition, and turn it into a valuable asset.

LIBERALISATION BONANZA

Direct communication, says McMinnm, was the way to do it:

> In the first year after I took over, we sent out over a million pieces of communications by email to our existing customer base. I made the decision that, if we had the customer's email address, we would touch them at least once every three months. It could be a simple message, reminding them that summer is coming and they could be better off on a fixed rate plan, or in the case of a potential emergency, such as a hurricane coming, we would despatch a safety warning.

He concludes, "What I wanted to avoid at all costs is that the only communication they ever got from us was the energy bill. I wanted our brand to relate to something positive in the minds of our customers."

When I ask Fitzpatrick about branding at the very beginning of our interview, he offers a perceptive distinction between the activity of branding and the brand itself. It is couched in a somewhat defiant reply. "I don't care about branding! It is something on the surface." A brand, however, is "something that's in the DNA of the company—and every company should worry very much about their DNA".

OVO started as a "challenger brand". Its early growth and cash-position were buttressed by Fitzpatrick's trading expertise. For five years prior to starting the company he had worked in the financial sector, leading him to realise that "risk management, trading and rigour were instrumental in OVO's success":

> Energy market is a very grown up business. It's highly political and highly socially relevant. It's something that touches everybody's lives. And there's lots of ways in which you can get it wrong. At the trading side there is the volatility of pricing, hedging . . . It's a very complex industry. And our aim was to make it simple for consumers— which doesn't mean that is easy to get right. So, with the two sides of the business in mind, the trading as much as the customer service side, we approached everything in the early days from a consumer perspective—but with a respect for the risk.

Fitzpatrick gives an example of how despite the best marketing strategy, the company could have been dragged under not long after it had begun trading:

> Within 18 months of our launch wholesale gas prices had doubled. If we hadn't been properly hedged, who knows what would have

happened. In the UK the gas price went from something like 36–37 cents to 75. We haven't seen that kind of volatility since. Without that respect for proper hedging and risk management, it's easy to imagine getting caught up in that.

Once customer numbers passed the 100,000 milestone in 2012, branding was back on the agenda:

> After our first four or five years it was easy to identify what we were against—as all challengers should. But, in 2014 to 2016 we went through a period when, I guess, we were trying to figure out what we were for. This is probably the biggest change in our perception, from where we were a challenger, challenging the incumbents, to being a leader, and being seen as being a company that was forward thinking, that was ahead of the competition, not just challenging the competition. So that's been the biggest change. But we are still a consumer champion.

In practice, as McMinn's believes, the attitude that you are in the customer's corner, fighting to get them the best possible deal, must develop from an understanding of your customer base—an understanding crucial to the success of energy retailers competing in an open market:

> We spent a lot of time doing our ABC socio-economic analysis, which helped us realise what kind of customer would be the right fit for us. This, of course, works both ways, as for certain customers, we might not be the right fit—we might not be able to give them what they want. From a brand perspective, you need to have the right offering for the particular customer stratum.

Such detailed analysis should feed into your communication strategy:

> I learnt so much about how our customer base reacts to communication, both as to type and frequency. Actually, I was truly amazed at the differences. Some customers just want to be customers, while others expect that email every three months. Then, there could be other groups in-between. You need to respect the different cadences of communications, and group customers accordingly.

LIBERALISATION BONANZA

Moving from US Gas and Electric to the job of Chief Sales Officer at Crius Energy was an opportunity for McMinn to further refine not just his ideas on customer acquisition, but his approach to corporate strategy. On LinkedIn he says that one of his accomplishments at Crius was "positioning of the company as an attractive target for acquisition". Duly, it was acquired by Texan energy company Vistra. From there he moved to Spark Energy and the first thing he did was to shut down the sales operation:

> Spark was facing both regulatory problems and high customer churn. But, at its core it's a fantastic brand, with a strong name and great recognition. We were doing primarily telemarketing and we decided that we were not doing it the right way. It's not that we don't believe in it telemarketing, it's just that it wasn't happening, particularly in terms of the quality of the customers we felt that we wanted to get. We made a commitment to step back and basically rebuild our entire marketing and sales infrastructure in the first six months of 2020.

McMinn applied a three-pronged approach to syncing marketing with sales. He aimed at improving the performance of the door-to-door sales force (for instance through regular daily feedback), and then reinforcing such improvements through a system of distinctions (special sales uniforms, praise at company meetings) and bonuses (for instance, a quarterly extra payment). The payment accrued not just on the strength of sales but also following "positive customer interactions", which "create a positive image of our brand".

What I found particularly interesting in McMinn's approach is the second prong of his marketing and sales strategy. It sounds like a reverse-engineered "brand-driving-sales" principle of modern marketing. In his interpretation it is "sales-driving-brand". This approach is necessitated by having a large sales force out in the field:

> You've got to be able to give salespeople a product they love and put them in an environment where they can make a sale every day. They shouldn't be running to the next door trying to beat the other guy. You need to look at the socio-economics of the sales catchment area and ensure, through combination of product and demographic analysis, that they can sell daily for the next year or two. That takes

an enormous amount of pressure off people. Agents can now take their time and interact with people, be polite and leave a meaningful response behind.

The final ingredient in improving brand penetration in a door-to-door sales drive is a marketing campaign timed slightly ahead of the sales force canvassing the area. McMinn mentions direct mail and billboards. It is the kind of collateral that changes the conversation at the door, boosting the agents' confidence, by giving them something they can readily reference.

These multi-layered and overlapping strategies are necessary because in a liberalised retail market a significant percentage of customer accounts is constantly in play. According to the Council of European Energy Regulators, in countries as culturally diverse as the United Kingdom, Portugal or Norway, the switching rate for electricity consumers is around 20 per cent.[11] This means that in a given year a full fifth of all consumers could be changing suppliers. It is similar across the Atlantic, In Texas, where, according to a report in the *Wall Street Journal*, "Deregulation of retail electricity went further . . . than any other state, nearly 60% of residents are required to shop for their electricity on the retail market, with no option of remaining with a traditional utility."[12] Despite mixed evidence on the benefits of switching suppliers (the *Wall Street Journal*, for instance, concludes that, "US consumers who signed up with retail energy companies that emerged from deregulation paid $19.2 billion more than they would have if they'd stuck with incumbent utilities from 2010 through 2019"), everyone now fully expects that they should have this option.

Fitzpatrick takes the view that consumer engagement in the energy sector was led by regulation, with the consumers following. Now, that liberalised markets are the norm this might change how consumers relate to energy brands:

> In industries where you have more consumer engagement and understanding, you'll probably find stronger consumer brands. Energy, historically has not been an industry that consumers have had very much enthusiasm for or understanding of—consequently, there has not been a lot of engagement. So you tended to find companies that have been successful, but not developed brands that were easily accessible to consumers, nor led by consumers.

That is starting to change now, but the fact is that when we think of brands we primarily think of our consumer brands. Of course, we are aware of industrial or commercial brands but the biggest brands, the ones that are best known tend to be consumer brands. Energy just hasn't had a lot of consumer champions. A lot of companies that have been successful or historically involved in the energy sector, did not have to invest a lot of money in branding.

Which might not have served to their advantage, "as the brand is who you are and what kind of company you are . . ." In the case of OVO "the brand is the culture that we have and it's one of our big competitive advantages".

This competitive edge was very much in evidence in 2019 as OVO purchased the retail arm of the energy giant Scottish and Southern Electricity (SSE). One of the UK's "big six" energy companies, SSE was formed in 1998, while the history of Southern Electricity can be traced even further back, to 1948 and the founding of the Southern Electricity Board company. In 2017, when SSE spun off its retail operation it had around 3.5 million accounts. That same year OVO held around 680,000 accounts, and at the point it made its offer to SSE two years later it had 1.5 million, thanks to buying out competitors and acquiring new customers. Still, it was a reverse take-over, as the smaller company gobbled up the larger, leapfrogged into double digit market share and became itself one of the "big six".[13]

But, what about the dangers of the SSE brand attributes overwhelming the OVO brand? After all, at its peak the energy giant held around 20 per cent of the UK's retail market and commanded 10,000 staff, while a few months prior to the SSE acquisition OVO was described in the media as an "energy minnow"—a small fish in the big pond of energy retail, one of the 15 new post-liberalisation start ups.[14]

The deal was not about something superficial like money. It is about values and behaviours. SSE is a bigger organisation, but looking, for example, at their retail operations in the big cities, their heritage in renewables and track record in customer satisfaction, you can see that they are closest to us. And it's a very well-run business. We like to move faster. We embrace the change, and we've embraced the changes much faster. But there's a lot that we can learn from each other.

Fitzpatrick concludes:

> The question in my mind is can we maintain the same focus on innovation and change on a larger scale. I think the answer is definitely yes, that's one of the things that technology allows us to do. When you look at other organisations, hundreds of thousands of people strong, you don't think of them as being too big. In the context of innovation—quite the opposite.

Harvesting synergies of size, wresting profit from companies through mergers and acquisition, is at the other end of the growth-strategy spectrum, and yet complementary to McMinn's micro-analytic attitude, of focusing on each individual account to ascertain its long-term profitability. It is a peculiar outlook because, taken to its logical conclusion, it might produce results that are, at first, difficult to swallow. As McMinn warns, you might actually end up shedding customers, in keeping with that old business adage "turnover is vanity, profit is sanity":

> When you start going down this journey, the board is the hardest to convince. Most of them get it, most of them want to do it, but they're afraid. You have to be willing to tell the board, that you're going to shrink. What board of directors wants to hear that? What investor wants to hear that? Here is where you have to use science to show the real economic, lifetime value of each customer, and why it's OK to let some of them go.

He continues:

> Once you have a local customer base in the same socio-economic bracket, you can build on that. In one example, I sent a very simple email saying, "the average consumer in your area uses 10 per cent less energy than you do". We sent that message three or four times and we saw that their usage in the summer peak hours went down compared to our other customers in that area that did not receive the message. I started showing the board that you can influence customers' behaviour, and strengthen that relationship.

McMinn noticed other positive outcomes of such "win–win" framing:

> Over the next 12 months customers that received emails were switching at a lower rate. And when we sent renewal notices they contacted

our call centre at a higher rate than other customers to acknowledge that they had gotten that renewal notice and were minded to renew contracts.

This leads to an intriguing question: to what degree can such brand building strategies be universalised. To put it another way, now that countries around the world are opening up their energy markets, what are the chances of entrepreneurial competition engendering a truly global energy brand—in the same way that competition in the IT market has created, among myriads of other well-known companies, Apple, Google and Microsoft. First, though, in building such a powerful brand, what are the mistakes to avoid?

Fitzpatrick thinks that the most prominent mistake was "trying to do too much, at the same time, under the same brand and not being clear enough on the things that we weren't going to do":

> It's not about being ambitious, rather we found ourselves in a world with lots of opportunity. I think it would have worked better for us to be more explicit about things that we were not going to do, because we didn't have to do everything. We should have been more focused on doing a small number of things well. You end up spreading yourself too thin.
>
> In terms of building a recognizable brand, I'm trying to think of a recognizable brand that is not good. I think that one of the challenges for OVO Energy is not about branding or creating a brand. I think that for us the question is on fame and how to be more famous, not just personally but for OVO to be better known. If you go into the high streets, a lot of people have never heard of it. I spoke to a person who suggested that I should care less about being famous, and instead ask myself "what I wanted to be famous for". Similarly, any energy company that's wondering about how to create an amazing brand should ask themselves, "What are we offering? What is it about our business, our company that is making the world a better place?" So if you can answer that, you've got a brand.

McMinn points at some prosaic reasons hampering energy start-ups, even in a liberalised market:

> It's very hard for an energy retail company to build a brand and part of the reason is that we're competing for customers against

the utility. The utility has no acquisition costs, while we're paying $200 to acquire a new customer. I'm already in the hole right there. The utilities are guaranteed a 12 per cent rate of return on their operations, and they never lose money on the commodity. If I'm in a position where nobody's making the calls, I'm not guaranteed a regular return on my operations. I have to liquidate ahead on a loss if the customer churns or reneges on their contract, as it takes more then a year to break even on that $200. To offset all of this, I have higher prices, and that ends up driving off my clients.

That is why, McMinn point out, the small energy retailer needs to be careful about the customers they choose:

You have to be sure that you're getting the customers who are going to see value in paying a little more per unit of electricity than they pay the utility. They are the customers that appreciate your mode of communication and believe in what you're doing. You have to bring them new services such as "100 per cent green" or price insurance. If I can give you the same unit price for the next three or five years I can embed a product there. I can give you a thermostat and every month I communicate advice on your energy consumption, if you're willing.

McMinn believes that once you have these specific types of customers who buy into the brand and believe in what you're doing, they will support you. They will follow you on social media and recommend your products. "Getting to that stage takes time, and it takes belief, and it takes investment."

From the point of view of energy retailers, then, the market needs more liberalisation, not less. Going back to Barrett's article and those five seductively simple steps to making it work (making it work for everyone, except, of course, former monopolies)—Step Two advises that "the control of monopolies/former monopolies over lawmaking designed to implement change should be limited and reduced". Explaining the logic behind the principle, Barrett says:

Change is difficult. In any drive for change, there are winners (i.e. those who benefit) and losers (i.e. those who lose something). The winners will inevitably be "for change" and the losers, inevitably "against change". With market liberalization, electricity monopolies are clearly the losers. They stand to lose assets, money, and power. So it's logical for them to try to lessen these losses as much as possible.

There is no reason why a truly global utility should not emerge from an open and global energy market, just as the openness of the internet has precipitated the emergence of internet platforms now available in every country on Earth. It can happen—but, will it happen?

Notes

1. Barrett, Eva. "Market Liberalization: Five Seductively Simple Steps to Making it Work." *The Electricity Journal*, Volume 30, Issue 3, April 2017, pp. 51, (doi.org/10.1016/j.tej.2017.01.007).
2. Ibid.
3. Hall, David et al. "Energy Liberalisation, Privatisation and Public Ownership." *Public Services International Research Unit*, September 2013, world-psi.org/sites/default/files/en_psiru_ppp_final_lux.pdf.
4. Joskow, Paul L. "Lessons Learned from Electricity Market Liberalisation." *The Energy Journal*, No. 29, Sep. 2008, p. 37, (doi:10.5547/ISSN0195-6574-EJ-Vol29-NoSI2-3).
5. The quip about the "one-armed" economist is attributed to Harry Truman on the strength of the references published on quoteinvestigator.com.
6. Barrett, "Market Liberalization", p. 51.
7. Hall *et al.*, "Energy Liberalisation, Privatisation and Public Ownership", p. 6.
8. "National Grid and SSE Move Offshore Over Labour Plans." *BBC*, 24 Nov. 2019, bbc.com/news/business-50536205. Labour Party's plans regarding National Grid were part of a wider set or pledges to renationalise key elements of the United Kingdom's infrastructure. Two weeks later, Labour lost the election with the party's vote-share shrinking by 7.9 per cent. Already in opposition at the time, it lost 60 places in parliament, prompting many analysts to conclude that nationalisation was a vote-loser.
9. Information on OVO Energy can be found on the company's website ovoenergy.com with a short statistical summary on the sub-page titled "OVO Energy Key Stats", at ovoenergy.com/ovo-newsroom/key-facts. For Spark Energy, see sparkenergy.com.
10. See Albert, Michel. *Capitalism vs. Capitalism.* Four Walls Eight Windows. 1993.

LIBERALISATION BONANZA 197

11. "Monitoring Report on the Performance of European Retail Markets in 2018—CEER Report." *Council of European Energy Regulators*, 4 Nov 2019, ceer.eu/documents/104400/-/-/5c492f87-c88f-6c78-5852-43f1f13c89e4.

12. Patterson, Scott and Tom McGinty. "Deregulation Aimed to Lower Home-Power Bills. For Many, It Didn't." *Wall Street Journal*, 8 Mar. 2021, wsj.com/articles/electricity-deregulation-utility-retail-energy-bills-11615213623.

13. See Domah, Preetum and Michael G. Pollitt. "The Restructuring and Privatisation of Electricity Distribution and Supply Businesses in England and Wales: A Social Cost–Benefit Analysis." *Journal of Fiscal Studies*, Vol. 22, No. 1, 2001, (doi.org/10.1111/j.1475-5890.2001.tb00036.x).

14. OVO Energy's take-over of the retail division of SSE has been widely reported in the UK press. See "OVO Energy Has 'Big Six' Potential Following the Latest Acquisition." *Power Technology*, 13 Dec. 2019, power-technology.com/comment/ovo-energy-has-big-six-potential-following-the-latest-acquisition. A statistical summary of OVO Energy post SSE transaction can be found on the price-comparison website Utility Switchboard, at https://utilityswitchboard.com/gas-electricity/providers/ovo-energy/.

16

FROM PRODUCT TO SERVICE

ANA BUSTO ON ENGIE POST-REBRAND

The great energy-rebranding wave of the past decade had in 2015 swept away a venerable name, whose resonances reach back to the early nineteenth century, and perhaps even earlier, to the time of the ancient pharaohs, the mighty kings of Persia and the emperors of Rome. For all of these figures shared a dream, that was rekindled by a young Frenchman in 1834, idling away his days in quarantine.

It was while detained in the harbour of Alexandria *en route* to assuming his position as the French vice-consul in Cairo, that the young Ferdinand de Lesseps had come across a book (written by another Frenchman, Jean Baptiste Lepère, head engineer in Napoleon's Egyptian expedition) describing the canal that had once connected, via the River Nile, the Red Sea with the Mediterranean. Lepère's interest in that legendary waterway, mentioned by Aristotle, Herodotus and Pliny the Elder, was not incidental. Napoleon had sent him to the Isthmus of Suez to explore the possibility of digging a direct canal across 100 miles of desert, that would cut around 10,000 nautical miles off the journey from Europe to the Far East.[1]

DOI: 10.4324/9781003351030-17

FROM PRODUCT TO SERVICE   199

In 1869, almost seventy years after the French Republic's Army of the Orient left Egypt (and with it the team of scholars, scientists and engineers that Napoleon brought in tow) the Suez Canal was completed. For Lesseps, who had conceived the project, secured political backing and raised the capital—forming in 1858 Compagnie Universelle du Canal Maritime de Suez—the grand opening was a day of triumph and universal vindication.

Among the guests at Port Said, anchored on their merchant vessels, yachts and frigates, were Empress Eugene of France, wife of Napoleon III; Emperor Franz Joseph of Austro-Hungary and his party; and the crown princes and princesses of the Netherlands and Prussia. Even the great Tsar of Russia sent a delegation; it was led by his son Grand Duke Michael. Accounts of the day mention countless Bedouin and Touareg tribesmen in their finest robes, joined on the shore by visitors from as far as America, Sweden and Sudan.

Egypt seized control of the canal and nationalised it in 1956, but the Compagnie, compensated for the loss of its crown jewel, stayed in business and diversified. It acquired a holding in Belgium's General Company, owner of road, rail and canal infrastructure (founded in 1822), and in Lyonese Water, one of France's largest environmental services providers. In 2004 Suez decided to focus on its five core businesses: power, gas and energy, water and environmental services, while in the same year the nation's gas company GDF was privatised. The next year it floated on the Paris Stock Exchange and by 2008 the two companies had merged into GDF Suez.[2]

The sprawling hybrid employed more than 150,000 people worldwide, with operations in 70 countries generating an annual revenue of €74.7 billion. It is considered to be the world's oldest still-operational multinational company, with a history spanning three centuries. You could say that it had everything except a snappy name, one that was in tune with the mood music of today's energy sector. As it stood, GDF was an acronym of Gaz de France, while Suez, the reminder of the past, carried little relevance for the company's future.

As we have seen elsewhere in this book, over the past ten years the trend for power companies has been to jettison the reference to fossil fuels in their names. Hence, Danish North Sea Oil and Gas (DONG) became Orsted, and Statoil became Equinor. It was a trend ignited by British Petroleum (BP) which—though it had the sensitivity to feel the winds of change blowing through the energy sector—did not at corporate level develop a coherent sustainability strategy, enabling a true transformation into a 'new energy' company.

Its 2000 name change to Beyond Petroleum, symbolically scheduled at the start of the new millennium, is now considered a rebranding fail (despite costing £133 million at the time)[3], and the design and colour scheme of the Helios sunflower logo an example of greenwash. After a decade of uncertain progress, BP divested itself of its solar business in 2011 and in 2013, with the sale of its wind energy subsidiary in the US, commenced a full scale retreat from the renewables sector. The company stated at the time that the sale was "part of a continuing effort to become a more focused oil and gas company".[4]

The example has reverberated through the industry and beyond, focusing attention on the crucial difference in modern marketing practice between visual branding (perhaps even "sensory branding", as sound is becoming an ever more important element of brand identity) and strategic branding. The former, which is branding in the colloquial or common sense of the word, includes logo, colour scheme, typography or sound, and other elements that establish brand identity at sensory level.

But, really, in modern branding practice visual branding is subservient to strategic branding, which develops out of a company's business strategy. Ideally, this strategy is based on prosocial convictions and values, which translate into a strategic business direction. As we have seen in Chapter 14 that direction has to make business sense, for example, energy company having to set out how it will replace its income from non-sustainable sources (if they are being phased out). It might sound like a Zen koan, but the transition to sustainability has to sustain itself.

As Eden Yin of University of Cambridge Judge Business School points out—calling his approach Strategic Branding 2.0—"Branding has to be based on delivering on the promises made to customers as part of the value proposition", while there also has to be "a focus on the strategic creation and execution of a branding chain; a shift from 'truth in advertising' to 'truth in delivering the promised value proposition'".[5]

If anything, the visual makeover of BP was a success. As Landor, the agency in charge of the new logo explained, "The Helios identity . . . captured BP's aspirations. A stylized sunflower symbolizes the sun's energy, while the colour green reflects the brand's environmental sensitivity."

According to Landor's case study "Nine months after launch, 97 percent of BP employees were aware of the brand idea, and 9 out of 10 agreed that BP was heading in the right direction." The agency extended the concept behind BP's new visual identity all the way into the company's interiors:

> We redesigned BP's physical environments right down to the plants—starting with its brand story the minute you stepped in the door. Aloe plants, the most efficient plant producers of oxygen, became fixtures in every office. For employees, they were inspiring. For visitors, they were conversation starters.[6]

On the other hand, the transformation of GDZ Suez to ENGIE at brand image level was somewhat less self-assured, but, arguably deeper rooted. As the UK's news portal *Energy Voice* reported at the time, "The rebranding was not trumpeted loudly by the Paris-based group on this side of the Channel", adding that a major marketing campaign was under way in key markets, particularly France and Belgium. It reported that "Engie has no specific meaning in French—websites describe it as a girl's name, a variant of Evangeline, of Latin and Greek origin and derived for words translating as 'good' and 'news'".[7] The Times, the United Kingdom's oldest daily newspaper, however, was more prosaic (and perhaps more accurate), claiming that the name was "a crunched-down version of énergie, the French for energy".[8] By the end of 2021, the company owned 34 gigawatts of renewable capacity worldwide.[9]

A year after the rebrand Ana Busto joined ENGIE as Senior Vice-President of Brand and Communication, after occupying a very similar role at food services and facilities management multinational Sodexo. She stayed at Engie until the end of 2020. Ana says she landed the job not despite the differences between the energy and the services sectors, but because of them:

> The sixteen years prior to being hired by ENGIE I worked either in legal, IT or food service companies. I think this is why Isabelle Kocher, the newly appointed CEO at the time, was interested in my profile. The energy sector is increasingly converting into a services sector, but those are still very different cultures. To be service-oriented requires a customer focus which is different from being focused on producing

goods or commodities. When I joined I found a company that was busy transforming itself.

According to Keller's standard textbook *Strategic Brand Management*, the challenge in marketing services compared to products, is that services are more intangible and "more likely to vary in quality depending on the particular person or people involved in providing the service".[10] Keller says that branding can be particularly important to service firms to address potential intangibility and variability problems and adds that, "brand symbols may be also especially important as they help to make the abstract nature of services more concrete". He concludes that, "Branding a service can also be an effective way to signal to consumers that the firm has designed a particular service offering that is special and deserving of its own name."[11]

Ana says that when she moved to ENGIE post rebrand she "experienced transformation":

> There were many people at the company who had worked all their career in the energy industry. They have a point of reference, which is specific to the energy sector. To some of them the transformation to a service-centred business model must have been a challenge.

Ana notes that you don't talk to customers in the same way:

> In the energy sector you could have long term contracts, such as power purchase agreements (PPA's), which, at a certain point, shift your corporate focus from communication to fulfilment. For the duration of the contract you would rely on engineering expertise to keep the customer satisfied. In the services sector, however, the nature of competition is different. There are frequent points of sale, even with the same customer, and all the while you have to be mindful of how your service is performing against that of your competitors. You are not being judged on price alone.

However, Ana also warns that when you look at the differences between industry sectors you need to be mindful of "comparing like with like". The comparison of the B2B aspect of the food services industry with the B2B aspect of the energy sector, does uncover some operational-level variance. But, frequent points of sale and customer contact could apply to both types of sectors, as energy companies could also have retail accounts, and food services companies sell to the public.

In marketing theory there are a number of frameworks that describe the difference between service and product. According to Lynn Shostack's spectrum of *intangible dominant* to *tangible dominant*—first set out in her influential 1977 article "Breaking Free From Product Marketing"—almost all industries have an offering that consists of both product (or tangible element), *and* service (or intangible element).[12] On the one side of the spectrum, something like a can of food would be a pure product. Once you have put it in your shopping basket, you would not expect from the manufacturer or vendor any kind of service to follow. At the other side, there are pure services, such as investment management, where there is no physical product. In the middle, between these two opposite ends, are most other industries with their various offerings.

Another way to understand the differences between product and service is through the generic categories of *intangibility, heterogeneity (variability), perishability of output* and *simultaneity of production and consumption.* However, these categories have been criticized as too generic and a list of eight differences has been offered to distinguish goods from services. Some of them are: *greater involvement of customers in the production process, absence of inventories, relative importance of the time factor* and *structure and nature of the distribution channels.*

When a company the size of Engie decides to rebrand, the implementation of a new corporate identity, both visual and conceptual, becomes as much a matter of marketing as corporate communication. It is a top-down approach, that—once agreed at board level—is communicated from the company's headquarters to subsidiaries around the world.

In terms of brand implementation—and as the trade press reported throughout 2015—the name change at parent-company level triggered a cascade from Romania to the United States. In some international markets, GDF Suez was a straight swap for Engie, while in others there was a deeper rethink which business are core to the new brand. Such considerations have continued to shape business strategy long after the rebrand. For instance, in 2018 the company incorporated three of its US businesses under the Engie umbrella, including an energy storage business, a data management service and an energy efficiency company.

Yet, though demanding, such internal communication and marketing campaigns are still of a significantly lesser order of magnitude in terms of financial outlay, compared to reaching your retail customer base. "Since being introduced in 2007, liberalisation has really taken off in France. There are now over 40 energy suppliers, aggressively competing for every customer. In such an environment the question of differentiation—key to successful branding—becomes crucially important", Ana concludes. Engie has over 11 million consumers in France alone, second only to EDF. But, EDF's example is a cautionary one as it has shed customers at a rate of 100,000 per month. *Le Figaro*, one of France's daily newspapers, offers a pithy explanation: "Many consumers are discovering the benefits of competition."[13]

"We shouldn't be naïve", says Ana, "the first criteria will always be price. But, in France retail prices are very much the same. Especially because when one company reduces prices others follow." This is confirmed by estimates that, despite an abundance of suppliers, the difference between lowest and highest retail electricity price is around 6 per cent.[14] "That is why brand is important. What it stands for and to what extent it is trusted by consumers. At Engie we generated trust and engagement by empowering customers to buy and use electricity more responsibly."

This store of goodwill, which protects the company from oscillations in turnover—as relative to competitors who might not have accrued it— underpins the confidence necessary for business-to-business (B2B) relationships. This is important because, in contrast to household energy sales, in B2B contract terms, credit limits and delivery schedules cover greater sales volumes, with both supplier and customer standing to lose more if things go wrong:

> The interesting thing with business-to-consumer (B2C) marketing is that if you implement your advertising strategy on a monthly basis you can clearly correlate your drop in sales, with the month when you ended your campaign, or scheduled an advertising hiatus. Then you need to start a new campaign to pick up business again.

But, as Ana continues, although B2B relationships don't need that constant mood music of advertising playing in the background, it would still be a mistake to think that you should not aim campaigns at business consumers. Visibility as an employer is not to be neglected when you wish to attract the top talent. "Since the rebrand we have noticed that the number of CVs we have been receiving has tripled." A strong brand will help attract the best employees and protect the company in times of crisis. All the more if it lies on a strong corporate *raison d'être*.

For Engie post-rebrand that *raison d'être* is an accelerated transition towards a carbon-neutral economy, through reduced energy consumption and more environmentally-friendly solutions:

> It is a turnaround from where we were. GDF Suez was a company that belonged to what was sometimes described as the "old world". Before you were part of the problem and now you are part of the solution. Hence, the branding challenge is not just to communicate that you will differentiate yourself with your new brand, but you need to say how and why you will do it.
>
> Our purpose—our *raison d'être*, if you will—is to be a carbon neutral company that generates progress in a harmonious way. Another way of putting this is that we want to bring progress in harmony not only with the environment but also with society as a whole. The question of branding revolves around the question of culture change. When focusing on the "how", we want to be "opening windows" within the company, working collaboratively and horizontally. This is a change compared to the more traditional way the company was run before.

But, what about the cost? How much of a challenge is it for the communication lead within an energy multinational to convince fellow executives—who might not be as convinced of the virtues of branding—on the need to spend money on brand?

> I see less of a challenge there compared to other sectors, because the energy sector is prone to high-visibility and high-stake crisis (take nuclear accidents, oil spills, gas explosions, renewables impact on the landscape), it makes sense to build a solid image that will protect you in difficult times.

The other thing energy companies should be grateful for, especially former state enterprises, is brand recognition. Few service providers can count on that kind of permanent brand capital, given the competition and the ever-shifting nature of the service business:

In France EDF has as a very high awareness rate. Everybody knows it, because EDF was the only provider of electricity for decades. And if you go around Europe I am sure you could find many other examples of companies which have evolved from state monopolies, and, as such, are in a much better position branding-wise than any new entrant to the energy market.

However, the legacy of privileged market access can be a liability when it comes to communicating with your customers:

Talking about energy is not easy—it is such a complex industry. It is technical and generally not top of mind for consumers. In order to differentiate Engie from its competitors, what we chose to do was to shift focus from the "what" we were doing and providing to the "why" we were doing it. The difference would not come from the product itself, which is pretty much the same across energy players, but from what we would bring to the customer (a more sustainable planet) and how we would do it.

Such is the power of 'why' that an article in *Entrepreneur* magazine (titled "'Why?' The Question That Changes Lives and Guides Success") claimed "the answer to the question, why? is the most important discovery you can make . . . it is the question that really exposes purpose".[15] Ana says that "The shift towards emotions in energy branding has not only resonated with younger audiences, but it has been long overdue in a sector dominated by an engineering mind-set":

You will always find executives in any industry that come across as conservative or simply old-fashioned. They might tell you that they don't have time for branding, but actually what they mean by that is they see value primarily in developing offers, rather than in investing in their brand. I am not sure this was the right approach even in the past, and even less so in our day and age.

Ana is also sceptical of the conventional wisdom, repeated by many CEO reluctant to loosen the purse strings for a branding campaign, that such spending, as a rule, takes years to pay off:

Actually, as I mentioned earlier you don't need to wait too long to see the feedback loop between marketing and turnover. The same goes for branding. If done properly, it does reinforce your brand and benefit your business. It might take six months or a year, but if you have good monitoring in place, you will be able to detect it.

We finish our interview on the question of whether energy companies of the future will be able to survive if they are not sustainable or "green". To illustrate the direction that the sector has taken Ana reminds me that some companies no longer have a sustainability department. The idea is that "sustainability" should not be in a separate box within the company, but that everything they do should have sustainability as an embedded goal:

You often hear that sustainability shouldn't be an "add on", or even less an optional extra. What this means at the level of brand is that it should be shaped with sustainability at its core. This is what Engie strove to do in order to build a neutral carbon society.

Notes

1. For information on the development and construction of the Suez Canal we have relied on Burchell, S.C. *Building the Suez Canal*. American Heritage Publishing, 1966.
2. The history of the GDF Suez company has been documented in the article "The History of the ENGIE Group", published on engie.com/en/group/history-engie-group, and also in Jacques, Derek and Paula Kepos, editors. *International Directory of Company Histories Volume 109*. St. James Press, 2010, pp. 256–263
3. The quoted cost of the BP rebrand at £133 million is from the article "BP Drops Shield in Favour of Sun." *Campaignlive*, 24. Jul. 2000, campaignlive co.uk/article/bp-drops-shield-favour-sun/11244.
4. David, Javier E. "Beyond Petroleum' No More? BP Goes Back to Basics." *CNBC*, 22 Apr. 2013, cnbc.com/id/100647034.
5. For an elevator-pitch summary of Dr Eden Yin's approach to brand management see "Strategic Branding 2.0: The Cambridge Approach" on the website of the Cambridge Judge Business School at jbs.cam.ac.uk.

6. The case study on Landor's rebrand of BP can be found on the company's website pages landor.com/work/bp, under the heading "Brand as a Beacon of Change".
7. "GDF Suez changes its name as the company rebrands." *Energy Voice*, 29 Apr. 2015, energyvoice.com/other-news/77875/gdf-suez-changes-its-name-as-the-company-rebrands/.
8. Hosking, Patrick. "GDF Suez Rebrands as 'Engie'." *The Times*, 25 Apr. 2015, by Patrick Hosking thetimes.co.uk/article/gdf-suez-rebrands-as-engie-oomwtgggmwh.
9. Engie generation capacity numbers are from the company's website engie.com, under the heading "Who We Are", subheading "Identity Card", document "Engie Key Figures", engie.com/en/group/who-are-we/identity-card.
10. Keller, Kevin Lane. *Strategic Brand Management*. Prentice-Hall, 1998, pp. 43.
11. Ibid.
12. The textbook by Christopher H. Lovelock (Lovelock, Christopher H. *Services Marketing*. Prentice-Hall, 1996.) opens with an extensive discussion on the distinction between products and services, in the sense relevant to marketing practitioners. Lynn Shostack's views on the issue are discussed on pp. 4, under the heading "Understanding Services". Other frameworks are then covered on pp. 14–19 under "Marketing-Relevant Differences between Services and Goods".
13. Guichard, Guillaume. "Pourquoi EDF perd près de 100.000 clients par mois." *Le Figaro*, 16 Dec. 2020, lefigaro.fr/societes/pourquoi-edf-perd-pres-de-100–000-clients-par-mois-20201216.
14. The datum on 6 per cent price differantiation comes from Rokicki, Tomasz et al. "Differentiation and Changes of Household Electricity Prices in EU Countries." *Energies*, Vol. 14, No. 21, October 2021, (doi:10.3390/en14216894). Further information on the French energy sector can be found on *cre.fr*, the website of the industry regulator Commission de régulation de l'énergie (CRE), which publishes, among other materials, regular statistical updates on the electricity and gas markets.
15. White, Thomas. "'Why?' The Question That Changes Lives and Guides Success." *Entrepreneur*, 16 Jun. 2015, entrepreneur.com/article/246847.

17

HARDER THAN ROCKET SCIENCE

KEVIN LANE KELLER ON THE THEORY AND PRACTICE OF ENERGY BRANDING

Browsing recently through the first edition of Kevin Lane Keller's *Strategic Brand Management* I was drawn once again to the case study some 760 pages in, under Appendix E "Nike: Building a Global Brand."[1] This part of the book is like a scaled-down diorama of Keller's work, demonstrating not merely his iron grip of the subject, but the breadth of his references, prodigious knowledge of popular culture and a nuts-and-bolts understanding of business strategy. Reading about Nike's ascent to one of the world's best known (if not the best known) brands is like looking at the cover of the Beatles' *Sgt. Pepper's* album.

Everyone and everything seems to be there: from pole-vaulter Sergei Bubka and the opera *The Barber of Seville*, to punk-rock star Iggy Pop and his band Stooges' song "Search and Destroy". Nike's two main competitors Adidas and Reebok are dealt with in passing, before we are moved on to the Argentinian football (or as Americans say "soccer") team Bocca Juniors, Germany's Borussia Dortmund and Paris St. Germain. A nametorrent of world-class footballers then follows: Romario, Bebbeto, Cantona,

DOI: 10.4324/9781003351030-18

Ian Wright and others. And yet overall, this is just a tiny portion of all the references in what is effectively the last 5 per cent of the book.

What I find fascinating about *Strategic Brand Management* is not just that it is authoritative. It is also very rich. And then there is something else. The quanta of information displayed therein are connected by a subtle understanding of what makes brands tick. As Keller explained in an interview, his goal in writing *Strategic Brand Management* was "to write an MBA-level textbook that maximized three key dimensions: breadth (covering all the important branding topics); depth (providing rigour and academic grounding); and relevance (offering practical recommendations and guidelines)". Putting it another way, the aim was to "provide a comprehensive and up-to-date treatment of the subjects of brands, brand equity, and strategic brand management". The latter, in his view, "involves the design and implementation of marketing programmes and activities to build, measure, and manage brand equity".[2]

A glimpse of how Nike went about managing brand equity and building a world conquering brand is given in the paragraphs devoted to the company's 1995 annual report. As Keller writes:

> In his letter to shareholders in Nike's 1995 annual report, Phil Knight [Nike's co-founder and CEO at the time] laid out the company's strategic objectives for the coming years as follows: "First, make strides toward becoming a global company, not just a company doing business internationally."[3]

It is on the understanding of such elusive conceptual differences ("a company doing business internationally" versus "a global company") that the success of Keller's textbook rests.

But, even if you accept the status of *Strategic Brand Management*—due to its omniscience and wealth of detail—as the "Bible of branding", it should be noted that Keller is no prophet in the desert. Rather, he is the archetype of the marketing *pracademic* (on the term see also discussion in Chapter 14). Parallel to an academic career at Berkeley, Stanford, University of North Carolina and most recently Tuck School of Business at Dartmouth—during which he co-authored another standard reference work, the textbook *Marketing Management* (now in its 16th edition)—Keller was also brand consultant to Exxon Mobil and Shell, and among non-energy sector companies to Unilever, Starbucks, Goodyear and others.[4] Recently, as I have found out in our interview, his branding practice has a strong communal flavour, with clients including local energy initiatives.

To this standard biographical fare, I can add my own impressions of our meetings, two of which were in Iceland. After our first meeting at the conference hosted by Iceland's Association of Marketing Professionals, Keller returned in 2016 to speak at my own Charge conference, presenting on the topic of *Building Strong Brands in Energy Markets*. At that point his 1993 article "Conceptualising, Measuring and Managing Customer-Based Brand Equity", which had, more or less introduced the concept of customer-based brand equity (CBBE), had been quoted literally thousands of times.[5] Much of Keller's academic work that followed, as well as his branding practice was built on that article. You could say that its findings had served him well. And, as they say in America, "if it ain't broke . . ."

But, in 2016, the year he attended Charge, Keller published the article "Reflections on Customer-Based Brand Equity: Perspectives, Progress, and Priorities". Its stated aim of was to "outline some of (Keller's) subsequent related branding research, as well as that of others" and "consider some future research priorities in branding".[6] It also looked at the origin of that influential 1993 article, generously crediting research partner David Aaker at Berkeley, as much as the work of Jim Bettman, whose study on memory factors in consumer choice, gave Keller the idea for his PhD thesis.[7] "Reflections . . ." was a revealing piece of writing, as it said more about Keller, than you could glimpse from his CV. I could not be but impressed by his ability to reflect on his own work with scientific seriousness and rigour, even more so because evidence thus far did not indicate anything wrong with the CBBE model. Then again, on a number of occasions, including our interview, Keller had said that branding is both an art *and* a science.

As it happens, the seed of such an ability might have been nurtured at an early age. "My father was a scientist", says Keller:

He was a nuclear physicist working for the US army and later at Westinghouse. There he got sucked into the business side of the nuclear industry. They were building reactors all over the place, but they made the mistake of throwing uranium into all the deals. They were promising long term supplies, but it turned out there was a uranium cartel, and the price of the material skyrocketed. There was a danger of the company going bankrupt and my dad had to focus on avoiding that. So at an early age I was made aware of both the science and the business behind energy.

Keller says that his father often jokes how branding is not rocket science:

To which I say, "it's actually harder than rocket science". We are not dealing with the laws of physics, there isn't a set of equations with a closed-form solution. The complexity of marketing, which is what makes it so interesting, comes from dealing with human nature, human psychology.

Initially, though, Keller's academic route was via an undergraduate degree in mathematics and economics:

I was going to go into finance. After my degree at Cornell I went straight to Carnegie Mellon business school. It is a quantitative program, which I thought would take advantage of my interest in math, economics and finance. But, I took a marketing course there and I just fell in love with the subject. I just thought it was the most interesting thing and I never looked back.

A doctoral thesis on memory factors in advertising, completed at North Carolina's Duke University, was to set Keller's research agenda for years to come. Inspired by Bettman's article "Memory Factors in Consumer Choice: A Review" (which presented the case-study of LIFE cereals, a product that suffered from poor ad recall, until the company put the scene from the actual TV advertisement on the packaging), it eventually led Keller to consider brand equity as a psychological nexus of "consumer response" and "perceptions, preferences and behaviours". As Keller sums it up, "Brand equity ultimately depends on what resides in the minds of the consumers."[8]

To understand why the model of consumer-based brand equity has proved such a breakthrough it worth noting that up until Keller, it was generally studied either as a function of the brand's overall economic value, or as a factor in improving marketing effectiveness. Essentially, it was as if brands were examined through the wrong end of a pair of binoculars. Once the study of brands was set right-side up, the interest in the subject

HARDER THAN ROCKET SCIENCE   213

spilled over from the consumer and luxury goods industries into such brand-agnostic sectors as energy:

In the 1980s and '90s branding sort of exploded, but even when it did it took a while to get to other industries like financial services and technology. All sectors now realize the importance of it. It is part of everyday vernacular; the way people talk about things.

Keller thinks that all this applies to energy companies:

They aren't that different, they also realize that branding matters. Like other businesses, energy companies think now about the big issues around their brands. Not just brand identity, the name and the logo, but what they stand for, the positioning, the meaning that they create, and most importantly, *the value they create*.

In fact, although the energy industry might not have been quick off the mark when it comes to branding, it was forced to consider issues around sustainability ahead of other sectors:

I don't think 30 years ago people thought about energy as much as they do now. They kind of just took it for granted. But, then again, if you are old enough to remember the oil crisis of the early 1970s, the lines at the gas stations and fuel rationing, you could argue that this is when energy got on people's radar.

Gradually, an awareness of the weight of branding and sustainability converged at both horizontal and vertical levels—regardless of business' catchment area or hierarchical complexity. Keller gives an example:

At Tuck, we have a programme with the New England Fuel Institute. It reaches more of the regional kind of energy providers. A lot of them are in the oil and gas business, for instance local guys who come to your house and install fuel tanks. Others are looking at renewable energy.

He was in charge of the marketing and branding section of the programme:

As these were mostly family businesses, named after their owners, we discussed things like "trust" and "heritage", and how to take advantage of these. They were keenly interested—I could sense that from the questions during the session. These family-run companies, that have been around for decades, also realise that marketing and branding matter.

But, how exactly does the CBBE model help a business? As a preliminary, it draws attention the value of brand equity. *Strategic Brand Management* gives quite a few definitions, either operational, analytic or descriptive, of brand equity value, the simplest perhaps, "the difference between the value of the brand to the consumer and the value of the product without that branding".[9]

At a more conceptual level CBBE itself is defined as "the differential effect that brand knowledge has on consumer response to the marketing of that brand".[10] As equity elsewhere, CBBE can be *positive* and *negative*, meaning that consumers of brands with positive CBBE are, for instance, less sensitive to product price increases or the withdrawal of advertising support, and more accepting of brand extensions or new distribution channels. These consumer dispositions are reversed where there is negative CBBE.

The interesting consequence of strongly positive CBBE is that the brand is impervious to rival advertising. Its adherents are so committed to it, that they are not just firmly entrenched in their purchasing habits to the exclusion of rival brands, but they are proselytisers, extoling the virtues of the brand to other consumers.

Regardless of how abstract the definition, however, numerous empirical studies (particularly those based on blind sampling or tasting comparisons) confirm the real effect of brand on product perception. And that perception, to a large extent, is the psychological basis of product value. In the simplest terms, if at home you are paying €0.0025 per litre of tap water, but in the shop €1 for a litre of your favourite bottled water, the difference of €99.9975 is brand equity. Of course, this is not the same as profit, as there are costs of manufacturing, advertising and distributing the branded product (as there are for an unbranded one), but in many product categories it is the largest contributor to "the bottom line".

What is specific to energy and technology companies, says Keller, is that they are engineering-driven:

> Engineers are very smart and they're very good at what they do, but they're not always that knowledgeable or savvy about how people

think and make decisions. That's not the way they were trained. A lot of times they'll think about things in real terms, whereas as marketers we think about them in perceptual terms. Reality matters for sure, but reality doesn't exactly map onto what people think. There is always a lot of other stuff that comes into play.

And this is where branding and marketing expertise helps energy companies specifically and technology companies in general:

Many technology companies in Silicon Valley learned the hard way that just because you have the best product doesn't mean you're going to be successful. In fact, there are lots of examples of companies with great products, that just did not market successfully. They did not close the gap from perceptions to reality. They neither educated nor persuaded people. They did not motivate them to get on board.

Keller says that large part of his work with business-to-business (B2B) companies is convincing them that having great products is not the whole story:

It is really important, and you should always make sure you are on the inside of that. But, thinking that a great product will automatically win in the marketplace—well, it's not how it works. The main points I would be trying to get across to these companies are, for example, on differentiation and relevance. This is where classic marketing concepts really come into play.

This assumption—that a great product will sell itself—is one that B2B marketers often make. Unfortunately, like the other—that emotions don't really matter in B2B marketing—it's plain wrong:

This actually comes up a lot, that business buyers are savvy, smart and rational, that they can figure out which is the best product. Again, it just doesn't happen. As a marketer, you still need to make sure you are doing a good job, because emotions affect everything we do.

According to Keller, emotions in play when one is making an individual-consumer purchasing decision, such as in buying a pair of sport shoes, are different to emotions in B2B transaction, but they are nevertheless easily recognisable:

> The big thing in B2B is a sense of security, the kind of comfort and confidence you should have when considering your decision. Also, how you feel about yourself when working with certain companies—the self-respect angle. That self that hosts trust, confidence, and a sense of respect and security has a big role in business purchasing decisions. What marketers tend to underestimate is how high the stakes are in B2B. If things fall apart, you will get the blame. You might even lose your job. If your shoes fall apart, nobody will know, unless you choose to tell them.

In 2009 Keller set out his other big idea (first being customer-based brand equity). The article "Building Strong Brands in a Modern Marketing Communications Environment" introduced the "brand resonance pyramid". Known colloquially among practitioners as "Keller's Pyramid", it is an extension of the CBBE model "that views brand building as an ascending series of steps, from bottom to top . . . Enacting the four steps means establishing a pyramid of six 'brand building blocks' with customers". Emphasizing the duality of brands, "the rational route to brand building is the left-hand side of the pyramid, whereas the emotional route is the right-hand side".[11]

Hence, at the first level of brand-building, that of *salience*, your concern along the emotional vector should be "deep, broad brand awareness" and on the rational side *identity*—the question of "who are you?". At the next level, that of *performance* and *imagery*, you should be focusing on "points-of-parity & difference" and conversely, on *meaning*—the question of "what are you?" Once you pass the level of *judgements* and *feelings*, you are at the top of the brand-building pyramid, in the realm of *resonance*.[12]

This is where a brand ideally wants to be. Emotionally, you are cultivating "intense, active loyalty" and considering, rationally, the question of "relationships"—"what about you and me?" As Keller points out, "Resonance reflects the intensity or depth of the psychological bond that customers have with the brand, as well as the level of activity engendered by this loyalty."[13]

In the energy sector, on the other hand, the elevated heights of resonance are still but a dream for many companies. The reason for this is partly due to the nature of what is being sold:

HARDER THAN ROCKET SCIENCE   217

Electricity is pretty intangible. But, actually, this is why it is so important to focus on branding—because you're trying to create clear meaning and understanding about your brand, particularly on the value it
creates for people. Your value proposition matters, as you've got to
convince people of the costs and benefits, in a very tangible way.

Keller continues, "We're thinking of branding here in a broad sense. Not
just the look, but more like 'how do I want people to think and feel about
me'. This includes positioning and all the other strategy components." Once
you broaden the discussion to encompass the modern notion of branding,
the whole equation becomes critical:

You've got to create, deliver and communicate value. If you don't do
that, I think you run the risk that people won't know who you are, what
you do, why you're different and why you're better. In brief, they
won't choose you.

Energy companies are faced with a different challenge. It is customer inertia. To give you an example, my neighbour emailed me
recently, to let me know that he would be installing rooftop solar
panels. As we live in an area of outstanding natural views, on the
border of New Hampshire and Vermont, he asked whether I would
be OK with that. I told him, yes, of course, but then I started thinking
why haven't I installed my own solar panels yet.

It's not as if I am unaware of the technology. I had actually helped
the town of Hanover, where Dartmouth College is located, to market
and brand the "Solarise Hanover" programme. Its aim is to get people to adopt solar power. I met with them five times over the last six
months, telling them what to do and I still haven't done it.

Keller's view is that sustainability programmes have to get over two
hurdles: the consumer has to back the value proposition. But once they
appreciate the value of the initiative, consumers have to be motivated to
act on it:

I think that energy companies have a more difficult job than companies selling products to consumers. Think about tennis racquets: they
are pretty much the same shape, and made of the same materials. Yes,
the manufacturers will talk about the graphite and the strings, but you

know they racquets are not that different. However, types of energies are hugely different, and you are asking the customer to make a fundamental choice and stick with it. To me that's a huge challenge.

Fortunately, the building blocks of the brand resonance pyramid, offer guidance in overcoming such a challenge. At the second level, that of "personality" and "images" the customer engages with the brand, among other issues, on cost and reliability on the rational side, and personality and values, on the emotional side. But, energy companies should pay particular attention to the next level, that of the building blocks of "judgements" and "feelings":

> The debate around energy goes back to the question of self-respect: "How do I feel about myself? Is this something that's consistent with my own identity and self-image?" Therefore, does it give me an emotional reward, because I'm making energy choices that reflect who I am, or who I want to be. Those questions are really important and have to line up with the rational and functional side.

But, Keller also gives the example of the Prius hybrid car, to draw attention to social approval as a sustainability-acceptance motivator:

> When the Prius came out some people bought it, because it was cool and hip. They wanted to signal that they were socially conscious. If they drove that vehicle, they could do all sorts of things that were terrible for the environment, or generally continue not to care a great deal, and still seem progressive. There's going to be a side of that with energy, too. I wouldn't play it up, but I can't ignore it because I know it plays a role. Functional and emotional drivers are probably dominant, but there may be a little social approval in there as well.

He goes back to the task of differentiation, which also applies to electricity, despite it being commonly considered a commodity:

> I would say that you can differentiate anything, because you are not really selling a product, you're selling a solution. It's about how to satisfy needs, how to solve problems. The key in differentiation is that it should typically complement the product on the non-product inventory side of things.

When it comes to considering return on investment in your brand and how long this should take, I've always been a believer that you want to try to do things that are good in the short run *and* in the long run. I would be always trying to figure out, how can I do anything in a way that's consistent with my brand; that somehow reinforces my brand even if I'm doing a promotion and a discount.

Keller says that ahead of any investment in your brand you should accept there would be a time-lag until your efforts pay off. But you shouldn't give up on short term results, achieved in a brand-centric and consistent way.

However, before prescribing a one-size-fits-all branding solution to the whole of the energy sector as a whole, a difference should be noted between traditional energy companies, that might suffer from an image problem, and the new energy companies, unencumbered by past burdens:

It's hard to lump them together, although, looking from the outside, they could appear similar. For both types of companies sustainability is huge. But, the traditional companies are approaching it in a more defensive way. They could be looking at mitigation, reducing emissions or improving efficiency. The new companies are strategically more offensive. In providing solutions and alternatives, they come across as progressive.

What marks energy out from other sectors when it comes to sustainability, is that it has become one of the industry's most significant "points of parity". This is an important concept in Keller's theory, which denotes a brand association that is equal in favourability with a competing brand association, and which serves to negate a "point of difference".[14] In other words, a point of parity will nix that particular reason a consumer has to choose a rival brand. But, in other sectors, companies might have other more urgent point of parity agendas.

Think about the rivalry between Nike and Adidas. If one of those companies launches a product which has a sustainability feature, before the other parries, it will have to consider how important that feature is as a differentiator. In the apparel industry that would not be immediately obvious because the consumers might be choosing a product on the strength of other features.

In the energy sector, however, there are a fewer points of parity, hence they gain in importance. These could be quality of customer service, cost, technological innovation and, of course, sustainability:

> Utilities probably never get as much credit as they deserve. We take them for granted and it's only when they screw up we really think about them. But, in addition to the technological and economic challenge of sustainability, if they are to retain customers utilities have to elevate a series of transactions to a relationship. That is not easy.

If you are just transactionally linked to long-term customers, then the success of future retention is based on building a stronger rapport. And given the significance of renewable energy as a point of parity, utilities might be already locked in a virtuous sustainability circle:

> Consumers attitudes to sustainability have changed for two reasons. One is that all these products have gotten better. You don't have to sacrifice anything if you are "going green". Secondly, people are willing to pay more money for it. Given that they will pay a premium, it is interesting to consider how this will impact the industry. There are so many dynamics playing out, the younger audience seems to be more pro-sustainability, as it is more concerned with climate change. Then there is that whole backlash against traditional fossil fuel companies.

And then, with curiosity and enthusiasm evocative of his entire approach to the subject Keller concludes, "Actually, energy branding is such a fascinating niche within branding and marketing. I am so interested to see where it goes."

Notes

1. See Keller, Kevin Lane. *Strategic Brand Management*, 1st edition. Prentice Hall, 1998.
2. Read, Debbie. "Guru Interview: Kevin Keller". *Emerald for Managers*, Sep. 2007, moam.info/guru-interview-kevin-keller-emerald_59d62e4f1723 dd3975ec7599.html.
3. Keller, *Strategic Brand Management*, p. 19.

4. For Keller's academic posts and CV, as well as bibliography and notable presentations see "About" pages on Tuck School of Business' website, at faculty.tuck.dartmouth.edu/kevin-lane-keller/.
5. Keller, Kevin Lane. "Conceptualizing, Measuring, and Managing Customer-Based Brand Equity." *Journal of Marketing*, Vol. 57, No. 1, Jan. 1993, pp. 1–22, (doi:10.2307/1252054).
6. Keller, Kevin Lane. "Reflections on Customer-Based Brand Equity: Perspectives, Progress, and Priorities." *AMS Review*, 6, 2016, pp. 1–16, (doi:10.1007/s13162-016-0078-z).
7. See Bettman, John R. "Memory Factors in Consumer Choice: A Review." *Journal of Marketing*, Vol. 43, No. 2, 1979, pp. 37–53.
8. Keller, *Strategic Brand Management*, p. 45.
9. Ibid., p. 43.
10. Ibid., p. 44.
11. Keller, Kevin Lane. "Building Strong Brands in a Modern Marketing Communications Environment." *Journal of Marketing Communications*, Vol. 15, No. 2–3, 2009, p. 143, (doi:10.1080/13527260902757530).
12. Ibid., p. 144, fig. 2.
13. Ibid., p. 143.
14. For a discussion of points of parity, see Keller, *Strategic Brand Management*, p. 53.

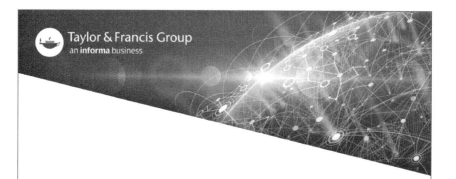